Great Books for Girls

More Than 600
Recommended Books
for Girls Ages 3–14

Kathleen Odean

Ballantine Boo
New York

Praise for *Great Books for Girls*

"When I was a girl, books were my teachers, my friends. They gave me hope, dreams, direction, and eventually power—power to become who I wanted to be. This guide-book, compiled by a knowledgeable, story-spirited woman, will allow adults to help girls find the great books that nourish the spirit. I recommend it for all those who want girls to grow up strong, free, bold, and kind."
—MARY PIPHER
Author of *Reviving Ophelia*

Praise for *Great Books about Things Kids Love*

"An invaluable resource for both fiction and nonfiction."
—*Minneapolis Star-Tribune*

"[Odean's] choices are superb. An excellent book."
—*Sacramento Bee*

"Kathleen Odean's compilation *Great Books about Things Kids Love* is an excellent resource for home and school libraries."

—*Denver Post*

"A strong parent's resource that also belongs on the professional shelf."

—*Booklist*

By Kathleen Odean

Great Books for Girls
Great Books for Boys
Great Books About Things Kids Love

Dedicated with love to my nieces and nephews, Autumn, Isabel, Rosalie, Graham, Andrew, Naomi, Shayla, Tyler, Noah, and Dana.

CONTENTS

CONTENTS

CONTENTS

Acknowledgments

I want to give my warm thanks to the following people: my fellow children's librarians and other friends in the children's book world for their suggestions and their dedication to children and books; the many children I've worked with over the years in schools and public libraries, for their excitement and honesty about books; the staff at the Barrington Public Library, for graciously helping me obtain so many books; my agent Lisa Ross, for her support; my editor Allison Dickens, for her help; my friends and colleagues Martha Wellbaum, Melody Allen, Karen Breen, Donna Good, Mary Lee Griffin, Pam Jenkins, Frances Martindale, Debby Neely, Elizabeth Overmyer, and Virginia Smith, for sharing their ideas and their love of children's books; and my husband, Ross Cheit, for his encouragement and love.

Introduction

"There are no heroines following the shining paths of romantic adventure, as do the heroes of boys' books. . . . Of course girls have been reading so-called 'boys' books' ever since there were such. But consider what it means to do so. Instead of closing the covers with shining eyes and the happy thought, 'That might happen to me someday!' the girl, turning the final page, can only sigh regretfully, 'Oh, dear, that can never happen to me—because I'm not a boy!' "[1]

Amelia Earhart wrote these word in the mid-1930s, after her own adventure flying solo over the shining path of the Atlantic. Looking at the books available, she was "struck with the fact that girls are evidently not expected to join in the fun."

[1] Putnam, George Palmer, *Soaring Wings: A Biography of Amelia Earhart* (New York: Harcourt, Brace and Company, 1939), 89.

INTRODUCTION

Today over four thousand children's books are published each year, far more than in the 1930s, but girls still get left out of much of the fun. Although publishers are more alert to this issue than when I wrote the first edition of this guide, published in 1997, there are still too few books that offer the kind of brave, strong females that Amelia Earhart longed to read about. Yet more than ever, girls need such heroines to offset the barrage of negative images society presents about females. In this updated version of the guide, which annotates 294 new books, I have brought together a total of more than 600 books about girls who defy the stereotypes about females in our culture. These books feature girls who are the ones slaying dragons—sometimes literally, more often figuratively. They face challenges and overcome them, just as parents hope their daughters will do.

If you are a parent, you want to be sure that your daughter has a fair start in life. You want her to be free to make choices, to be active, to pursue a range of interests, and to speak her mind. But these goals are undermined by what psychologist Mary Pipher calls "our girl-poisoning culture." Movies, television, magazines, and popular music give short shrift to strong, active women and instead place enormous emphasis on women's looks and sexuality. Few females can reach the standards of beauty set by advertisements and the fashion industry, leaving teenage girls with a constant sense of failure. They are increasingly prone to depression and eating disorders, and are pressured to use drugs and alcohol.

Sexism starts young. Research shows that even preschoolers harbor negative views of females and positive ones of males. In one troubling academic study, three- and five-year-olds viewed a videotape of two infants playing side by side. Half of the children were told that the infant on the left was female and the one on the right, male; the other half were told the opposite. The children proceeded to describe the infant they thought was female as "small, scared, slow, weak, quiet, dumb, and soft." They described the one identified as male as "big, mad, fast, strong, loud, smart, and hard." The *same* infant was rated in negative terms when the children believed it was a female, in positive terms when they believed it to be male.[2]

Myra and David Sadker, authors of *Failing at Fairness: How America's Schools Cheat Girls*, found that even as they got older, boys continued to hold a low opinion of what it means to be a girl. Of eleven hundred Michigan children who wrote essays between 1988 and 1990 on what life would be like if they were a member of the opposite sex, 95 percent of the boys saw no advantages and many disadvantages, which they described in disparaging terms. Forty-two percent of the girls articulated the advantages of being male: "They would feel more secure and less worried about what other people thought, they would be treated with more respect, they looked forward to earning more money at better jobs."[3]

Children constantly have the idea reinforced that males are important, while females are unimportant and sometimes almost invisible. A 1998 analysis of thirty-three popular video games revealed that 41 percent of the games had no female characters, and women were portrayed as sex objects in 28 percent of the games.[4] The children's advocacy organization, Children Now, issued a report in 2001 saying that 65 percent of adult characters on prime-time television and 60 percent of young characters are male, a continuing trend that emphasizes men and boys on television.[5]

[2] Susan Golombok and Robyn Fivush, *Gender Development* (Cambridge: Cambridge University Press, 1994), 28–29.

[3] Myra Sadker and David Sadker, *Failing at Fairness: How America's Schools Cheat Girls* (New York: Maxwell Macmillan International, 1994), 84.

[4] Tracy L. Dietz, "An Examination of Violence and Gender Role Portrayals in Video Games: Implications for Gender Socialization and Aggressive Behavior." *Sex Roles: A Journal of Research* 38 (1998): 425–442.

[5] "Fall Colors: Prime Time Diversity Report." Children Now, 2001.

Unfortunately, schools often intensify the problems facing girls. Research has revealed that most schools sustain gender stereotypes to the detriment of female students. Teachers give more attention to boys and give them more constructive criticism. According to the Sadkers, boys are twelve times more likely to talk in class than girls, and teachers reprimand girls who call out or interrupt more often than they scold boys who do the same thing. Although their research was some time ago, anecdotal evidence suggests that many of the problems persist.

One unintentional but insidious practice of many educators is to perform tasks for girls instead of expecting girls to do it themselves, a mistake parents also make. The Sadkers give an example from a kindergarten in which a male aide showed boys who wanted to play a VCR tape how to insert it, a task the boys quickly learned to do themselves. But when girls wanted to play a tape, the aide simply put it in for them—throughout the entire school year. Presumably the boys got the message that they are competent and able to try new technological tasks, while girls learned to be dependent.[6]

The good news since the 1997 edition of this guide is that girls are taking more math and science courses than they used to take, and doing better on standardized tests in those areas. (Girls also continue to do significantly better on certain national tests in reading and writing, a fact that raises concerns about boys and education.) However, girls still lag badly behind boys in computer science and related courses. According to *Tech Savvy: Educating Girls in the New Computer Age*, a report published by the American Association of University Women in 2000, girls represent only 17 percent of the Computer Science Advanced Placement test takers, and less than

[6] Sadkers, 80.

one in ten of the Computer Science "AB" test takers (AB is an advanced placement test). Related statistics show that women receive less than 28 percent of the computer science bachelor's degrees, down from a high of 37 percent in 1984. Computer science is the only field in which women's participation has actually decreased over time. Women make up just 9 percent of the recipients of engineering-related bachelor's degrees. Clearly, girls and women still have a long way to go in certain academic areas that lead to well-paying, challenging jobs.[7]

Another problem girls face that has received publicity in the last few years is sexual harassment in schools, particularly as they get older. The American Association of University Women's 2001 publication *Hostile Hallways: Bullying, Teasing, and Sexual Harassment in School* surveyed students in eighth through eleventh grades and found that both girls and boys experience considerable harassment, but girls report more incidents of harassment and describe themselves as more negatively affected by it than boys do. [8]

What can you do to help your daughters thrive in this adverse environment? Many factors are out of your control. Schools change slowly even under pressure from concerned parents, and the media shows little sign of changing. But you *can* take one important step toward safeguarding girls' sense of self by reading your daughters (and sons) books about strong females, and helping them find similar books for their own reading and school research. This guide will lead you to such books.

I was inspired to seek out these books by my seventeen years as a children's librarian, during which I read to groups

[7] *Tech Savvy: Educating Girls in the New Computer Age.* American Association of University Women, 2000.

[8] *Hostile Hallways: Bullying, Teasing, and Sexual Harassment in School.* American Association of University Women, 2001.

of children ages three to eleven, helped them find books to check out, and advised teachers and parents about books for children. I made it a priority to promote books that feature strong girls, but even for someone knowledgeable about children's literature, it continues to be a challenge to find a wide range. Far too many books present boys as leaders and girls as followers. Boys go exploring, girls stick close to home. Boys take things apart, girls watch. Men are praised for accomplishments, women for being supportive.

Picture-story books, the mainstay of the preschool and lower elementary crowd, most often have main characters—human or animal—who are male. Even when gender makes no difference to the plot, the "default setting" is male. Many of the best picture-story books such as *Dr. DeSoto*, the Frog and Toad series, and *Harry the Dirty Dog* deserve their popularity, but unfortunately they have only supporting females or none at all. The only female in the ever-popular *Winnie the Pooh* is Kanga, the overly protective mother. These are fine books to read to children, but we owe it to both sexes to find equally appealing books about adventurous females.

Older children want "chapter books," as they call them, meaning longer fiction and informational books. Fiction books are more likely to have female protagonists than picture-story books are, but even then, those girls are not always strong characters. Most often they are caught up in problems about relationships or are focusing on friendships, family problems, or everyday life in school. Girls are still far less likely than boys to be setting off on a quest or pursuing a goal outside of relationships.

Nonfiction is even more problematic, since it includes history and biography, areas traditionally dominated by books about men. Most sports books are still geared to boys; library shelves still hold far more biographies of men than women. The list goes on.

What About Boys?

Of course, boys as well as girls need to read about strong women. In order to treat girls as equals, boys must grow up believing females are as important as males—a message that is not getting through, as the documentation about teenage boys sexually harassing their female schoolmates clearly indicates. Boys are not going to learn to treat girls and women with respect by watching MTV or sitcoms. But parents can give their sons books in which younger and older females play dynamic roles and are honored for them.

Currently 9.1 million women own a total of 38 percent of businesses in the United States, employing millions of people.[9] As women gain power in the workforce, even more men will work for women, yet very few children's books show a man working for a woman. A handful of valuable books show boys who look up to the daring girls who are their friends or sisters. In a few novels, boys who initially scoff at the idea of girls' being courageous change their minds by the book's end. I have included as many books like these as I could find.

The widespread belief that boys do not want to read books in which the main character is a girl, whereas girls are willing to read about boys, needs to be reexamined. In my experience, if a book sounds appealing enough, a boy will be interested. For example, I knew a middle-school boy—a dedicated ice hockey player—whose favorite book was *The True Confessions of Charlotte Doyle* by Avi, a novel in which a girl on a ship gets involved in a mutiny. Many third-grade boys I've known kept

9 "1999 Facts on Women-Owned Business: Trends in the U.S. and the Fifty States." National Foundation of Women Business Owners, 1999.

reading in the Ramona series by Beverly Cleary after hearing the first one read aloud in class. I have found with younger children that one reading of *The Adventures of Isabel* by Ogden Nash, with hilarious pictures by James Marshall, had the boys as well as the girls eager to check out the book. Present the right book in the right way and most children will want to read it.

Parents may also like to consult my guide, *Great Books for Boys: More than 600 Books for Boys 2 to 14*. In it, I brought together books that I know from my experience boys enjoy, books that get boys reading and keep them reading, including many books with girls as main characters as well as biographies about exciting women.

Parents of boys *and* girls may also be interested in *Great Books About Things Kids Love: More than 750 Recommended Books for Children 3 to 14*. Based on the fact that many children choose the books they read by topic, books in this guide are organized into fifty-five popular categories. Within each category are a variety of books, including nonfiction, picture-story books, fiction, and biographies. The guide also offers about fifty pages of ideas and activities to encourage children to read.

Brave Girls, Strong Women: The Criteria

In selecting the books in *Great Books for Girls*, I looked for strong girls and women who faced the world with courage, either from the first or after overcoming their fears. I found female characters who are creative, capable, articulate, and intelligent. They solve problems, face challenges, resolve conflicts, and go on journeys. These girls are not waiting to be rescued; they are doing the rescuing. Nor are they waiting for a male to provide a happy ending: they are fashioning their own stories.

I sought out characters who have attributes too seldom associated with girls, such as bravery, athleticism, and independence. These girls take risks and treat setbacks as ways to learn. They differ from other girls in fiction by liking machines, insects, snakes, rocks and dirt, and large dogs. Some of them enjoy fixing things, some are good with numbers, and a few even get into fist fights (as do so many boys in books).

In picture-story books, the adventures might seem mundane—a trip to the pond or a bicycle ride—and the acts of independence small—refusing to leave a mud puddle or playing the drums loudly. The problems the girls solve may seem commonplace, but it is the very act of a girl having an adventure, asserting her independence, or puzzling out her own solution that sets her apart from more traditional fictional girls. For in books, as in real life, adults tend to do things for girls, while they challenge boys to do things on their own. These seemingly mild books compare favorably indeed to the many books about girls learning to please their parents and friends.

9

Girls don't need any more lessons in being nice; they need lessons in making decisions for themselves.

I was pleased when I found stories about girls working well together and cooperating to reach a goal, solve a problem, or defeat an enemy. Too many books about girls deal with jealousy between friends, and too few show the sort of easy companionship found in books about boys.

I looked for fictional mothers who encouraged strong traits in their daughters and even modeled them. It is all too easy to find portraits of mothers who protect their daughters to the point of holding them back from exciting opportunities. Frequently, lively girls must disobey their mothers to pursue activities that their brothers are free to try.

When adults are the main characters, mostly in the picture-story books and folktales, the stories I selected center around women who are happy living alone and traveling alone. Breaking grandmotherly stereotypes, older women travel far and wide, ride motorcycles, pilot airplanes, and prove fearless in the face of adversity. Women in these books work at a variety of jobs, sometimes running their own businesses.

Since folktales often perpetuate the passive role of females, it was exciting to discover dozens that break the mold. These tales tend to end in marriage, but it is only after the heroine has accomplished difficult deeds to win the husband, rather than the other way around.

Inevitably some of the "villains" in these stories are female, although I avoided those who embodied the worst traits most often associated with women. On the other hand, some female antagonists are complex, interesting characters who make worthy opponents.

Inevitably and unfortunately, many of the main female characters are pretty or beautiful. Authors apparently feel obliged to supply their female heroes, especially in novels, with good looks—sometimes unconventional beauty, but beauty nonetheless. It is unusual to find a protagonist with a weight or complexion problem. Even when an author has broken free of clichés and described an ordinary girl, the book jacket is likely to show a pretty one. A welcome exception is *Yolonda's Genius* by Carol Fenner, about a strong black girl who considers herself "queen-sized" rather than overweight and enjoys feeling physically powerful. In another exception, *Rules of the Road* by Joan Bauer, the narrator feels physically awkward like she's been "glued together with surplus parts," but she's a smart risk taker who has a natural aptitude for the business world.

Historical fiction and fantasy figure heavily in the fiction sections for several reasons. One of the best fictional devices to send girls on adventures is to have them disguise themselves as boys. Many of the historical novels hinge on such a disguise and give the girls a taste of the freedom available only to males of the time. Frontier settings, where men and women work side by side, also provide more opportunities than modern life does for girls to be daring or heroic. In updating this guide, I was struck by the large number of new historical novels for children, many of them in series. You will find the sections on "Historical Fiction" for middle and older readers to be noticeably longer than the other genre listings because there is so much more to choose from now.

Fantasy writers can create new times and places, including cultures where females and males are more equal. In some fantasy stories women have magical abilities that give them power equal to that of men. Sometimes science fiction writers hypothesize about future societies where sex differences matter less than they do now. Fantasy listings are not as long as those for historical fiction, but still longer than other areas.

Modern fictional girls have fewer chances in their everyday lives to test themselves than girls in historical fiction or fantasy do. Being stranded in the wilderness, of course, is a good plot device for pushing a character to her limits, which happens to two girls—who must survive in the woods in winter—in *Tracks in the Snow* by Lucy Jane Bledsoe. Sports are another good arena for testing character. In several books with contemporary settings, girls get involved with civil rights or other, sometimes dangerous, political causes. *Running on Eggs* by Anna Levine combines sports and politics in its story about an Israeli girl and a Palestinian girl on the same track team who forge a friendship in a hostile environment. In a few cases, the protagonist pushes herself to excel in music. I chose certain books about modern girls because the main character has a strong, often funny voice and a nonconformist view of the world.

Very few of the books are about a girl with serious emotional or family problems, even though such problems may build character. Some readers would consider *The Great Gilly Hopkins* by Katherine Paterson to be about a strong girl. Yet Gilly's tough exterior is the result of the pain she feels about being a foster child whose mother deserted her. She is smart but ends up hurting herself with her clever ideas. This outstanding novel, which isn't included, seems to me to be more about sadness than strength.

In most of the books in this guide, the main character is a female. Sometimes, though, the narrator is a boy even though the strongest character is female. For example, in the picture book *Anna Banana and Me* by Lenore Blegvad, a young boy emulates his friend Anna and describes a day with her in the park. In Richard Peck's novel *A Long Way from Chicago*, the narrator is a boy who spends summers with his Grandma Dowdel, a self-sufficient, strong-minded woman who keeps things lively in her small town. I haven't included books like the Harry Potter series—popular as they are—where the main character is a boy, even though in those books Hermione is important and participates in some of the action. My goal was to find books where a female is the main focus of the story, not a sidekick or good friend of a main male character.

The informational books I've listed show women in active roles. Fortunately, far more biographies than ever are being published about important women for younger readers as well as older ones. Books on history have begun to emphasize girls and women, and more and more sports nonfiction books feature female athletes, the history of women in sports, and how-to sports books aimed specifically at girls.

Making the Choices

I read or reread every book in the list as well as a few hundred that I chose not to include. I read many of the picture-story books and folktales aloud to groups of children, and asked older children to read and react to the novels. This second edition of the guide contains 294 annotations of books not found in the earlier version. The new titles replace books that are now out-of-print, those that contain dated information, or books whose subject is better covered in a more recently published book.

To find the books, I drew on my seventeen years of experience as a children's librarian in schools and public libraries, and also elicited ideas from librarians, teachers, friends, and children. I searched through reference books, publishers' catalogs, and lists from libraries, browsed through bookstores and library collections, and surfed the Internet. Not every book that meets my criteria is listed. I could have added more books, especially historical fiction and biographies, thanks to the greater number now published, but I wanted to keep the guide a reasonable length and affordable price.

In general, the books listed are well written, with illustrations of high quality. However, a limited number are strong enough in their theme and content that they are included despite their obvious flaws. For example, a few books that focus on women in the workplace are pedestrian in text and design, but admirably serve their purpose of showing many women at many jobs. Biographies tend to vary the most in quality, particularly in terms of photographs and illustrations. I could not avoid including a few less than stellar biographies that were the only ones available about certain women, and I have indicated weaknesses in the annotations.

Many excellent books do not appear in this guide simply because they center around boys or around traditional girls. Some types of books presented me with hard decisions, such as books about girls who make difficult sacrifices for other people, giving up something important to themselves. Such acts take a great deal of moral courage, but I believe that girls have plenty of examples of women giving of themselves for others. Females are taught to please and help others, to put themselves and their desires aside. Far more difficult for girls is finding the moral courage to face conflict to pursue their own paths and dreams, a plot element I did look for.

I found that at first glance certain books seemed to fit the criteria but then proved disappointing upon a closer reading. For example, many people suggested that I include *Madeline* by Ludwig Bemelmans. However, although she is *described* as fearless, Madeline does not actually *do* anything in the first book about her. Worse, her fellow students spend an awful lot of time crying. In *Madeline's Rescue*, however, which I did include, a female dog displays courage and Madeline shows admirable persistence.

Some readers will be surprised not to find their favorite childhood novels about girls. For example, *Anne of Green Gables*, which is not included, is a novel about an energetic and intelligent girl who initially seems to defy some of the restrictions put on girls. Yet at the end of the book, she consciously sacrifices her education to help her beloved relative. Even before she makes this decision, Anne has become dreamier and less given to speaking her mind than when she was young. It's a heartwarming book, but the lesson it ultimately offers girls is a very traditional one. While Anne gains in independence in later books in the series, many readers may read only this, the most famous title in the series, which I don't find meets my criteria.

Caddie Woodlawn by Carol Ryrie Brink has similar problems, yet its strengths outweigh its weaknesses. Caddie herself is far bolder than most girls in children's books and promises to become a strong-minded woman. True, her parents are out to make her less wild and she seems to acquiesce. But as soon as she takes up the womanly art of quilting, she gets her brothers involved, too. Near the end, Caddie's sedate mother chooses the American frontier over a genteel life in England, a vote for adventure that sends a strong signal to her daughter.

For some reason, certain types of books about girls rarely get published. I was disappointed five years ago in my attempts to find much sports fiction about girls' sports teams, even though more than two million girls play high school sports. There still are not enough novels, or picture-story books, about girls involved in sports. However, the number of biographies of female athletes and instructional books specifically for girls about sports has increased noticeably, a welcome addition.

Despite the popularity of mysteries, too few mystery novels have strong girl detectives like Herculeah Jones in the series by Betsy Byars, who actually solves the problem rather than have the solution fall into her lap. Another weak area is animal fantasies of novel length, most of which have male central characters. A fantasy with a host of female animals along the lines of *The Wind in the Willows* does not seem to exist. Almost no books tell stories about mothers and daughters having adventures together, or stories about several girls going on quests or journeys together.

How to Use This Guide

The guide is divided into six main chapters that list books: "Picture-Story Books"; "Folktales"; "Books for Beginning Readers"; "Books for Middle Readers"; "Books for Older Readers"; and "Poetry." Each book entry contains the author, the title, the illustrator, the publishing information, an age range, and a description. The publishing information includes the original year of publication and the publishers of whichever editions are currently in print—hardcover, paperback, or both. (Since hardcover and paperback status changes rapidly, check with a bookstore for updated information if you want to buy a book.) If the book has sequels or related books featuring strong females, I have mentioned those, too.

If a book won a Newbery or Caldecott Award, I have mentioned it in the annotation. These are annual awards given to the most distinguished children's books of the year by the American Library Association. The Newbery Award is for writing, and the Caldecott Medal is for illustration. Several other outstanding books of the year are named Newbery or Caldecott Honor Books. I have chaired the Newbery Committee, and served on both committees, and I know the great care put into the selection each year.

The books listed in "Picture-Story Books" typically consist of thirty-two pages with pictures on every page. Most but not all have a short text. At many libraries these are labeled "E," which technically stands for "easy," but often a sign is posted that reads "E Is for Everyone" because the appeal of these books spans such a wide age range. Many of them have surprisingly sophisticated vocabulary—don't be deceived by the pictures. Preschoolers and early readers will enjoy listening to picture-story books read aloud and, as they become stronger readers, they will enjoy these books on their own.

Some of the books in "Folktales" are collections with just a few illustrations, but most are single tales with pictures on every page. They also have a wide age range and are good for reading aloud.

The "Books for Beginning Readers" are for children who are learning to read and those who are ready for short chapter books, typically children ages six to eight, although the age of beginning readers varies a great deal. The books may also suit older children, particularly those reluctant readers who find long books intimidating. The section includes Easy Readers, Short Novels, and Biographies, most of which have many illustrations. Easy Readers are specifically aimed at children who are at an early stage of reading, who may be sounding out words and relying on pictures to supply clues about the story. Short Novels are for children who have a wider sight vocabulary and greater fluency. The Biographies range from heavily illustrated thirty-two-page books to sixty pages with much more text.

The chapter on books for middle readers gives ideas for children roughly nine to eleven years old, while the chapter on books for older readers covers roughly ages twelve to fourteen. Again, there is a lot of variation in the age ranges within each chapter; I've specified an age range for each book. Entries in "Books for Older Readers" generally have more challenging writing in terms of style or content or both than the entries for middle readers. *Lyddie* by Katherine Paterson is a good example of a book for older readers. Most books in "Books for Middle Readers" have congenial main characters, but Lyddie is a young woman whose poverty and hardship harden her in some ways. The reader needs to make a leap of understanding to sympathize with Lyddie and her choices. The unusually dense, carefully crafted writing is challenging, while the theme of employer sexual harassment requires emotional maturity from the reader. Not all books in this section are this sophisticated. Some are simply longer, have more demanding vocabulary, or concern older characters. Some include romance, and a few deal in part with abuse. Within these two chapters, the lists are divided into fiction (subdivided into genres), and biographies and nonfiction.

Most parents will want to browse through the appropriate sections, read book descriptions, and decide what sounds good. Do not be limited by the age ranges, which are loose guidelines, and don't confine yourself to only one chapter. Early elementary children who are strong readers and reluctant older readers present real challenges for parents. Look at the sections before and after your child's age for ideas. The annotations can also guide you to books for independent readers further along than your child that you might want to read aloud.

Older children may want to browse through the guide themselves, reading the annotations and choosing books that sound appealing. Voracious readers are always looking for new ideas, and less enthusiastic readers may have a strong sense of topics that interest them.

Keep in mind that older children still benefit from listening to books read aloud. Often parents will conclude that once a child can read to herself, reading aloud serves no purpose. Not true. Even most older children understand far more words when hearing them spoken than they can recognize on the page. Think of the conversations full of long words you have with a young child. Books tend to use even more complex vocabulary, so reading aloud introduces a multitude of new words in context. Later, when your child runs across such a word on the page in her own reading, she will have heard the word before and have a sense of what it means.

Even if reading aloud did not enhance vocabulary and knowledge of grammar, it would be worth continuing past the early grades because it is such pleasurable time spent with a child. In a busy world, reading aloud offers a quiet, cozy interlude, and a way to wind down at the end of the day. It also offers the perfect chance to discuss values and opinions about issues raised in the books.

Many of the novels in this guide are so wonderful that you should consider reading them on your own. Three of my favorite examples of beautifully written books, one from each fiction section, are *Sarah, Plain and Tall* by Patricia MacLachlan, *Tuck Everlasting* by Natalie Babbitt, and *Toning the Sweep* by Angela Johnson. It's easier to recommend a book to a child if you have read it yourself and can describe it enticingly. Equally important, the sight of parents reading is one of the strongest incentives for children to read. The annotations for each book highlight outstanding books.

If you find at some point in your daughter's life that she quits heeding your advice about books, you might buy or borrow some of these books and leave them lying around. Or enlist the help of a favorite teacher or librarian to promote books about strong females. Mother–daughter book groups have sprung up everywhere in recent years, leading to shared reading and lively discussions, a wonderful way to bring two generations together around good books.

Two chapters near the back of the book draw on current trends of interest to girls. "Nonfiction Books in Series" is based on the fact that many publishers now produce specific series about famous girls and women, or women in the workplace. While I didn't have the space to list each book separately, I have described several series and given examples for readers who might want to pursue them further.

"Magazines and Web Sites for Girls" highlights a few magazines directed specifically at girls, and an even greater number of Web sites created with girls in mind. These offer articles, information, and resources that encourage girls to expand their view of the world and the roles they can play in it.

The last chapter in this guide gives other ideas of book-related activities, listing possible tie-ins to specific books such as craft projects or field trips. It also gives tips on reading aloud, as well as information about locating books through bookstores and libraries and keeping up with children's book publishing. I have included an annotated list of other books and resources of interest to parents concerned about their daughters, a list of children's books on sex and growing up, and some ideas for parents who want to encourage their daughters' strength and independence.

My Hopes

Psychologists use the metaphor of girls losing their voices as they grow up surrounded by sexism and stereotypes. All too soon, the research shows, the girls start doubting what they have to say and so quit saying it. We need to give them books about girls and women who have found their voices or kept them strong and clear all along.

"You tell a story because a statement would be inadequate," Flannery O'Connor once wrote.[10] Conveying a message through a book can be more effective than giving direct advice. You can tell your child to be brave or strong, but she is more likely to know what that means through immersing herself in a novel about a courageous girl. You can tell her that she should reach high in her professional goals, but it's more helpful to back up that advice with concrete examples of successful women and how they accomplished their goals. These books will help girls internalize the message that they can be the heroes in their own stories, overcoming obstacles—slaying dragons—and making their dreams come true *themselves*.

As I read through hundreds of books about strong girls and women, I regretted that I had so few of them available to me growing up in the late fifties and the sixties, when most books I read showed boys as leaders and girls as accommodating followers. Yet even now, I love reading these books and find them exciting and inspiring. I also have a great time sharing them with the children in my life.

"Writing and reading decrease our sense of isolation,"

[10] Flannery O'Connor, *Mystery and Manners: Occasional Prose* (New York: Farrar, Straus, and Giroux, 1969), 96.

wrote Anne Lamott in *Bird by Bird*. "They deepen and widen and expand our sense of life: they feed the soul."[11] I hope that the books I have chosen to list here expand the dreams of young girls, decrease the isolation of adolescents, and widen the sense of life for all who read them.

[11] Anne Lamott, *Bird by Bird* (New York: Vintage Anchor Publishing, 1995), 237.

1

Picture-Story Books

Picture-story books really are for everyone, but they find their greatest audience among preschoolers and early elementary grade children. These thirty-two page gems can be read in one sitting, making them perfect for reading at bedtime or for entertaining a group of children. Most of the books in the following list are geared toward children three to seven. (Note that the age ranges in this section indicate ages for listening, not independent reading.) But, do not be strictly limited by the age-range suggestions. A two-year-old book lover would probably enjoy many of the books marked "3–6," while eight- and nine-year-olds may independently read books marked for younger children.

The best thing about reading these books with children is sharing their enjoyment of the story and pictures. You'll laugh together and bask in the warmth of happy endings. You'll find that favorite books become part of your family conversations and folklore. Along with the fun come the educational benefits of reading picture-story books with your children. Children absorb new vocabulary, hearing it in context and storing it away for the day when, as readers, they see it in print. They begin to understand the structure of stories and hear the beauty of well-written prose. Beginning writers can use these books as models for tightly crafted short stories. For adults as well as children, the illustrations are a special treat. Poring over the superb artwork in many of these books is like having an art museum at home.

When choosing books, be sure to check other sections of the guide for more suggestions, even for young children. Most of the folktales in the next section are also thirty-two pages long and filled with pictures. The collections at the end of the Folklore section also include some stories suitable for reading aloud to children four and older. The Easy Readers in "Books for Beginning Readers" are short illustrated books that can be read in one sitting; they appeal to preschoolers as well as beginning readers. "Books for Beginning Readers" also offers possible read-alouds in the list of novels and in the biography section.

Aller, Susan Bivin. *Emma and the Night Dogs.* Illustrated by Marni Backer. 1997. Hardcover: Albert Whitman. Ages 5–9.

Before the start of this story about a girl who rescues a little boy with the help of search-and-rescue dogs, an author's note sets the stage by describing the role of canine search and rescue, how they behave and what they do. In the story, a girl named Emma learns about a little boy who is lost in nearby woods. Because Emma's aunt owns a search dog, the rescue team gathers at Emma's house after a day of searching. Emma helps serve the dogs kibble and the adults hot chocolate, then everyone gets some sleep. But when Emma wakes in the night and hears the dogs barking, she decides to take them out on her own and, sure enough, together they find the little boy.

Anderson, Laurie Halse. *Ndito Runs.* Illustrated by Anita van der Merwe. 1996. Hardcover: Henry Holt. Ages 4–8.

Ndito, who lives in a Kenyan village, runs to school one morning, barefoot and clad in a white blouse and green skirt. Although her older brothers tease Ndito as they pass her, she pays them no attention. After waving to people in the village, she runs across the highlands. She imagines herself as different animals as she runs along: gazelle, goat, dik-dik, wildebeest, and others. Textured illustrations in warm colors show the animals she imagines as she hops under a baobab tree and gallops up a hillside. The energetic pictures render her joy in running palpable. Nearing the schoolhouse, Ndito passes her tired brothers and enthusiastically enters the school's open doors.

Asch, Frank. *Just Like Daddy.* 1980. Hardcover: Simon & Schuster. Paperback: Aladdin. Ages 2–5.

A bear child, dressed like its father but not identified as a boy or girl, imitates all the father's actions throughout the morning as the family prepares to go fishing. "Just like Daddy," goes the refrain. But in the twist at the end of this simple story, the little bear catches a large fish, "Just like Mommy," while Daddy catches a tiny one. Most children are caught by surprise the first time they hear the end, and see the picture of the mother and child with big fish and the father with a tiny one.

Atkins, Jeannine. *Get Set! Swim!* **Illustrated by Hector Viveros Less. 1998. Hardcover: Lee & Low. Ages 4–8.**

It's time for Jessenia's first swim meet, the first year she is on the swim team. As she rides on the bus with her mother, brother, and teammates, Jessenia worries and gets impatient with her mother's reminiscences about Puerto Rico. Her opponents live in a wealthier neighborhood and practice at a bigger pool, but her coach reassures his team and tells them to concentrate on their own performance. In her first race, Jessenia gets distracted by an opponent, but she has a second chance later and makes the most of it. Her teammates' encouragement of one another and Jessenia's support from her mother and brother add a dimension to the competition, and although they lose this time, Jessenia's last words are, "We'll be back." It is an upbeat story about a young athlete and her first big competition.

Baker, Karen Lee. *Seneca.* **1997. Hardcover: Greenwillow. Ages 3–7.**

The narrator loves everything about her horse Seneca, whom she visits every day before and after school. No task daunts her: cleaning the stall, feeding him, fetching water, taking stones from his hooves, grooming him. She rides him through the woods, where she sometimes falls as the horse jumps over logs. She and Seneca like galloping best, as an exuberant double-page spread conveys. Expressive watercolors in fall tones show a jeans-clad girl and her large white horse enjoying their time together in a rural setting. The simple story, well told, is certain to appeal to young animal lovers.

Barber, Barbara E. *Allie's Basketball Dream.* **Illustrated by Darryl Ligasan. 1996. Hardcover: Lee & Low. Paperback: Lee & Low. Ages 4–8.**

Allie is thrilled when her father brings her a basketball one Friday evening. The next day, he walks her to the playground and leaves her to shoot baskets while he does errands. Allie, wearing a basketball jacket, a T-shirt, shorts, and sneakers, starts practicing but misses. Older boys nearby laugh at her, and her friend Keisha tells her, "My brother says basketball's a boy's game." Allie hears this refrain more than once, but argues that her cousin Gwen has won more than ten trophies on her high school basketball team. Finally, Allie convinces three of her friends to shoot baskets with her and when she swishes one through, even the older boys applaud. Computer-enhanced colored-pencil illustrations reinforce the sense of Allie's excitement and determination.

Barton, Byron. *I Want To Be an Astronaut.* **1988. Hardcover: Harper. Paperback: Trophy. Ages 2–5.**

Simple in text and pictures, this book takes the bold step of having the cover show a female proclaiming that she wants to be an astronaut. She then appears in many of the pictures, at a control panel, putting on a space suit, and sleeping in zero gravity. Her fellow crew members have short hair and are not distinguishably male or female. Not an outstanding contribution, but a nice inclusion of women that could lead to a discussion of Sally Ride and other female astronauts.

Bell, Lili. *The Sea Maidens of Japan.* **Illustrated by Erin McGonigle Brammer. 1996. Hardcover: Ideals. Ages 5–9.**

In Japan, women known as *ama* dive for the prized sea delicacy abalone. In this story, the narrator Kiyomi comes from a family of female abalone divers including her mother Okaasan, her grandmother, and great-grandmother. At first when Kiyomi learns to dive, holding her breath for over a minute, her mother ties a rope around the girl's waist for safety. But the day comes when Kiyomi is to dive on her own. Dressed all in white, with white cream to protect her face, she is deeply scared. Ultimately, Kiyomi overcomes the fear and her success makes her part of a group of women divers who surround her when she emerges. Soft-edged pictures add information and atmosphere.

Bemelmans, Ludwig. *Madeline's Rescue.* **1953. Hardcover: Viking. Paperback: Puffin. Ages 3–7.**

Madeline is certainly one of the best-known personalities in children's books. Many children know that "To the tiger in the zoo / Madeline just said, 'Pooh pooh!' " In the original book named after her, Madeline's main adventure is a case of appendicitis. In this sequel, she creates excitement when she walks along a bridge railing and plunges into the water below. When a female dog jumps in and rescues her, Madeline and her classmates take the dog back to their boarding school, name her Genevieve, and enjoy her many talents. The school board makes the dog leave, but she comes back and provides a puppy for each of the girls. Madeline's popularity has endured a long time along with her reputation as an unusually brave and feisty girl. The delightful pictures were honored with the Caldecott Medal.

Best, Cari. *Last Licks: A Spaldeen Story.* **Illustrated by Diane Palmisciano. 1999. Hardcover: DK Ink. Ages 5–9.**

Annie loves her Sky-High Super Pinkie, a fuzzy pink ball used for stickball, handball, punchball, and other urban street games. She can't resist throwing it in school, which gets her in trouble, and throwing it around at home. But best of all are Sundays, when her apartment house superintendent is gone, and all the kids gather to play. The Super has collected all the balls that have hit his window, and Annie's is one of the few left. Her excitement about the Sky-High Super Pinkie jumps off the pages as she bounces it everywhere, punches it, slaps it, jumps over it, claps it, and catches it. On Sunday she and her friends play all day. Just as their mothers call, Annie insists on her "last licks," one more chance to play, and throws her ball farther than ever before, drawing in a surprising reaction from the Super. A lively book in word, picture, and spirit about a dedicated ballplayer.

Blake, Quentin. *Mrs. Armitage and the Big Wave.* **1997. Hardcover: Harcourt. Ages 3–7.**

Hurray for the energetic Mrs. Armitage. As this zany story opens, she and her dog Breakspear set off to do some surfing. Her self-confidence shines forth as she strides along with her big yellow surfboard. She and Breakspear swim out to wait for the Big Wave, but as they wait, Mrs. Armitage repeatedly thinks of things they need, starting with her comment to Breakspear, "What we need here is something to keep a faithful dog afloat." She swims to the beach, where she gets a series of items, and then swims back to wait for the wave. They end up with a sun umbrella, food, a wind kite, and much more. Their equipment comes in surprisingly useful when Mrs. Armitage catches a big wave, rescues a little girl, and does a string of hotdog swerves and flips on her surfboard. Irresistible.

Blake, Robert J. *Akiak: A Tale from the Iditarod.* **1997. Hardcover: Philomel. Ages 4–8.**

The sled dog Akiak has run the 1,151 miles of the Iditarod many times. Now she is ten years old and it's her last chance to run and win. Mick, the woman who drives the sixteen-dog team, starts the race off with Akiak in the lead. Snow-filled paintings with heavy brush strokes depict the immense, empty landscape and the excited dogs running through it. But Akiak hurts her paw and Mick leaves her behind to be carried out by helicopter. Akiak escapes and runs after her team, finally catching up to them at a key juncture in the race. The rules say Akiak can't run after a break, but she can still help the team cross the finish line first.

Blegvad, Lenore. *Anna Banana and Me.* **Illustrated by Erik Blegvad. 1985. Hardcover: McElderry. Paperback: Aladdin. Ages 3–6.**

A boy narrates the adventures he has when he follows the lead of his spirited friend Anna Banana. She leads him into dark places, tells him goblin stories, and inspires him with her example of boldness. Overcoming his fear at the end, he proclaims, "I'm just as brave as Anna Banana!" In the appealing illustrations, Anna appears as a messy-haired girl in blue jeans, who incidentally wears glasses. She leaps down stairs, dances, swings, and runs—full of life. Another one of the welcome but rare stories in which a boy emulates a girl.

Borden, Louise. *The Little Ships: The Heroic Rescue at Dunkirk in World War II.* **Illustrated by Michael Foreman. 1997. Hardcover: McElderry. Ages 6–10.**

In this excellent picture-story book for older children, a fisherman and his daughter risk their lives to help evacuate Allied forces at Dunkirk in 1940. The girl has always helped her father on his fishing boat, the *Lucy*, so she volunteers to help him on this mission. They cross the English channel to the beach where a half million British and French soldiers wait, hoping to escape the Germans. Although the story is fictional, it is true that more than eight hundred little ships ferried soldiers from the beach to larger ships that took the soldiers back to England. Told through the eyes of a brave girl, this is a moving story of great courage, beautifully told in word and in sweeping, action-filled watercolors.

Brett, Jan. *Trouble with Trolls*. 1992. Hardcover: Putnam. Paperback: Puffin. Ages 3–8.

A hardy Scandanavian girl named Teva decides to visit her cousins on the other side of a mountain. She puts her skis on her back and starts to hike up to the top, but soon she and her dog, Tuffi, are accosted by trolls, who want to take Tuffi. Teva tricks the first troll into taking her mittens instead. She encounters several more trolls, including two females, and ends up giving away her hat, sweater, and boots. But she manages to get them back at the top of the mountain, claiming she needs them to fly with her skis. A double-page spread shows Teva holding her dog and swooping happily down the mountain on her skis, having escaped the angry trolls. The pictures alone develop a subplot in the trolls' underground home where they are lovingly preparing a bed for a dog, they hope. Detailed pictures with a needlepoint border show the young heroine completely at home on the mountainside and on skis.

Brown, Marc. *D.W. Rides Again*. 1993. Hardcover: Little, Brown. Paperback: Little, Brown. Ages 2–5.

D. W. is back, and in a hurry to master riding a bike. She's willing to practice a lot when necessary, and to her delight, her persistence pays off. There's nothing shy or shrinking about the irrepressible D. W., who keeps readers laughing with her sharp (but not too disrespectful) remarks. For example, when her overly worried father concentrates on D. W. instead of where he's going, he winds up in the creek. So, D. W. offers him her training wheels, which he has just agreed she no longer needs.

Brusca, María Cristina. *On the Pampas*. 1991. Hardcover: Henry Holt. Ages 4–8.

Told in first person, this short memoir recalls a girl's summer on her grandparents' ranch in Argentina. She spends most days with her younger cousin Susanita, who knows all about horses, cows, and the other ranch animals. Susanita, an accomplished rider, teaches the narrator how to groom horses and persuades her to swim in the creek with their horses, a scary exploit. The gaucho Salguero teaches the girls to use a lasso, and they persist despite setbacks. The girls run carefree on the pampas, as the plains are called, having adventures and enjoying their friendship. Just before the narrator has to return to the city, she brings in the horses by herself and herds them to the corral. There her grandmother is waiting to give her a gaucho belt decorated with silver coins, recognition of the girl's new ranching skills. The action-filled watercolors combine with the details of ranch life to convey a magical time in a girl's childhood. Outstanding.

Burton, Virginia Lee. *Katy and the Big Snow*. 1943. Hardcover: Houghton. Paperback: Houghton. Ages 3–7.

Katy, a bright red tractor, was "very big and very strong and she could do a lot of things." The appealing illustrations show her in the summer working as a bulldozer and pulling a steamroller out of a pond. In winter she is converted to a snowplow and proves her worth to the city during an enormous snowfall. She clears the way for all the workers: police, mail carriers, telephone repair trucks, firefighters, and doctors. Only when all have reached their destinations, thanks to Katy, does she stop to rest. The pictures have an old-fashioned feel, but they and the story hold up beautifully regardless of their age.

Bynum, Janie. *Altoona Baboona*. 1999. Hardcover: Harcourt. Ages 2–5.

A pleased baboon looks out from the basket of her hot-air balloon on the cover of this jaunty book. Altoona Baboona, whose story is told in rhyme, is bored one day in her home near the beach. What better solution than to take to the sky in a hot-air balloon? Color pictures show her flying to Cancun and Rangoon, and later picking up a lonely loon for company. Reading a book one day in the balloon, she hears music and follows it to find a saxophone-playing raccoon, who also joins her in the balloon. With her new friends, Altoona returns home, happy after her journey. One of the few female baboons in children's books, Altoona exudes self-reliance and a sense of adventure.

Caines, Jeannette. *Just Us Women*. Illustrated by Pat Cummings. 1982. Hardcover: Harper. Paperback: Trophy. Ages 3–7.

The narrator and her Aunt Martha set off on a road trip together, packing the food they like and planning to do whatever they feel like along the way. They walk in the rain in different states, shop at roadside markets, and thoroughly enjoy themselves together. A strong sense of independence pervades this short book, in which the illustrations show the characters as African-American. Great fun.

Caple, Kathy. *The Purse.* **1986. Paperback: Houghton. Ages 3–7.**

In this humorous story, an enterprising girl buys a purse to replace the metal Band-Aid box she had kept her money in. Once she has thrown away the box, she realizes how much she misses the clanging of coins against the metal, so she sets out to earn enough money to buy another box of Band-Aids. She clearly has the makings of a future businesswoman who pursues her goal diligently, carefully adds up her earnings, and openly enjoys the sound of money.

Carlson, Nancy. *Harriet and the Roller Coaster.* **1982. Hardcover: Carolrhoda. Paperback: First Avenue. Ages 4–7.**

When Harriet's class plans a trip to the amusement park, her classmate George describes the scary roller coaster and then suggests that Harriet will be too scared to ride it. She stoutly asserts she will try it, then worries all night and the next morning. But, predictably, Harriet finds the ride exciting, while it scares George and makes him sick. Harriet ends up riding the roller coaster all day; George spends the day sitting unhappily on a bench. The jacket cover shows a smiling Harriet in a roller-coaster car, so the end is no surprise. Unfortunately the only boy shown is a bully, but the message to girls is admirable, encouraging them to try activities that seem scary.

Carlson, Nancy. *Louanne Pig in Making the Team.* **1985. Hardcover: Carolrhoda. Paperback: Carolrhoda. Ages 3–7.**

In this sweet story, Louanne decides to try out for the cheerleading squad, while her smaller friend Arnie wants to try out for the football team. When they practice together, Arnie coaches Louanne on the split jump and cartwheels, which he does much better than she. Louanne, however, excels at football, unlike Arnie. They try to keep up each other's spirits, and even after Louanne fails to make the squad, she swallows her tears to show Arnie a few football tricks. When the coach sees her, he asks her to try out for the football team and she makes it. Inspired, Louanne drags a tearful Arnie over to the cheerleading tryouts. The final pictures show Louanne leading the football team to victory with Arnie leading the cheers. The tidy, colorful pictures work well for this story about characters who find the activity that suits them best, regardless of stereotypes.

Chandra, Deborah. *A is for Amos.* **Illustrated by Keiko Narahashi. 1999. Hardcover: FSG. Ages 2–6.**

A young girl, who appears on the title page in overalls and a cowboy hat, imagines that her hobbyhorse is the real thing and starts riding. Structured as an alphabet book, each page shows the two of them on their journey, with rhythmic lines such as "B for the bumpity bridge we cross. C for the clippety clop of his trot." The girl and her horse ride across pastures and fields, galloping and jumping fences. Going past pigs in a puddle for the letter "P," the girl gets off and walks with her pant legs rolled up. A rainstorm sends them trotting back home to the warm, dry barn. Lovely watercolors capture their day in the countryside and the many animals they meet on their energetic outing.

Cole, Babette. *Princess Smartypants.* **1987. Hardcover: Putnam. Paperback: Paper Star. Ages 3–7.**

The cover shows Princess Smartypants zooming along on a motorcycle with an alligator seated behind her, a clue to her personality. She enjoys doing just what she wants, living in a castle with a collection of outlandish pets. Despite her parents' wishes, she has no interest in getting married: "She enjoyed being a Ms." Inevitably, though, princes appear and she must ward them off with difficult tasks, such as feeding her pets or riding her wild horse. No one succeeds until the arrival of Prince Swashbuckle. In a series of zany pictures, he meets all her demands, to her dismay, for she is sincere in her wish to stay single. So, she must resort to a magic kiss, which sends the smug prince away as a gigantic warty toad. In the last picture, the princess lounges happily among her pets, knowing she has rid herself of suitors forever. A humorous counterbalance to the many stories that end with the princess getting married; instead, this one makes single life look very attractive.

Cole, Brock. *No More Baths.* **1980. Hardcover: FSG. Paperback: FSG. Ages 3–7.**

Jessie McWhistle, who likes to play in dirt and read with her shoes propped up on the wall, runs away from home one day to avoid taking a bath. She visits her animal friends Mrs. Chicken, Mrs. Cat, and Mrs. Pig one by one. When she complains about the bath, each friend offers her another way to get clean. Jessie joins Mrs. Chicken in frazzling in the sand but ends up itchy and dirtier than before. She tries to lick herself clean like Mrs. Cat with no success, then joins Mrs. Pig in the mud hole. Looking cranky the whole way, she marches back home to bathe. She ends up clean but still stubborn. When her mother suggests there are worse things than a bath, "aren't there?" Jessie's answer is "Nope." Deliciously messy pictures add to the fun.

Cole, Joanna. *The Magic School Bus in the Time of the Dinosaurs.* **Illustrated by Bruce Degen. 1994. Hardcover: Scholastic. Paperback: Scholastic. Ages 3–8.**

Ms. Frizzle, the most dynamic schoolteacher ever, drives a magic school bus on extraordinary field trips in a series of books. In this one, she takes her class back in time to study dinosaurs. As always, she is adventurous, knowledgeable, and brave. Her students describe her as loving science, lizards, test tubes, slime, mold, and experiments. She has clearly inspired her female students to be as excited about science as she is herself—the girls are every bit as involved as the boys. Although the series is aimed at a slightly older crowd than three-to-five-year-olds, the topic of dinosaurs will appeal to them as will the bright and cluttered pictures. Don't forget to look closely at Ms. Frizzle's amazing clothes! Other wonderful books include *The Magic School Bus at the Waterworks*, *The Magic School Bus Lost in the Solar System*, and more.

Cooney, Barbara. *Miss Rumphius*. 1982. Hardcover: Viking. Paperback: Puffin. Ages 3–8.

Miss Rumphius, who is great-aunt to the narrator, resolved as a girl to travel to faraway places, to live by the sea, and—on her grandfather's advice—to do something to make the world more beautiful. She accomplishes all three, fulfilling her last goal by spreading lupine seed on her piece of the world. One of the most beautiful and inspiring of children's books, which every child should know.

Corey, Shana. *You Forgot Your Skirt, Amelia Bloomer!* Illustrated by Chesley McLaren. 2000. Hardcover: Scholastic. Ages 4–9.

Dashing, richly colored illustrations set the tone for this story about Amelia Bloomer, who campaigned for women's voting rights in the mid-1800s. One day she had a visit from a friend who was wearing baggy pantaloons under a short skirt. In a time when women's clothing weighed as much as forty pounds and often constricted women's breathing, Bloomer wrote enthusiastically about the new clothing in the women's newspaper she edited. The outfit, which came to be called bloomers, freed girls—and women—to run and jump and climb. This charming account of how Bloomer changed women's fashions relies heavily on the pictures, with minimal but snappy text. Today's girls unfamiliar with this aspect of history will rejoice in their own freedom to wear shorts and pants.

Cousins, Lucy. *Maisy Drives*. 2001. Hardcover: Candlewick. Ages 2–4.

This board book, which is shaped like a car, shows the popular mouse Maisy at the wheel of a series of vehicles. The paintings, which use rich colors in strong black outlines, begin with Maisy driving a car. "Maisy drives a train. Toot, toot!" reads the first page where Maisy waves from an old-fashioned green and red steam engine. She goes on to drive a tractor, fire engine, and bus, as well as pilot a plane and ride her tricycle. Each simple illustration includes animals other than Maisy as passengers or onlookers. The white mouse glows with pride and pleasure in each vehicle in this jaunty book that young children will love.

Cowen-Fletcher, Jane. *Mama Zooms*. 1993. Hardcover: Scholastic. Paperback: Scholastic. Ages 2–5.

In this very brief story, an attractive, smiling mother zooms a young boy around on her "zooming machine." Told from the child's perspective, the story portrays the mother as adventurous and fun-loving. It is only near the end that the audience realizes the zooming machine is a wheelchair. The mother with her "very strong arms" gives her child love and excitement, all the while erasing stereotypes about the disabled.

Crew, Gary. *Bright Star.* **Illustrated by Anne Spudvilas. 1997. Hardcover: Kane/Miller. Ages 5–9.**

In 1861, amateur Australian astronomer John Tebbett discovered a great comet, which became visible even in the day. In 1881, he discovered another one. This fictional story set in his hometown of Windsor, Australia, introduces a girl named Alicia who lives near Tebbett. She is a hard-working farm girl who excels in school, and who can't help but notice how much more freedom boys and men have. When John Tebbett visits the school to talk about comets, he is impressed with Alicia's quick mind and he invites her to come to his observatory. Although her father pays no attention, Alicia's mother sees to it that the girl seizes the opportunity. Once there, Alicia peers through the huge telescope at the moon, stars, and a comet, and talks to Tebbett about space. In the end, it's clear she will be back to use the telescope again. Glowing, impressionistic paintings add details to the setting and a sense of wonder about the night sky.

Crowley, Michael. *Shack and Back.* **Illustrated by Abby Carter. 1993. Hardcover: Little, Brown. Ages 4–8.**

The Spurwink Gang of four girls and three boys breaks up the day "Crater" Creighton says, "Cooking is for sissy-girls." The girls, who had suggested making minipizzas, stalk off in disgust. The other two boys aren't too pleased with Crater, especially when the Broad Cove Bullies challenge them to a bike race. The best Spurwink racer is one of the girls, T-Ball, so the boys go to plead with her to join them again. Crater even grumbles that he's sorry, but the girls, who are busy swinging, won't commit themselves to the race. In the end, the gang is reunited, the fierce T-Ball has shown how unfounded Crater's remark was, and Crater has reluctantly recognized his mistake. These scruffy children in their jeans, T-shirts, and bike helmets seem believable, as does their argument.

Davol, Marguerite W. *The Loudest, Fastest, Best Drummer in Kansas*. Illustrated by Cat Bowman Smith. 2000. Hardcover: Orchard. Ages 3–8.

Maggie comes out of the womb drumming and never quits, perhaps because a parade was going by the hospital when she was born. She drums on her crib and, after she breaks it, on the floor. She drums on steps, chairs, pans, and finally on the drum her parents give her. When she is too noisy for the house, she drums outside. Maggie's drumming has its uses, such as scaring off a plague of killer wasps. But the little town of Serena isn't prepared for the noise, and the mayor outlaws drumming. After a period of uncanny silence, the town needs Maggie's drums once again when a new danger arrives. Lively illustrations create a small town with an old-fashioned look and a girl who defies all stereotypes about quiet, meek females and follows her noisy dream.

de Paola, Tomie. *Strega Nona*. 1975. Hardcover: Simon & Schuster. Paperback: Aladdin. Ages 4–8.

This tale set in Italy tells of Strega Nona, which means "Grandma Witch," an old woman whom the town relies upon for cures for their ills and troubles. When she hires a young man, Big Anthony, to do domestic tasks for her, he overhears her speak to her magic pot to produce a meal. But when Strega Nona leaves one day and Big Anthony tries the magic words, he fills the whole town with pasta because he doesn't know the words that will stop the pot. Strega Nona returns and saves the day, then metes out due punishment: Big Anthony must eat up all the pasta. What a woman: wise, clever, and just. A Caldecott Honor Book.

Dodds, Dayle Ann. *Sing, Sophie!* Illustrated by Rosanne Litzinger. 1997. Paperback: Candlewick. Ages 2–7.

"I bumped my knee, I scratched my nose, / I lost my shoe, I tore my clothes. / Whenever trouble passes by, / I don't worry, I don't cry. / 'Cause I'm a cowgirl, don't you see? / Yippee-ky-yuu! Yippee-ky-yee!" Sophie loves to sing the crazy songs she makes up, like this one. She likes to sing them loud, strumming her guitar. But one day, no matter where she goes to sing, someone in her family asks her to sing somewhere else. With a huge cowboy hat and red cowboy boots, she keeps moving around the farm, singing a different, funny song at each stop. Clever, cartoonlike pictures show her followed by a cat that changes size, some chickens, and a few other creatures. Only when Sophie quiets the screaming baby with a catchy song does her family finally recognize her talent.

Dorros, Arthur. *Abuela.* Illustrated by Elisa Kleven. 1991. Hardcover: Dutton. Paperback: Puffin. Ages 3–7.

A girl imagines that she and Abuela, her grandmother, fly above New York City together one day. In this splendid trip, they visit the Statue of Liberty, spot friends, and race sailboats. Abuela, with her billowing star-studded skirt, revels in the flying as much as her granddaughter does because she is a woman who "likes adventures." The warmth of the relationship, the bustling beauty of the city, and the joyful romp through the air are perfectly conveyed by extraordinarily vibrant pictures. The simple text weaves in Spanish words and phrases, defined in a glossary at the back. In the sequel *Isla,* the two take another flying trip, this one over the Caribbean island where Abuela grew up.

Duke, Kate. *Archaeologists Dig for Clues*. 1997. Hardcover: Harper. Paperback: Harper. Ages 5–9.

Two boys and a girl accompany an archaeologist to her local dig, where they learn about archaeology. At first, the children are disappointed that the dig looks like a hole in the ground. But as the day goes on, they get drawn into the digging process and especially the discovery of an archaic awl, a needle without a hole that was used for sewing. Cheerful pictures along with diagrams and sidebars deliver plenty of interesting information. Besides the archaeologist, a number of other women are working on the dig and at the archaeology lab. The visiting girl plays an active role, digging in the dirt, lifting buckets, and making scientific notes. One of the high-quality "Let's-Read-and-Find-Out Science" series, this shows females competent and at home in a hands-on scientific setting.

Erdrich, Louise. *Grandmother's Pigeon*. Illustrated by Jim LaMarche. 1996. Paperback: Hyperion. Ages 4–8.

A magical grandmother and a gray-haired ornithologist provide two strong female role models for a girl and her brother. The grandmother ends a visit to the children by riding off on the back of a porpoise, leaving behind her a nest of eggs. The three eggs hatch, and the children feed the newborn pigeons with an eye-dropper. When their mother cannot identify the birds, she calls in the ornithologist, who is shocked to find they are passenger pigeons, which were thought to be extinct. Now the children need to decide if they will release the birds to the wild or turn them over to scientists to study. Expansive, light-filled illustrations add mystery and charm to the tale.

Ernst, Lisa Campbell. *Bubba and Trixie.* **1997. Hardcover: Simon & Schuster. Paperback: Aladdin. Ages 3–7.**

Bubba, a shy, nervous caterpillar, learns to enjoy life with the help of Trixie, a brisk, outgoing ladybug. Undeterred by a broken wing that means she can't fly, Trixie knows how to have a good time in the garden and urges Bubba to join her. They zip down water slides on iris leaves and play hide-and-seek among the snapdragons, shown in large-scale pictures. Trixie's greatest wish is to touch the stars, while Bubba just hopes that nothing ever changes. Bubba, however, cannot avoid changing into a butterfly, although for a while he thinks he has prevented it. His change, which he grows to like, allows Trixie to get her wish. While sentimental in places, the story offers a reassuring note to shy children who dread change, and reverses stereotypes about adventurous males and shy females.

Falconer, Ian. *Olivia.* **2000. Hardcover: Atheneum. Ages 3–8.**

The young pig Olivia has star quality, as does this Caldecott Honor Book that introduces her with such aplomb. Olivia's priceless facial expressions and body language perfectly convey her energy and strong-mindedness as she refuses to nap, insists on five books at bedtime, and generally wears out her parents. Whether at the beach, art museum, or home trying on seventeen pieces of clothing before choosing, Olivia bursts with personality. "She is good at lots of things," it says, followed by pictures of her hammering, using a yo-yo, kicking a ball, baking, and jumping rope. A remarkable debut about an unforgettable pig, followed by *Olivia Saves the Circus.*

Falwell, Cathryn. *Word Wizard*. 1998. Hardcover: Clarion. Ages 3–8.

Cheerful collage artwork introduces an energetic girl named Anna who loves words. Playing with her cereal letters one morning, she discovers the pleasures of anagrams, using the same letters to form different words. She starts with "dawn" and turns it into "wand." Donning a wizard's hat and taking her spoon as a magic wand, she proceeds to change other words. She finds a practical outlet for her fun when a younger boy named Zack needs help finding his way back home. Anna transforms the "ocean" of his tears into a "canoe," then the "shore" into a "horse," and takes him home again, defeating a beast on the way. A note at the end gives more suggestions for playing with words. A colorful and engaging celebration of words with a confident girl in charge of the magic.

Fleischman, Paul. *Lost!: A Story in String*. Illustrated by C. B. Mordan. 2000. Hardcover: Henry Holt. Ages 4–9.

A blackout from a lightning storm leaves a grandmother and granddaughter in the dark, with no television, VCR, or computer for entertainment, to the girl's distress. The grandmother, though, knows how to tell a good story and even illustrate it with string figures she makes with yarn. The story concerns another girl, who lived in the mountains with few worldly goods. But that girl also knew how to make string figures, starting with a barn gate, followed by a dog's head to show the stray dog that arrived one day. As the story progresses, the girl goes out into the woods to look for her dog and gets caught in a snowstorm. She draws on her resourcefulness to survive a night in the winter wilderness, scavenges for food, and fashions snowshoes for walking home. On each page, hands shape string into different pictures of elements in the story, while dramatic black-and-white pictures show the girl and her adventure. A long appendix tells more about string figures and shows how to form them. An intriguing book about a self-reliant girl.

Fleming, Candace. *When Agnes Caws*. Illustrated by Giselle Potter. 1999. Hardcover: Atheneum. Ages 4–9.

In this tongue-in-cheek tale, eight-year-old Agnes and her mother, Professor Octavia Peregrine, an ornithologist, live a life steeped in birds. Agnes not only knows a lot about them, she also has an uncanny ability to imitate birdcalls. The World Bird Society selects Agnes and her mother to travel to the Himalayas to find the rare pink-headed duck. Thanks to Agnes's birdcalling, they succeed. But the villainous bird-hunter Colonel Edwin Pittsnap, who kills and mounts birds, wants a dead pink-headed duck for his collection. He has nearly ruined their expedition when Agnes defeats him with her quick wits and saves the day. The fresh illustrations provide a sense of time and place, and add visual humor about birds. Full of bird lore and bird calls, this is an entertaining story about a clever mother–daughter team.

Franklin, Kristine. *Iguana Beach*. Illustrated by Lori Lohstoeter. 1997. Hardcover: Crown. Ages 3–7.

Reina begs to go to the beach with her cousins and her uncle, Tío Benito. Reina promises her doubtful mother that she will stay away from the waves. Off they go in a red pick-up truck, with the boys and Reina in the back. After a hot trip, the tropical sea and its big waves, which Reina is seeing for the first time, look irresistible. She tries to follow her cousins into the water, but Tío Benito catches her and makes her sit with him as he reads the newspaper. She plays by herself and looks at the crabs, iguanas, and monkeys nearby. Then she takes off down the beach at a run, with her cousins and uncle behind her. They end up at a lagoon with no waves. Since Reina said she'd stay out of the waves, not out of the water, Tío Benito joins her and the boys in the lagoon. Thick brush strokes of rich colors add texture to this story about a persistent young swimmer.

Friedman, Aileen. *The King's Commissioners.* **Illustrated by Susan Guevara. 1994. Hardcover: Scholastic. Ages 3–7.**

This humorous tale with its vivid illustrations concerns a king who is confused. He has appointed so many royal commissioners, such as the Commissioner for Things That Go Bump in the Night, that he can't keep track of them. With the help of his two advisors, he tries to count them as they file into the throne room. Interrupted by his jaunty red-haired daughter, the king loses track and then cannot understand his advisors' tallies. One has counted by twos, the other by fives. So his daughter has the commissioners line up in rows of ten, then explains how the same results can be reached by twos or fives. Her confused father finally understands, thanks to the princess. A long note for adults discusses how children learn mathematics, and how to use the book with them. A highly palatable way to reinforce counting skills, complete with funny pictures and a smart princess.

Gardella, Tricia. *Blackberry Booties.* **Illustrated by Glo Coalson. 2000. Hardcover: Orchard. Ages 4–8.**

A girl learns the value of bartering in this attractive picture-story book. Mikki Jo needs a gift to give her baby cousin, and she wants it to be special. Coming home with her dog from picking blackberries, Mikki Jo spots a neighbor, Mrs. Lozano, with wool she has just sheared from one of her sheep. Mikki Jo trades a pail of blackberries for the wool, but can't make anything out of it. Luckily, she sees another neighbor spinning yarn from wool and barters blackberries to have her wool spun. Finally, Mikki Jo gives a third neighbor blackberries as payment for knitting baby booties out of the yarn. All the while, Mikki Jo dashes around her rural neighborhood in shorts, T-shirt, sneakers, and a baseball cap, bargaining to reach her goal. A final scene shows the creative addition she makes to the booties themselves.

Gardella, Tricia. *Casey's New Hat*. Illustrated by Margot Apple. 1997. Hardcover: Houghton. Ages 3–8.

Casey, who appears on the book cover riding a rearing horse, is a dedicated cowgirl. She wears cowboy boots, and her room is full of toy horses. So it's a problem when she discovers that her cowboy hat is getting too small. She and her cowboy father go to town to find her a new hat, but nothing suits her. The people they encounter, men and women, take Casey's quest seriously, but it isn't until she hops into a truck to go feed horses with her grandfather that she finds the perfect hat—Grandpa's crumpled, old, dusty cowboy hat. In the final picture, Casey and her grandfather perch on the back of his pickup truck, each happy in a cowboy hat. Appealing colored-pencil illustrations show an energetic girl who knows what she wants and who feels completely at home on a ranch.

Garner, Alan. *The Well of the Wind*. Illustrated by Hervé Blondon. 1998. Hardcover: DK Ink. Ages 4–8.

In this original fairy tale, a fisherman finds a floating crystal box with a girl and boy inside. He takes them in, but dies, leaving them on their own. One day a witch comes and tells them about a magical silver spring. Embarking on three magical tasks, the boy brings home an endless jug of water, then gets acorns of gold. But when he sets out for the magical Well of the Wind, he doesn't return, so his sister sets out after him. Whistling all the way, she makes all the right choices, even when they are dangerous, and rescues her brother. Her final idea leads them to their long-lost parents and a happy ending. Poetic language with rhythmic refrains is matched by evocative illustrations and a graceful book design.

Gelman, Rita Golden, reteller. *Queen Esther Saves Her People*. Illustrated by Frané Lessac. 1998. Hardcover: Scholastic. Ages 6–10.

Richly colored folk art dominates this retelling of the biblical story of Queen Esther, who risked her life to save her people. Palm and orange trees, minarets, archways, detailed fabrics, and elaborate decorations create an exotic Persian setting. When the vain, temperamental King Ahasuerus banishes a wife who disobeyed him, his courtiers gather the most beautiful women in the empire as potential wives. A Jewish woman named Esther catches his fancy and becomes his wife. When Ahasuerus's advisor plans to put the Jews to death, Esther risks her own life and the king's anger to save her fellow Jews. The Jewish people still celebrate Esther's heroic act on the holiday of Purim.

Greenfield, Eloise. *Africa Dream*. Illustrated by Carole Byard. 1977. Hardcover: Harper. Paperback: Trophy. Ages 3–7.

"I went all the way to Africa / In a dream one night," begins this poetic book about an African-American girl and her imaginary journey. Soft-edged, timeless black-and-white drawings create a magical atmosphere as she visits cities and villages, dances and sings. A particularly warm picture shows her meeting her grandfather, who forms a circle for her with his long arms. More poetry than story, but poetry about a brave girl on an adventure.

Grimes, Nikki. *Meet Danitra Brown*. Illustrated by Floyd Cooper. 1994. Hardcover: Lothrop. Paperback: Mulberry. Ages 6–10.

This poetry collection about a "splendiferous" girl named Danitra Brown looks like a picture-story book, with one poem and a glorious picture on each double-page spread. An admiring friend of Danitra Brown's supplies the voice for each poem, and appears with Danitra in the pictures. The two jump rope and bicycle together, share problems and pleasures. They both prefer wearing jeans to wearing dresses, and Danitra likes to wear purple because it's the color that queens wear in Timbuktu. Maybe, says her friend, Danitra is a princess. Aiming high, Danitra plans to win the Nobel Prize someday for her writing. An outstanding combination of art and poetry about two splendid African-American girls.

Grossman, Bill. *My Little Sister Ate One Hare*. Illustrated by Kevin Hawkes. 1996. Hardcover: Crown. Paperback: Random House. Ages 3–8.

What a girl! "My little sister ate one hare. We thought she'd throw up then and there," opens this riotously funny counting book. As the book moves from one to ten, the narrator's sister, a small girl with a large mouth, eats increasingly disgusting foods, mostly rodents, reptiles, and insects. In each of the outrageous scenes, she is in a different costume: a pirate eating mice from her sword, a vampire eating bats, a snake charmer eating snakes. Lurid colors and exaggerated features perfectly suit the words. She has no trouble eating all of the creatures—but a plate of peas defeats her, leading to a surprise ending and a great final picture. Here is a girl who not only breaks stereotypes about girls and squirmy creatures, she actually welcomes the little critters. A hilarious book that might teach children to count if they can stop laughing long enough.

Haas, Jessie. *Hurry!* Illustrated by Joseph A. Smith. 2000. Hardcover: Greenwillow. Ages 4–8.

The picture on the cover of this book shows a girl driving a load of hay, the reins in her hands attached to two huge workhorses. On top of the hay, a woman and man are working with pitchforks in their hands. Nora and her grandparents have been waiting for just the right time to harvest the hay. On the first page, Nora drives the team of horses harnessed to the hay tender, a machine that turns the grass over to dry. Then she and her grandfather wait and worry. The grandfather sends Nora out to check the hay and she makes the decision that it's ready. Gram gets the pitchforks and they are off, determined to beat the rain clouds gathering overhead. Nora helps with everything, and the three of them succeed in getting the load of hay to the barn just in time. A simple, satisfying story that takes it for granted that women and girls play key roles on a farm.

Hallensleben, Georg. *Pauline*. 1999. Hardcover: FSG. Ages 3–8.

The young weasel Pauline lives with her parents in a tall tree where they look down at the jungle and its animals around them. One day Pauline is old enough to go down to the jungle by herself, where she discovers that the animals that looked small from a distance are bigger than she is. She and an elephant named Rabusius become friends, despite their size difference. But one day hunters appear and trap Rabusius in a net. Hearing that they're going to put the elephant in a truck, Pauline quickly devises a plan and carries it out with help from her parents. Her scheme scares the hunters and saves her friend, to the joy of all the other animals. The large illustrations with thickly laid paint and luscious colors have a childlike air that suits this jungle story.

Hamanaka, Sheila. *I Look Like a Girl*. 1999. Hardcover: Morrow. Ages 3–8.

Richly colored oil paintings set the scene on the title page with three girls jumping rope: one black girl, one white, and one with Asian features. On the next page, three girls are walking along the top of a fence. "I look like a girl," reads the book's first line, with an illustration that shows a girl holding a romantic fairy tale but gazing into the distance. She's thinking that she's really a tiger, and her thoughts appear in a striking double-page spread of a leaping tiger. The rest of the book features different girls in action and the animals they resemble. "Throw out those glass slippers" advises the ending, inviting girls to be much more than "sugar and spice." An inspiring message told in simple words and vivid illustrations.

Hayes, Sarah. *Lucy Anna and the Finders*. 2000. Hardcover: Candlewick. Ages 2–6.

Black outlines filled with bright colors show the Finders, cuddly striped monsters who steal a little red horse and some toys from Lucy Anna. They come to her cottage, take things, and then flee back to the woods. Furious, Lucy Anna puts on her backpack and marches off to the woods to get back her possessions. But when she catches up with the Finders, she sees that they are much bigger than she is. She uses her wits to distract them while she plans her escape. After a few tricks, she fools them into playing hide-and-seek, and while they hide, she hops on her red horse and heads for home. Lucy

Anna, who wears hefty red sneakers, has a look of determination on her face that matches her actions in this simple story.

Hearne, Betsy. *Seven Brave Women*. Illustrated by Bethanne Andersen. 1997. Hardcover: Greenwillow. Ages 7–11.

To show that history is more than men fighting in wars, this slim, illustrated book looks at seven women from the time of the Revolutionary War until now. "My great-great-great-grandmother did great things," opens the first, two-page chapter. The first brave woman described crossed mountains and an ocean to come to this country. Each generation has her own contribution, through farming, homemaking, raising children, teaching, painting, and more. One great-grandmother became a doctor who traveled to India to provide medical care to women. Each description gives lively details about the things each woman did. Large, flowing paintings show each woman in action. A welcome approach to history for younger children, which puts women solidly in the picture.

Hendrick, Mary Jean. *If Anything Ever Goes Wrong at the Zoo*. Illustrated by Jane Dyer. 1993. Hardcover: Harcourt. Paperback: Harcourt. Ages 3–6.

Leslie and her apparently single mother go to the zoo each Saturday. There Leslie tells all the zoo workers she sees that if "anything ever goes wrong at the zoo," they should send the animals to her house. Sure enough, one night when the zoo floods, the workers bring the animals to Leslie's house. The monkeys perch on the swing set, the alligator stretches out in a bathtub full of water. The elephant keeper Joanna drives up in a huge truck with three elephants, who go into the garage. When the zookeepers come the next day to retrieve the animals, women are shown handling the lion and the goats. The presence of so many women working with the animals is gratifying, as is the tolerant spirit of Leslie's mother as she asks her daughter to check with her first the next time she asks friends home.

Henkes, Kevin. *Chester's Way*. 1988. Hardcover: Green-willow. Paperback: Puffin. Ages 3–7.

One of the best books in this section, this story opens by introducing Chester and Wilson, two rigid but likable mice who are best friends. Then the flamboyant Lilly moves into the neighborhood. She likes to wear Band-Aids all over herself to look brave; she always carries a loaded squirt gun. The two friends ignore Lilly until one day she saves them from some bullies, thanks to one of her many disguises. From then on the three are great friends and Lilly puts a new sparkle into their safe but dull routines. She is the daring and inventive one of the threesome, the leader in their adventures, and one of the liveliest picture-book characters ever, male or female.

Henkes, Kevin. *Julius, The Baby of the World*. 1990. Hardcover: Greenwillow. Paperback: Mulberry. Ages 4–8.

The mouse girl Lilly from *Chester's Way* is back and as incorrigible as ever. Witness the dust jacket: Lilly, wearing her Groucho Marx disguise along with red cowboy boots, is leaning over her brother's crib trying to scare the peaceful baby. Some adults will find Lilly too negative about poor Julius, "the germ of the world" as she calls him. But others will howl at her distinctive voice as she yells out to a pregnant woman, "You will live to regret that bump under your dress." In the end she charges to the defense of her brother when someone else insults him—and the last picture shows both of them in Groucho glasses. An outstanding combination of great story and illustrations. In a third delightful book, *Lilly's Purple Plastic*

Purse, Lilly can hardly contain her excitement about school, her teacher Mr. Slinger, and her new plastic purple purse.

Henkes, Kevin. *Sheila Rae, the Brave*. 1987. Hardcover: Greenwillow. Paperback: Puffin. Ages 3–7.

Sheila Rae is the idol of her younger sister Louise. When Sheila Rae eats fruit cocktail, she makes believe the cherries are the "eyes of dead bears" and eats five at a time. She giggles at the principal and steps on every crack on the sidewalk. But even Sheila Rae has her weaknesses and one of them emerges when she walks home from school a new way and gets lost. Her normal refrain of "I am brave, I am fearless" fails to raise her spirits. Luckily the more timid Louise has secretly followed her and knows exactly how to get home. Louise leads the way, stepping on every crack herself, and when they get home she has the joy of Sheila Rae's praise, "Louise, you are brave. You are fearless." As if such an outstanding plot weren't enough, charming pictures add detail and humor to the story.

Hest, Amy. *When Jessie Came Across the Sea*. Illustrated by P. J. Lynch. 1997. Hardcover: Candlewick. Ages 5–8.

Children often get the impression that until recently men worked for pay and women didn't. In this story of a thirteen-year-old Jewish immigrant, three generations of women earn their living. Jessie's grandmother in the old country sews lace, saves her money, and teaches her orphaned granddaughter to sew. Jessie has an unexpected chance to immigrate to the United States, where she works for her rabbi's sister in her dress shop. Jessie goes to school but also saves money to bring her grandmother to New York. After three years have passed, Jessie gets engaged to a young man she met on the ship. The unusually large illustrations vary between dramatic close-ups of faces and expansive vistas of the village, the ocean, and New York City.

Hoban, Russell. A *Birthday for Frances*. Illustrated by Lillian Hoban. 1968. Hardcover: Harper. Paperback: Trophy. Ages 3–7.

The intrepid Frances resents all the fuss over her little sister Gloria's birthday, but then she herself makes a fuss because she hasn't bought Gloria a present. When she does buy her a Chompo candy bar, she finds it difficult not to eat it or at least squeeze it a lot. In the end, Frances rises above most of the temptation and gives Gloria the whole bar. Frances is very funny, making up little songs and spelling out words incorrectly but expecting her parents to recognize them. Fun for adults and children, this is one in a series of books about Frances and her escapades.

Hoffman, Mary. *Amazing Grace*. Illustrated by Caroline Binch. 1991. Hardcover: Dial. Ages 3–8.

The jacket introduces the reader to the exuberant Grace, grinning on the front and dancing on the back. She is a girl who loves playacting as Joan of Arc, Anansi the Spider, or Aladdin. Charming watercolors also show her as an explorer, a warrior, a pirate, and a doctor. But when her classmates tell her she cannot be Peter Pan in the school play because she is a girl and because she is black, Grace needs all the encouragement her mother and grandmother can give her. She regains her self-confidence when her grandmother takes her to see a talented black ballerina. "I can be anything I want," the girl thinks, and goes on to be a stunning Peter Pan. An outstanding story followed by *Boundless Grace* and *Starring Grace*.

Hopkinson, Deborah. *A Band of Angels: A Story Inspired by the Jubilee Singers.* **Illustrated by Raúl Colón. 1999. Hardcover: Atheneum. Ages 6–10.**

Extraordinary textured illustrations in browns and golds set a warm mood for this story based on the Jubilee Singers. As a narrative device, an aunt is telling her young niece about the girl's great-great-grandmother Ella, starting with the words, "Grandma Ella was born into slavery, but no one could chain her voice." The character Ella, inspired by the real Jubilee Singer pianist Ella Sheppard Moore, seeks an education after the Civil War at Fisk School, later to be Fisk University. When this school for former slaves runs low on money, Ella and several other music students travel with a music professor around the country to raise money through their concerts. This story focuses on the chorus's switch from singing mainly popular songs to singing spirituals. The dedication of the students and the excitement of their success comes across strongly in this inspiring historical tale of African-American courage.

Hopkinson, Deborah. *Birdie's Lighthouse.* **Illustrated by Kimberly Bulcken Root. 1997. Hardcover: Atheneum. Paperback: Aladdin. Ages 4–9.**

Told in diary form, this tall, slim picture-story book encapsulates the year 1855 in the life of a girl named Birdie Holland. Birdie's father has given up his dangerous work as a fisherman to become a lighthouse keeper on an island in Maine. Life is bleak and isolated so far from the mainland, but the work is important. When Birdie's brother Nate leaves to become a fisherman, Birdie learns to assist her father in keeping the lights going. Then one stormy night when her father is sick, Birdie alone keeps the lights burning and unknowingly saves her brother's life. The pen-and-ink and watercolor illustrations add darkness and danger to this fictional tale of courage that echoes real tales about girls and women who kept lights burning in lighthouses.

Hopkinson, Deborah. *Maria's Comet*. Illustrated by Deborah Lanino. 1999. Hardcover: Atheneum. Ages 5–9.

Maria Mitchell, America's first female astronomer, discovered a comet when she was nineteen, and later taught at Vassar College. In this picture-story book based loosely on her childhood, the young girl's father is an astronomer who looks through a telescope on the roof of their house on Nantucket Island. The poetic text describes what he sees, including comets, while the girl works down below sweeping and tending the fire for their large family. She plays in the attic with her brother Andrew, where she reads her favorite stories about early astronomers like Copernicus and Galileo. When Andrew runs away to sea, Maria finds the courage to follow her father to the roof to learn about the heavens. An author's note tells more about Maria Mitchell and astronomy.

Hopkinson, Deborah. *Sweet Clara and the Freedom Quilt*. Illustrated by James E. Ransome. 1993. Hardcover: Knopf. Paperback: Random House. Ages 5–8.

Striking paintings in rich colors illustrate this story of a girl who escapes slavery through her own ingenuity and daring. Taken from her mother to another plantation, Clara finds a friend in fellow slave Rachel who treats her like a daughter. Rachel, worried that fieldwork will wear Clara out, teaches her to sew and gets her a job in the Big House as a seamstress. From her chair in the sewing room Clara overhears bits of information about the layout of the plantation and the countryside around it, and stories about the Underground Railroad. In a stroke of brilliance, she thinks of fashioning a quilt that will serve as a map, and she adds landmarks and roads as she hears about them. Not only does it enable her to escape, rescue her family, and follow the North Star to Canada, but the map serves as an aid to others around the plantation. An inspirational story about a resourceful girl and the others who take risks to help her.

Howard, Elizabeth Fitzgerald. *Virgie Goes to School with Us Boys*. **Illustrated by E. B. Lewis. 2000. Hardcover: Simon & Schuster. Ages 5–9.**

This engaging story, inspired by the author's great aunt and five great uncles, takes place in Tennessee during the Reconstruction. A girl named Virgie wants to go to the school that Quakers have opened for blacks after the end of slavery. Her older brothers, who spend each week away from home at the school, warn her that she's too young and, as one of them says, "Girls don't need school." But the narrator, C. C., stands up for her. Virgie persists until her parents say she, too, can go. On the seven-mile trek, Virgie proves she is strong enough to walk the long way. Once at school, she shows she is brave enough to spend the week away from home. Glowing watercolors show the children on their journey and in a classroom where Virgie takes up a quill to "learn to be free."

Isadora, Rachel. *Sophie Skates*. **1999. Hardcover: Putnam. Paperback: Puffin. Ages 3–8.**

Sophie has loved to figure skate since she was three, when she started skating on the pond near her house. Now eight years old, Sophie dreams of becoming a professional ice skater, watches skating on television, and attends ice shows when she can. She takes lessons five mornings a week at five A.M. and three afternoons after school. A double-page spread shows her clothing and equipment, then the book shows different children performing a variety of moves and jumps on the ice. One section compares movements from ballet, which Sophie also studies, with movements in skating. The illustrations incorporate a lot of information and show many skating costumes. No one can doubt the seriousness of this girl in trying to reach her long-term goal.

Jeram, Anita. *Daisy Dare*. 1995. Paperback: Candlewick. Ages 2–5.

The young mouse Daisy, dressed in overalls and polka-dot shirt, does things that her three friends—two boys and Contrary Mary—don't dare to do. She climbs trees to get apples, walks along a high wall, and eats a worm. On a dare she takes a bell off the collar of a huge cat. After a scary moment, she escapes into the house with her friends, who sing her praises. Daisy, hoisted on their shoulders, beams with pride and doesn't mind admitting she is scared sometimes. The short text, small format, and jaunty little mice will appeal to young children.

Johnson, Angela. *The Girl Who Wore Snakes*. Illustrated by James E. Ransome. 1993. Hardcover: Orchard. Ages 3–7.

When a zookeeper visits Ali's class with a snake, Ali immediately volunteers to hold it. In fact, she wears it all day long, to the consternation of some of her classmates. Radiant paintings show a smiling African-American girl who revels in her role as "the girl who wore the snake." Soon she buys her own snakes and wears them at home. Her parents, friends, and teacher tolerate her new pleasure but don't share it. Then one day she discovers that one of her aunts also understands the attraction of snakes. The story aptly contradicts stereotypes about girls being afraid of snakes, while the illustrations make the snakes Ali loves look beautiful.

Keats, Ezra Jack. *Maggie and the Pirate*. **1979. Hardcover: Four Winds. Paperback: Scholastic. Ages 4–8.**

Maggie, who lives on a river and paddles wherever she goes, treasures her cricket Niki and the house her father made for him. But then Niki is stolen by someone who leaves a note, "The pirate was here." Maggie leads her two faithful friends, a boy and a girl, through the darkening evening in search of the thief. When she finds him, she launches herself at the pirate— an unhappy boy—"trying with all her strength" to rescue Niki. Though the cricket dies, the book ends on a peaceful note. Terrific pictures show Maggie as a wild-haired, expressive heroine who is fearless in her search for her pet.

Keller, Holly. *Geraldine's Blanket*. **1984. Hardcover: Green-willow. Paperback: Mulberry. Ages 2–5.**

Geraldine has no intention of giving up her blanket, no matter what her parents want. When her exasperated mother tells her that the frayed blanket looks silly, Geraldine replies, "Then don't look at me." But when she receives a new doll meant to replace the blanket, Geraldine supplies her own solution: she makes the blanket into a dress for the doll. This very simple story creates a strong female character, a plot that engages young children, and a clever resolution. A gem, this is the first in a series about strong-minded Geraldine.

Ketteman, Helen. *Heat Wave*. **Illustrated by Scott Goto. 1998. Paperback: Walker. Ages 4–9.**

"My big brother, Hank, used to tease me that girls couldn't be farmers," opens this tall tale about a girl who changes her brother's mind on the day that the Heat Wave hits. The Heat Wave roasts geese in midair and pops the corn while it's still on the stalk. Luckily, the narrator has a series of clever ideas to combat the damage. On her suggestion, the family takes the popcorn, drenches it in the butter that the hot, jumpy cows give instead of milk, and sells it in town at the drive-in movies. That's just the first of her successful schemes. The large, wildly exaggerated paintings, which show a girl wearing overalls and a baseball cap, suit the story to a tee.

Kimmel, Eric A. *Four Dollars and Fifty Cents.* **Illustrated by Glen Rounds. 1990. Hardcover: Holiday House. Paperback: Holiday House. Ages 4–7.**

Widow Macrae intends to get the four dollars and fifty cents that cowboy Shorty Long owes her. She cannot run her Silver Dollar Café if customers don't pay up, so she picks up her rolling pin, hitches up her horses, and heads out to the Circle K ranch. When his pals see her coming, they whip together a coffin for Shorty to climb into. Widow Macrae is suspicious, so she offers to take the coffin back to town for a burial. The ragged sketches smudged with color, perfectly suited to the story, show the widow and Shorty's coffin at the graveyard where she announces that she intends to watch the body all night. The midnight arrival of robbers leads to an unpredictable ending. Rollicking pictures and homespun language tell an action-packed story about one determined businesswoman in the Old West.

Kroll, Virginia. *Girl, You're Amazing.* **Illustrated by Mélisande Potter. 2001. Hardcover: Albert Whitman. Ages 3–8.**

Girls can do most anything, declares this poetic celebration of today's girls. Each stanza starts with the phrase, "Girl, you're amazing," and continues to describe the many possible aspects of a girl's life. Whimsical mixed-media illustrations extend the text, showing a wide range of activities and girls. They are building sand castles, jumping on trampolines, writing, stargazing, and creating different kinds of art. They are playing saxophones, dancing, feeding puppies, standing up to bullies, shooting baskets, and climbing trees. Girls are praised for being kind and being brave. The joyful text closes with a litany of girls' names, and the final line, "Girl, you're amazing! I'm glad that you're YOU!"

Lasky, Kathyrn. *Pond Year.* **Illustrated by Mike Bostock. 1995. Paperback: Candlewick. Ages 3–6.**

Two six-year-old girls who call themselves "pond buddies and scum chums forever" love to spend time at the shallow pond near their houses. Not the least bit squeamish, they like to catch bugs, make mud cookies, and braid friendship rings from dried scum. Appealing watercolors show them wading during the summer, looking for muskrats at night in the fall, and skating in the winter. They collect frogs' eggs and crawdaddies, examine dead bugs under a magnifying glass, and let salamanders crawl up their arms and legs just for fun. Lovely illustrations, poetic text, and two terrific girls make this an all-around winner.

Lattimore, Deborah Nourse. *Frida María: A Story of the Old Southwest.* **1994. Paperback: Voyager. Ages 4–7.**

Frida María longs to ride the horse Diablo in the upcoming fiesta, to her mama's horror. Her mother wants Frida María to be ladylike, and the girl tries, but she finds it hard to get interested in sewing and baking. When the fiesta finally arrives, Frida María seizes the chance to ride Diablo, racing to win a bet and save her family a lot of money. In the end even her mother recognizes that Frida María has important talents, ladylike or not. Vigorous, colorful paintings, filled with the architecture of the Southwest, match Frida María's strong character.

Lee, Milly. *Nim and the War Effort.* **Illustrated by Yangsook Choi. 1997. Hardcover: FSG. Ages 5–9.**

Set in San Francisco during World War II, this story focuses on the efforts of a Chinese-American girl named Nim to win a newspaper collecting contest. Her only serious rival in collecting papers for the war effort is a sneaky boy named Garland, who takes papers he knows people have left for Nim. With daring, Nim ventures outside Chinatown to wealthy Nob Hill and has unexpected luck in her quest. But with her luck comes an angry reaction from her revered grandfather for her boldness. In the end, though, her grandfather acknowledges Nim's efforts and accomplishment. Glowing paintings show Nim, her family, and San Francisco's Chinatown.

Levitin, Sonia. *Boom Town.* **Illustrated by Cat Bowman Smith. 1998. Hardcover: Orchard. Ages 4–8.**

Amanda's family has moved to California in search of gold, but the girl's business sense becomes the key to the family income. With only a wood stove to bake in, Amanda is determined to make a gooseberry pie in a skillet. After two disasters, the third pie comes out right. The next time her father comes home from the gold fields, he takes a pie back with him and sells it. Thus begins Amanda's business, which eventually expands into a bakery. By then, she has her brothers and sisters working for her and, once a school opens in the town, she turns the main baking over to her father. Meanwhile, she has given business advice to several men, who adopt her ideas and open a trading post, laundry, stable, and more, until their little settlement is a real town. Energetic watercolors paint a freckled, red-haired girl hard at work in this terrific story.

Lewis, J. Patrick. *Night of the Goat Children.* **Illustrated by Alexi Natchev. 1999. Hardcover: Dial. Ages 5–9.**

This tale comes loosely from a real occurrence in seventeenth-century Germany when a town defended itself by disguising children as goats. In this version, a princess known as Birgitta the Brave comes up with the idea when outlaws surround the town of Beda, which is protected by thick walls. When the outlaws try to climb the walls, the people cut their ropes. But the outlaws know that all they have to do is outwait the townspeople, whose animals will die, leaving them to starve. Birgitta enlists the help of five children and disguises them as goats. Then she disguises herself as an old woman and lets herself be captured by the outlaws. She misleads them, telling them the animals of Beda never die. When the outlaws shoot the goats they see on the top of the walls, the animals appear to live, since they are really children thickly padded with goatskins. Birgitta then tricks the enemy into thinking she has magically been turned into a goat, and they flee in fear. Slightly exaggerated pictures add a touch of humor to this story of courage and cleverness.

Luenn, Nancy. *Nessa's Fish.* **Illustrated by Neil Waldman. 1990. Paperback: Aladdin. Ages 5–8.**

When Nessa and her grandmother, who appear to be Inuits, are ice fishing away from home, the grandmother falls ill. Nessa protects her and their catch of fish, scaring away a fox and warding off a bear with a song. Particularly impressive is the way she dominates the lead wolf of a pack by making herself tower above it and stare it in the eye. Beautiful, luminous watercolors make this a pleasure to look at as well as read. In the sequel, *Nessa's Story*, the girl encounters a legendary beast and finds a story of her own to tell.

Lyon, George Ella. *Together*. Illustrated by Vera Rosenberry. 1989. Hardcover: Orchard. Paperback: Orchard. Ages 2–6.

Two girls imagine having lots of good times together, "dreaming the same dream." Joyful watercolor and ink pictures expand the simple poem, showing one dark-haired, dark-skinned girl and another blond, light-skinned one. When the poem says they are fighting a fire together, the pictures show one driving a fire truck and the other putting out a fire from a dragon's mouth. They also sail, fish, and ride dolphins together. At the end we see them driving horse-drawn chariots into the sky, as always, having a great time together. A tribute to friendship and imagined adventure.

MacGill-Callahan, Sheila. *To Capture the Wind*. Illustrated by Gregory Manchess. 1997. Hardcover: Dial. Ages 5–10.

Dark, dramatic paintings set the stage for this original tale with a Celtic flavor. The heroine, Oonagh, has a good life, successful at her farming and sheep herding, and happy to be engaged to the weaver Conal. But when she hears that Conal has been kidnapped by a pirate, Oonagh summons her impressive wit and strength to defeat the pirate Malcolm. Pretending to seek Malcolm's son in marriage, she agrees to solve four riddles, answering one each week. To prepare for the final riddle, "How do you capture the wind on the water?" Oonagh enlists the help of Conal and the other captive weavers. In the end, Oonagh draws her sword on Malcolm, defeats him in an unexpected way, and is reunited with Conal. Lyrical language and an exciting plot make this a good read-aloud.

Mahy, Margaret. *Boom, Baby, Boom, Boom!* Illustrated by Patricia MacCarthy. 1997. Hardcover: Viking. Ages 2–7.
In this cheerful story, Mama settles her baby in a high chair with lots of good food for lunch, then turns her back to play her drums. Although Mama looks conventional, she declares, "Beating those drums makes me feel at ease with the world." What the baby and the reader know, and Mama doesn't, is that a group of animals has heard about the lunch and comes in the door. The baby obliges them by dropping her food bit by bit on the floor, to the cat, dog, chickens, sheep, and finally the cow: "Boom-biddy-boom-biddy MOO-MOO-MOO!" The mother sighs with happiness just as the cow races out, then turns to her smiling child and gives her a banana, not knowing she hasn't eaten the rest. Large, rounded, colorful pictures suit the happy spirit of this bouncing book about a drum-beating mother.

Maloney, Peter, and Felicia Zekauskas. *The Magic Hockey Stick*. 1999. Hardcover: Dial. Paperback: Puffin. Ages 4–8.
The narrator, a girl who loves everything about hockey, including playing, is thrilled when her parents buy Wayne Gretzky's hockey stick at a charity auction. Although her father tells her not to, she cannot resist using it in hockey games, and finds she has magically become a great player. She scores in every game, often twice. But when she reads in the newspaper that Gretzky, the Great One, has hit a slump, she knows she must get the stick back to him. Even though her own game will suffer, she returns the stick and saves the day. Her father complains, but her mother gives her a high

five. The rhyming text sometimes strains, but it succeeds in capturing the spirit of fun also seen in the humorous pictures. A rare book about a girl dedicated to ice hockey.

Marshall, James. *The Cut-Ups.* **1984. Hardcover: Viking. Paperback: Puffin. Ages 5–8.**

In this slight story illustrated with comic pictures, Spud Jenkins and Joe Turner are the cut-ups, incorrigible boys who drive adults crazy. But Mary Frances Hooley, who drives a sports car she built and named after herself, impresses even these two hard cases. She offers them a ride in the spaceship she has constructed and gets them into trouble by having them land in a nasty neighbor's yard. While the angry man pursues the boys, Mary Frances rescues some sports equipment that he had confiscated from her and other neighborhood kids. She has tricked the tricksters, who richly deserve it. Mary Frances, shown as a redheaded, sturdily built girl with green sunglasses, is a force to be contended with.

Marshall, James. *George and Martha.* **1972. Hardcover: Houghton. Paperback: Houghton. Ages 3–8.**

The hippos George and Martha experience the give and take of friendship in a spirit of equality, with Martha every bit as strong as George. For example, in the third of "Five Stories about Two Great Friends," Martha objects to George peeking in the window when she takes a bath. One day she cures him of the habit by turning the bathtub over on his head, saying, "There's such a thing as privacy." The other stories also deal with small problems and joys of life and friendship. The priceless pictures of these large hippos in their dapper clothes and cozy houses are full of humorous details. A modern classic, this is the first in an outstanding series that every child should get to know.

Martin, Bill, Jr., and Michael Sampson. *Swish!* **Illustrated by Michael Chesworth. 1997. Hardcover: Henry Holt. Paperback: Henry Holt. Ages 4–8.**

In this fast-paced book, two girls' basketball teams are battling it out in the last minute. The story, told in rhyme, describes the game play-by-play as the girls dribble, pass, shoot, rebound, and score. When one team ties the game with a basket, the word "Swish" fills the page. With sixteen seconds left, the game is tied. A successful jump-shot brings another big "Swish," and the other team takes a time-out. Will they try a three-point shot to win? Lively watercolors convey the excitement of the game and the tension of the last sixty seconds. Sure to appeal to young sports fans, this is one of the few picture books on basketball.

Martin, C. L. G. *Three Brave Women.* **Illustrated by Peter Elwell. 1991. Hardcover: Atheneum. Ages 3–7.**

Caitlin, her mother, and her grandmother, who share a fear of spiders, each tell a story about being afraid. Then Caitlin decides to overcome her fear and asks the other two for help. They wrinkle their noses but pitch in. They all crawl under the porch where Caitlin discovers a huge, black spider. Though a bit scared, they persist and capture the spider. "We are three brave women," Grammy declares. Caitlin quickly digests the lesson that confronting fear can overcome it, and plans to catch a mouse and dig up some worms, also with the help of her mother and grandmother. The theme that girls learn their timidity, sometimes from their mothers, and can unlearn it is summed up in Caitlin's last comment that "my grandchildren aren't gonna be afraid of anything!" Expressive illustrations record Caitlin's transformation from a sobbing child to a girl proudly flexing her muscles and leaping through the yard. Terrific.

Mayer, Mercer. *There's Something in my Attic.* **1988. Hardcover: Dial. Paperback: Puffin. Ages 2–5.**

Like the better-known *There's a Nightmare in My Closet,* this concerns a girl confronting her fears. Her bugaboo is a large, almost cuddly creature who has stolen her teddy bear. Wearing her nightgown, cowboy boots, and a cowboy hat, she successfully lassoes the creature, but it manages to escape before her parents see it. "I'll just have to get my bear back tomorrow," she concludes. Persistent, brave, and good with a lasso—what more can you ask?

McCully, Emily Arnold. *Beautiful Warrior: The Legend of the Nun's Kung Fu.* **1998. Hardcover: Scholastic. Ages 5–10.**

This story about two talented women opens long ago in China's Forbidden City, where a baby girl is born and named Jingyong or "Quiet Courage." The girl's father decides to educate her like a son and soon Jingyong excels at the martial art of kung fu. After an invasion, she enters a monastery, where she becomes a nun called Wu Mei, or "Beautiful Warrior." One day Wu Mei saves a girl named Mingyi from bandits. When another bandit insists Mingyi marry him, the girl apprentices herself to Wu Mei to learn kung fu. After a challenging year, Mingyi fights the bandit and saves herself. Instead of marriage, the girl vows to devote her life to kung fu. Glorious dramatic watercolors show the two strong females in action.

McCully, Emily Arnold. *The Bobbin Girl.* **1996. Hardcover: Dial. Ages 7–10.**

This picture-story book deals with a subject most appropriate for older children: the working conditions for female millworkers in the mid-1800s. It focuses on a ten-year-old girl named Rebecca who works in a textile mill removing full bobbins of yarn and replacing them with empty ones. Her mother runs a boardinghouse for the workers, so Rebecca hears a lot of talk about the mills and their problems. When one of the workers who lives at the boardinghouse gets injured by a machine, the mill owners fire her. Next, the owners announce that wages will be cut. Judith, a young woman whom Rebecca admires, calls a meeting to fight back against the owners and leads a walkout. When the workers in Rebecca's workroom hesitate to follow Judith, Rebecca speaks out and leads the way. A lot of information, such as why various women came to work at the mills, is packed into this story. Elegant illustrations add to the sense of time, place, and character. An author's note explains that Rebecca was based on a real girl, and gives more details about the mills and the women who fought against unfair working conditions.

McCully, Emily Arnold. *Mirette on the High Wire*. **1992. Hardcover: Putnam. Paperback: Putnam. Ages 5–9.**

This gloriously illustrated book, which won the Caldecott Medal, is set in Paris a hundred years ago. Mirette, whose mother runs a boardinghouse popular with performers, becomes determined to walk the tightrope when she sees a guest named Bellini practicing in their courtyard. The guest, a world-famous tightrope walker who has lost his nerve, agrees to teach her because he is impressed with her perseverance. Her belief in him inspires Bellini to attempt a dangerous crossing high above a nearby street. When he freezes at the last minute, Mirette saves the day by starting to walk from the opposite end of the rope. The brilliant paintings make this story of a daring girl unforgettable. In *Starring Mirette and Bellini* and *Mirette and Bellini Cross Niagara Falls*, the remarkable girl continues her high-wire adventures.

McDonald, Megan. *Insects Are My Life.* **Illustrated by Paul Brett Johnson. 1995. Hardcover: Orchard. Paperback: Orchard. Ages 3–7.**

The budding young entomologist Amanda Frankenstein is crazy about all insects. She collects them, studies them, tries to protect them, and even imitates them sometimes. She argues with her brother, whose passion is dinosaurs, declaring, "Insects are fascinating. Insects are my life!" When Amanda starts school, she trades inventive insults with an unpleasant boy who teases her, but finally finds a promising friend, another girl with a strong interest in nature. The apt illustrations capture Amanda's enthusiasm and add touches of humor and interest. Amanda is an endearing character with a mind of her own. A companion book is *Reptiles Are My Life.*

McDonald, Megan. *The Night Iguana Left Home.* **Illustrated by Ponder Goembel. 1999. Hardcover: DK Ink. Ages 4–8.**

Although reptiles who talk in children's books are rarely female, this tale provides a terrific exception. Iguana lives with her friend Alison Frogley, who first appears at her computer keyboard with Iguana draped on her shoulder. Although Iguana has a comfortable life with her own heating pad, library card, and e-mail address, and plenty of pizza and ice cream, something just isn't right. When she sees travel posters of warm places, she realizes that the problem is the snowy winters where they live. So Iguana packs her bathing suit, library books, and suntan lotion, and takes a bus to Key West, Florida. Irresistible illustrations show her sunbathing and surfing until she runs out of money and has to take up dish washing. After averting a danger, Iguana returns home but with plans to catch a few rays the next year. A jazzy combination of picture and story with a modern twist and a great iguana.

McKissack, Patricia C. *Flossie and the Fox*. Illustrated by Rachel Isadora. 1986. Hardcover: Dial. Ages 3–8.

This irresistible tale features a little girl named Flossie who must deliver a basket of eggs to a neighboring farm. Her mother warns her about a fox who will do "most anything to get at some eggs." Sure enough, Flossie meets him immediately and proceeds to distract him with her teasing. She claims not to be afraid of him because, she says, she doesn't believe he is a fox. Indignant, the fox tries again and again to convince her. Unafraid, Flossie keeps him at bay until she reaches her destination, where a hound is waiting to pursue him. Told in a readable dialect and accompanied by appealing pictures, this is a wonderful story.

McKissack, Patricia C. *Nettie Jo's Friends*. Illustrated by Scott Cook. 1989. Hardcover: Knopf. Paperback: Knopf. Ages 4–8.

Joyful, slightly blurred pictures evoke a time past in this story about a resourceful girl. Nettie Jo needs to sew her doll a dress that will be presentable at a wedding, but she has no needle. While she is looking for one and gathering stray things into a burlap sack, Nettie Jo helps three animals solve their problems. She happens to have the perfect answer for each in her sack. As in many folktales, her cleverness and kindness lead to a happy ending. The final picture shows a smiling African-American girl dancing in the moonlight with her doll and her sewing needle, while three comical animals dash away in the background.

McLerran, Alice. *Roxaboxen*. Illustrated by Barbara Cooney. 1991. Hardcover: Lothrop. Paperback: Puffin. Ages 5–8.

This is truly a gem among books, combining a poetic, evocative text and stunning illustrations. Roxaboxen is a city some children have created near their homes in the desert. Dominant among these friends is Marian, who serves as mayor and sometimes as general. Although boys play at Roxaboxen, girls seem most important. The pictures show girls gathering rocks, "driving" steering wheels, riding stick horses (for which there is no speed limit), and holding down their Fort Irene. One fine picture shows a girl, Frances, relaxing with an air of propriety and confidence in her own spot outlined by colored glass: "a house of jewels." Based on a true story about the author's mother and her friends in Yuma, Arizona, seventy years ago, this beautiful book describes a magical place with room for girls to lead and create.

McMillan, Bruce. *My Horse of the North*. 1997. Hardcover: Scholastic. Ages 3–8.

In this informational photo-essay, a nine-year-old Icelandic girl named Margrét has her own horse and important tasks to accomplish while riding. A skilled rider, she practices for the big sheep roundup at the end of the summer by herding cows and geese while on horseback. The large, vibrant photographs then show Margrét and two of her friends on horseback, helping with the roundup. Sweeping shots of the countryside, some fifty miles below the Arctic Circle, give a flavor of Iceland, and an author's note adds more information about the country and its unique horses. A delightful introduction to Iceland and to a competent girl joining in an important task.

McNaughton, Colin. *Captain Abdul's Pirate School*. 1994. Hardcover: Candlewick. Paperback: Candlewick. Ages 4–8.

In this zany picture-story book, told in diary format, Maisy Pickles's parents send her to Pirate School because she likes art and books too well, and she isn't tough enough. The faculty at Captain Abdul's Pirate School are scruffy male pirates with names like Poop Deck Percy Ploppe and Riffraff Rafferty. The children, boys and girls dressed in pirate uniforms, make cannonballs and swords in arts and crafts class and learn how to read treasure maps in geography. The pirates encourage them to lie, cheat, and cut in line. But when Maisy overhears the pirates' plan to kidnap and ransom them just before parents' day, the children mutiny under Maisy's leadership. Maisy ends up as the swashbuckling captain of her own pirate ship, who steals only from other pirates. Animated cartoonlike pictures cluttered with funny details fill the large-book format, just the right accompaniment to this story, which turns the idea of school on its head.

McPhail, David. *Ed and Me.* 1990. Paperback: Voyager. Ages 3–6.

The little girl who tells this story appears on the title page sitting on the roof of a truck. The truck, known as Ed, used to belong to a family friend, then "came to live with us." She tells of all the enjoyable times she has with Ed, going into town for ice cream, sitting on his tailgate for picnics, decorating him for a parade. In the cozy pictures, she is shown helping her father load Ed with hay and later with firewood and then pumpkins. She even pitches a tent in the back of the truck one night and stays until her flashlight batteries run out. As winter approaches, she helps her father build a shed for Ed. Encouraged by her father, this small girl does everything you would expect a farm boy to do, even swinging on a rope to jump into a pond. A unique portrayal of a young girl and the truck she loves.

Meddaugh, Susan. *Beast.* 1981. Paperback: Houghton. Ages 2–5.

Anna is the youngest in her family and the bravest. When she spots a big, furry beast coming out of the forest, the rest of the family immediately declares it a dangerous, bad beast. Her father tries to shoot it unsuccessfully and decides it must be tricky as well as dangerous. Anna, however, wants to know more before she makes up her mind. Like a scientist, she tries to learn more about it and discovers the beast is far from dangerous. It cries and Anna comforts it, then sends it off home. Anna, who has red hair and wears a red dress, is a girl who promises to go far thanks to her inquiring spirit. Simple drawings of the small, determined girl and the huge furry beast will delight readers.

Meddaugh, Susan. *Hog-Eye*. 1995. Hardcover: Houghton. Paperback: Houghton. Ages 3–7.

A young pig is telling her family the story of why she didn't go to school that day. Cartoon balloons add the funny comments of her family as she tells the tale. After getting on the wrong school bus, she says, she was captured by a wolf who decided to make her into soup. Children will enjoy the discrepancy between what the pig describes and what the cartoonlike pictures show; for example, she reports they went to the wolf's "terrible, gloomy cave," but the pictures show a cozy little house. The pig, a quick thinker, goads the wolf into using a recipe he can't read. Each ingredient she mentions causes him big problems when he goes to fetch it, especially the "green threeleaf" that gives him a terrible rash. She convinces him she has the power to release the wolf from the itching, and so escapes. A tale very high in child appeal with droll illustrations.

Meddaugh, Susan. *Martha Calling*. 1994. Hardcover: Houghton. Ages 3–7.

The first page of this funny book shows the dog Martha up in the air catching a frisbee thrown by her owner, Helen.

Martha, amazingly enough, can speak when she has been eating alphabet soup, and she loves to talk, especially on the telephone. One day she answers a radio quiz correctly and wins a free weekend for four at the Come-On-Inn. Because the inn doesn't allow dogs, Martha goes dressed as an old lady, a disguise she almost gives away when she leaps to catch a Frisbee at the inn. When Martha's pose is revealed, she complains loudly about the hated words "No Dogs Allowed," wringing the hearts of visiting dog owners. The inn changes its policy—and hires Martha as the dining-room hostess. Martha rates high as a canine heroine: She's energetic, talented, and far from shy. The cartoonlike pictures, with plenty of talk balloons, are hilarious. Martha first appears in the funny *Martha Speaks*.

Merriam, Eve. *Mommies at Work*. Illustrated by Eugenie Fernandes. 1989 revised edition. Paperback: Aladdin. Ages 3–7.

A useful look at the jobs, blue-collar and professional, that some mothers hold outside their homes. Typical of the text are lines such as "Mommies with telescopes. Mommies punching tickets on trains." Women appear working in grocery stores, offices, auto plants, and airports. There are dancers, teachers, doctors, truck drivers, and even tightrope walkers. The cheerful illustrations are multicultural and show warm relationships between the mothers returning from work and their children.

Moss, Lloyd. *Zin! Zin! Zin! A Violin*. Illustrated by Marjorie Priceman. 1995. Hardcover: Simon & Schuster. Paperback: Aladdin. Ages 4–8.

This wonderful introduction to an orchestra combines a witty rhymed text and outstanding illustrations. Five of the ten orchestra members are women who play the trumpet, cello, flute, oboe, and harp. The players in the multicultural group resemble their instruments: The trumpeter's skirt flares out like a trumpet, while the flute player herself is long and thin. A subplot with a dog, two cats, and a mouse will delight younger children, while older ones will effortlessly absorb information about musical instruments. Named a Caldecott Honor Book for Priceman's clever, highly original illustrations. Bravo!

Moss, Thylias. *I Want To Be*. Illustrated by Jerry Pinkney. 1993. Paperback: Puffin. Ages 4–7.

Glorious watercolors combined with poetic text celebrate a girl's dreams of what she wants to be. Pinkney's light-filled illustrations show her running, leaping, dancing, flying a kite, swinging, and poised at the top of a slide. A magical quality pervades the book as the girl jumps rope "with strands of rainbow" and flies her kite far beyond the earth. She wants to be everything: big and strong, fast and tall, wise but willing to learn. The pictures show her as African-American, although the text doesn't specify, a glowing child in overalls and dresses. A joyful celebration with memorable illustrations.

Munsch, Robert N. *The Paper Bag Princess*. Illustrated by Michael Martchenko. 1980. Hardcover: Annick. Paperback: Annick. Ages 4–7.

This story of a princess who rescues a prince certainly conveys a worthy message. When a dragon steals the prince and ruins all the princess's pretty clothes, she resorts to wearing a paper bag and sets off to rescue her fiancé. She tricks the dragon and releases the prince, only to have him grouse at her about what a mess she looks. She replies that he looks like a prince but is acting like "a bum," and they part ways with the princess romping off into the sunset. Although the writing is choppy and the pictures unexceptional, the theme is right on target.

Murphy, Stuart J. *The Best Vacation Ever*. Illustrated by Nadine Bernard Westcott. 1997. Hardcover: Harper. Paperback: Harper. Ages 5–8.

In this entry in the "MathStart" series, the narrator's family keeps very busy, and she decides they need a vacation. In order to choose where to go and what to do, she starts asking opinions and keeping charts. She collects data on what kind of weather the five family members, including herself, would like, if they want to go far or near, if they want excitement or a quiet rest, and if it's important that their cat Fluffer comes with them. Then she spreads out her four charts, adds up the numbers, and comes up with a clever solution to the problem. Westcott's characteristic colorful, upbeat watercolors, with the cat Fluffer in every picture, make this feel more like a story than a math challenge. An afterword suggests other topics children might like to chart. An entertaining lesson with a smart girl.

Murphy, Stuart J. *Game Time!* Illustrated by Cynthia Jabar. 2000. Hardcover: Harper. Paperback: Trophy. Ages 4–8.

It's game time for the Huskies, a girls' soccer team that hopes to beat the Falcons the following week. They spend the intervening time practicing. With their mascot dog Oliver and fans on the sidelines, the girls plunge enthusiastically into the game. At halftime, the Falcons are up one and the Huskies do a cheer to boost their spirits. Girls dribble, kick, head, defend, and run energetically up and down the field until the close ending. In addition to portraying a tense soccer game, the book highlights math concepts on each page, emphasizing units of time such as minutes in the quarter, fractions of the game hour, scores, and more. Cheerful cartoonlike pictures capture the excitement of the game as the girls throw themselves into their sport.

Narahashi, Keiko. *Is That Josie?* **1994. Hardcover: McElderry. Ages 2–5.**

This simple book asks questions about a little girl named Josie, and answers by comparing her to an animal. "Is that Josie running fast through the grass?" "No, it's a cheetah. There she goes—wait for us." In the watercolor picture, the girl is running, with a more transparent cheetah beside her. As the story progresses, the animals named become larger and more powerful, from a fox and turtle to a hippopotamus and a crocodile, strong images for a young girl to aspire to. Take note of the wonderful endpapers, with Josie on one side in various positions and different animals on the other imitating her.

Narahashi, Keiko. *Two Girls Can.* **2000. Hardcover: McElderry. Ages 2–5.**

Using simple words and well-designed watercolor illustrations, this book describes lots of different things that two girls can do together, many of which go beyond stereotypes of young girls as friends. For example, they can dig a hole, make a tunnel, and fly a kite. Pictures show them playing leap frog, seesaw, and tug-of-war. On one page, one of them declares, "Two girls can get really, really mad, then make up and be brave together"—a welcome sentiment. They climb walls and trees, dance and sing, and enjoy each other's company throughout. A celebration of girls' friendships and the range of the activities and emotions they share.

Nash, Ogden. *The Adventures of Isabel.* **Illustrated by James Marshall. 1991. Hardcover: Little, Brown. Paperback: Little, Brown. Ages 3–8.**

Two great humorists come together to create one of the bravest, most entertaining girls in children's books. No fearful creature can get the best of Isabel, who conquers a bear, witch, giant, doctor, and nightmare in this wonderful poem. Marshall's red-haired Isabel perfectly suits Nash's words. She is an inspiration to all readers, as she teaches them how to "banish a bugaboo." Appropriately, she is surrounded in the pictures by admiring, even dumbfounded, children who clearly look up to her. Girls and boys could use dozens more role models like Isabel. A book with very high child appeal.

Newman, Leslea. *Heather Has Two Mommies.* **Illustrated by Diana Souza. 1989. Hardcover: Alyson. Paperback: Alyson. Ages 3–7.**

In this story about a girl whose two caring mothers are lesbians, the women serve as strong role models. One is a doctor who lets Heather listen to her own heartbeat with a stethoscope; the other is a carpenter who gives Heather a small hammer to use on the table they are building together. While a bit stilted in picture and text, this is valuable for its attention to a neglected topic and its warm spirit.

Nolen, Jerdine. *Raising Dragons.* **Illustrated by Elise Primavera. 1998. Hardcover: Harcourt. Ages 3–8.**

The narrator, a farm girl who already knows a lot about raising young animals, finds a dragon egg and tends to the dragon that emerges. She names him Hank, feeds him and reads to him, and goes on grand flights on his back at night. At first, her mother objects to Hank, but slowly she relents as the dragon helps out around the farm in surprising ways. He grows enormous, with an irresistible toothy grin, but when he starts to get attention from outsiders, the girl realizes it's time for a change. She finds the answer to his future in a library book, and the two take a trip to a dragon-land in the middle of the ocean where Hank immediately feels at home. Fortunately the narrator goes home with new dragon eggs. "The same way Pa knew that farming was in his blood, I knew that raising dragons was in mine," she declares in this magical book about a girl who knows what she wants.

Numeroff, Laura. *What Mommies Do Best/What Daddies Do Best*. Illustrated by Lynn Munsinger. 1998. Hardcover: Simon & Schuster. Ages 2–5.

Here are two books in one. After starting at one cover and reading to the middle of the book, you turn the book upside down and start reading at the other cover. Each offers the same, simple text, with either the words "mommies" or "daddies" at the opening of each sentence. "Mommies can teach you how to ride a bicycle," begins one half of the book, showing a mother bear and little bear both riding bikes. The other half opens, "Daddies can teach you how to ride a bicycle," with a father hippo on foot lunging after a child on a bike. Both parents appear with their children making a snowman, baking, sewing, giving piggyback rides, gardening, playing in the park, reading a bedtime story, and more. The message that mothers and fathers can do the same parenting tasks comes across gently through the cozy, lighthearted illustrations of happy animal families.

O'Neill, Alexis. *Loud Emily*. Illustrated by Nancy Carpenter. 1998. Hardcover: Simon & Schuster. Paperback: Aladdin. Ages 3–7.

"LOUD HELP NEEDED. NOW" reads the sign on a ship, offering a much-needed haven to young Emily, whose loud voice doesn't suit her sedate nineteenth-century life. In her family's wealthy world, the little girl with the enormous voice is a problem. Illustrations show her beautifully furnished home and restrained, well-dressed relatives, with Emily looking out of place. But on the ship, she is invaluable, bellowing the captain's commands and delighting the whales. Charming folk-art paintings portray a colorful seaside town, the changing conditions at sea, and an energetic girl with a mouth that is usually wide open. Great fun, with a heroine who believes that girls should definitely be heard as well as seen.

Oppel, Kenneth. *Peg and the Whale*. Illustrated by Terry Widener. 2000. Hardcover: Simon & Schuster. Ages 4–8.

Sunny illustrations with rounded shapes and touches of humor help tell the tall tale of Peg, a "big, strapping lass" who excels at fishing from her parents' ocean-going boat. After great success catching fish, she resolves to catch a whale. "Well, Peg was pushing seven, and she figured it was high time she made something of herself," reads the text. The girl signs on to a whaling ship, where she finds the crew unfriendly and unwilling to let her do more than swab the deck. But when the captain's hat flies into the water, she fishes it out with her handy pole. The same fishing pole hooks onto a whale the next day, but a nasty sailor cuts the ropes holding Peg to the mast and the girl goes flying after the whale, holding onto her pole. After Peg ends up inside the whale where it's cozy and full of fish to eat, the two of them head for shore and all ends well, with the whale free and Peg ready to try her hand at another challenge. An outstanding tale with wild exaggeration and an impressive young heroine.

Peet, Bill. *Encore for Eleanor*. 1981. Paperback: Houghton. Ages 3–6.

Eleanor the elephant has been a star performer in the circus, accustomed to crowds roaring "Encore" after her act.

But she has grown old and unsteady, and finally the circus boss sends her off to live in a zoo. Unhappy without a job to do and missing her fancy circus clothes, Eleanor mopes in her barn all day. But one afternoon a teenage girl sets up an easel near Eleanor's fence and starts to draw. The artist loses her temper when the rhino she is sketching rolls over. She stomps away, leaving her materials, and Eleanor decides to try drawing. She picks up charcoal with her trunk and quickly sketches a clown face. The returning teenager exclaims with delight, but the officious zoo director insists that a "dumb animal" could not have drawn the picture. The "super-intelligent" Eleanor proves him wrong with a quick, skillful drawing of a lion, and she becomes a star once more. One of the few books about a female by this popular author.

Pérez, Amada Irma. *My Very Own Room/Mi Propio Cuartito.* Illustrated by Maya Christina Gonzalez. 2000. Hardcover: Children's Book Press. Ages 4–8.

Virginia Woolf wrote that a female writer needed to have a "room of one's own." In this book, an eight-year-old girl in a large family shares the same sentiment. She declares that she is getting too big for the crowded room she shares with her five little brothers. "I just needed a place of my own." Although it takes some persuading, the narrator convinces her mother to let her fix up their storage space behind a curtain into a room. The girl enlists the help of the whole family in her project, cleaning and painting. To celebrate, she gets books from the public library to read to her brothers and to read herself to sleep. Told in English and Spanish, with vibrant illustrations, this charming book portrays a girl who combines determination and thoughtfulness.

Pinkney, Brian. *JoJo's Flying Side Kick*. 1995. Paperback: Aladdin. Ages 3–7.

The jacket picture of JoJo in her Tae Kwon Do clothes performing a flying side kick will attract readers immediately. JoJo must break a board with a flying side kick in order to earn her yellow belt. The challenge makes her so nervous, she tells her granddaddy, "I'm freakin' out." Remembering his boxing days, he advises her on footwork. A friend with Tae Kwon Do experience says to yell loudly. And her mother, clad in a tennis dress, advises her to visualize her goal. JoJo puts it all together and a forceful picture shows her triumph. JoJo and her supportive family are African-American in this unusual story about a girl mastering a martial art while she also masters her own fears. A real winner by an award-winning illustrator.

Polacco, Patricia. *Mrs. Mack*. 1999. Hardcover: Philomel. Paperback: Puffin. Ages 8–11.

This nostalgic picture-story book, based on the author's childhood, will have young riders cheering and crying. Ten-year-old Patricia, who longs to ride horses, is disappointed when her father takes her to a run-down stable. But she soon realizes that the manager, Mrs. Mack, knows all there is to know about horses. With the kind woman's help, Patricia learns to ride through trial and error, getting back onto horses after she has fallen, and riding faster horses when she gets the chance. She learns lessons from Mrs. Mack that apply to much more than horses, such as the need to make mistakes on the way to mastering anything important. Patricia also figures out how to make friends with a variety of people as the summer progresses. Polacco's warm illustrations, many of horses, add color and drama to this story about a brave, believable girl.

Pomerantz, Charlotte. *The Piggy in the Puddle*. Illustrated by James Marshall. 1974. Hardcover: Macmillan. Paperback: Aladdin. Ages 2–7.

A rollicking, rhyming story about a naughty girl pig who won't get out of a mud puddle. No matter how much she is scolded by her parents and brother, she won't budge. She ignores their complaints and their pleadings and their advice to use lots of soap (to which she answers, "Nope"). In the end, she is having such a merry time that her family decides to join her. A "squishy-squashy, mooshy-squooshy" story that is almost a tongue twister, this little book is not to be missed. As always, James Marshall's illustrations add character and humor to the text.

Porte, Barbara Ann. *Ma Jiang and the Orange Ants*. Illustrated by Annie Cannon. 2000. Hardcover: Orchard. Ages 5–9.

Lovely illustrations set this story long ago in rural China, where a girl named Ma Jiang lives happily with her parents, her older brothers, and her baby brother Bao. The family makes a living by selling insect-eating ants to orange farmers who need harmful insects in their orange trees destroyed. Ma Jiang's father and brothers climb trees to get the ant nests, then put them in bags her mother weaves. When her mother takes the ants to sell at market, Ma Jiang baby-sits Bao. When her father and older brothers are forced to join the army, Ma Jiang and her mother lose their income from the ants. Then one day Ma Jiang has an inspiration and invents a way to trap ants that doesn't entail climbing trees. Her ingenuity restores their income and impresses her father and brothers when they finally return. A fine combination of expressive watercolors, an intriguing story, and a smart girl.

Porte, Barbara Ann. *Tale of a Tadpole*. **Illustrated by Annie Cannon. 1997. Hardcover: Orchard. Ages 3–7.**

Francine is fascinated with her new tadpole, feeding it every day and waiting for it to get feet, which she learned about at a nature center. Light-filled watercolor illustrations show Francine, her parents, and her older sister gathered around the aquarium. Although her sister teases Francine about kissing a frog, both girls follow the creature's progress as it gets back feet, then a tail, and then arms. Even Francine's grandparents get caught up in the excitement when they come to visit. They also realize something about Fred, as the pet is called, that surprises the family. Francine comes across as an enthusiastic young girl who likes amphibians and doesn't at all mind getting dirty.

Priceman, Marjorie. *Emeline at the Circus*. **1999. Hardcover: Knopf. Paperback: Dragonfly. Ages 3–8.**

What if you bought peanuts at the circus and an elephant picked you up in order to eat them? This is exactly what happens to Emeline when she goes to the circus with her teacher Ms. Splinter and the rest of the second grade. While Ms. Splinter recites facts about elephants, Emeline finds herself wrapped in an elephant's trunk in the circus ring. Next thing she knows, a clown has put a red nose and a clown's hat on her, just as Ms. Splinter's explaining the origin of the word *clown*. Wildly energetic paintings in vibrant colors show Emeline flying off a seesaw into the air, landing on a galloping horse, hanging from the tightrope, and other dangerous acts. At first she looks scared, but after the strongman rescues her from a hippo's mouth, Emeline starts enjoying herself, snarls at the tiger, and happily grabs a trapeze, which lands her back with her fellow students. A girl's daredevil romp through a circus ring, illustrated with appropriate liveliness.

Priceman, Marjorie. *How to Make an Apple Pie and See the World.* 1994. Hardcover: Knopf. Paperback: Dragonfly. Ages 3–7.

An outstanding book, this tells about a girl who wants to make an apple pie but finds the grocery store closed. So she takes a journey around the world to fetch the various ingredients she needs. She cuts a dashing figure in many countries on all sorts of transport, from bicycle to balloon to airplane. Lively pictures, witty prose, and a great sense of adventure fulfill the promise of the dust jacket, on which the girl is merrily parachuting through the air with a cow and a chicken and her cooking supplies.

Pulver, Robin. *Axle Annie.* Illustrated by Tedd Arnold. 1999. Hardcover: Dial. Paperback: Puffin. Ages 3–7.

Axle Annie is the best school bus driver ever. She does magic tricks, sings songs, and tells jokes, and nothing stops her, not even a snowstorm. When a winter storm comes up, the school superintendent in Burskyville calls Axle Annie to get her opinion. If she thinks she can drive the bus up the steepest hill in town, then there'll be no snow day. Axle Annie always answers, "Do snowplows plow? Do tow trucks tow? Are school buses yellow? Of course I can make it up Tiger Hill." But a lazy school bus driver and the new owner of a local ski resort conspire to keep Annie from succeeding, because they want snow days. Nothing stops the sturdy, enthusiastic Axle Annie, though. A light-hearted book about a competent woman at the wheel of a big vehicle.

Quindlen, Anna. *Happily Ever After.* Illustrated by James Stevenson. 1997. Hardcover: Viking. Paperback: Puffin. Ages 4–9.

Kate is a baseball-loving fourth-grader who also loves fairy tales. When her aunt gives her a special baseball mitt on her birthday, Kate doesn't suspect that it is magic, and only finds out when she makes a wish near it. Her wish to be a princess turns out differently than she could have predicted. She finds herself in a tower with a boring prince who fights for her, but later leaves her when a frightful witch appears. The witch, however, loves the games and songs that Kate teaches her and loves Kate's breezy style. Kate later travels to a castle, where she teaches the Ladies-in-Waiting and the Serving Maids to play baseball. She introduces useful slang like "wimp," "princess, schmincess," and "Cheers, big ears," to the court, but when the king and prince appear, she wisely wishes to be back home. A funny, clever story, perfectly accompanied by funny, scrappy pictures. Highly recommended.

Rappaport, Doreen, and Lyndall Callan. *Dirt on Their Skirts: The Story of the Young Women Who Won the World Championship.* **Illustrated by E. B. Lewis. 2000. Hardcover: Dial. Ages 5–9.**

During World War II, when many male ball players joined the military, women started playing professional baseball in the All-American Girls' Professional Baseball League. This fine book recounts the 1946 world championship game between the Racine Belles of Wisconsin and the Rockford Peaches of Illinois. Through the eyes of a girl named Margaret and her family, the reader watches the final inning during overtime when Sophie Kurys of the Belles hits a single, steals second base, and slides in for the winning run. Everyone in the family—Margaret, her parents, and her brother—root passionately for the Belles, a team Margaret hopes to play for someday. Large, light-filled watercolors show the players in action in this terrific story.

Rathmann, Peggy. *Officer Buckle and Gloria.* **1995. Hardcover: Putnam. Ages 3–7.**

Officer Buckle is an earnest, boring safety officer who puts schoolchildren to sleep with his safety tips. But when he teams up with the dynamic police dog Gloria, children sit up and pay attention. Behind Officer Buckle's back, Gloria acts out the dire consequences of ignoring his tips. When he advises children not to swim during electrical storms, she soars in the air with her hair on end. Her acrobatics delight the audience but dismay Officer Buckle when he finally realizes she is upstaging him. The clever, funny pictures, which won the Caldecott Medal, show Gloria's antics, which are never mentioned in the text. Young readers enjoy being in on the secret well before Officer Buckle is. A sure-fire hit.

Riggio, Anita. *Beware the Brindlebeast.* **1994. Hardcover: Boyds Mills. Paperback: Boyds Mills. Ages 3–7.**

On All Hallow's Eve, Birdie, a poor but optimistic old woman, is walking home past the old burying ground where, to her surprise, she almost trips over a kettle full of gold. She starts pulling it home through the dusk and suddenly realizes the pot of gold has turned into a barrel of apples. But she sees this has benefits, too, and cheerfully continues on her way. When the apples become a pumpkin, Birdie again sees the transformation in the best light. Outside her cottage, the pumpkin turns into a terrible monster, the Dread Brindlebeast that all her neighbors fear. Fearless, Birdie is even slightly amused by the monster and her courage brings unexpected rewards. Bold oil paintings show a hearty, white-haired woman who enjoys life. Perfect for children who enjoy being scared— a little.

Ringgold, Faith. *Tar Beach.* **1991. Hardcover: Crown. Paperback: Dragonfly. Ages 4–8.**

Rich illustrations in a folk-art style show eight-year-old Cassie Lightfoot flying through the night above the George Washington Bridge. As she says in the poetic narrative, she feels powerful in the air and magical when she sleeps out on Tar Beach, the rooftop of their apartment building. Most of all she feels free. She wishes she could use the power she feels to save her family from hard times. But if she cannot do that, Cassie can at least take her brother with her and teach him to fly. The strength of this unusual book is the extraordinary artwork, based on a story quilt shown at the back of the book. A Caldecott Honor Book.

Robertson, Bruce. *Marguerite Makes a Book.* **Illustrated by Kathryn Hewitt. 1999. Hardcover: J. Paul Getty Museum. Ages 8–11.**

Set in the 1400s in Paris, this lovely book tells the story of Marguerite, a girl whose father, Jacques, illuminates manuscripts. Marguerite has learned the craft, from purchasing vellum and gold leaf to mixing dyes and, finally, executing the exquisite paintings. Large pictures full of details about the time and place show the father and daughter going on errands together, gathering materials to finish a book for a wealthy woman. But when Papa Jacques's glasses get crushed, Marguerite must finish the beautiful prayer book herself, shown in a series of pictures. An intriguing story about a strong girl mastering a craft.

Rosenberg, Liz. *The Carousel.* **Illustrated by Jim LaMarche. 1995. Hardcover: Harcourt. Ages 4–8.**

Two sisters, remembering words their mother had said when she was alive, visit a carousel on their way home one day in winter. When they hear horses whinnying inside, they venture in, mount their favorites, and race into the sky, with the other horses galloping behind. The horses act wild, because the carousel is broken, so the girls fetch their mother's toolbox, for she "had been someone who could fix anything" and who sometimes took apart appliances just for fun. The narrator, pictured sitting among the pieces of the dismantled carousel machinery, carefully inspects it until she fixes the problem. Then her sister lures the mad horses back by playing a song their mother used to play on the flute. The final picture shows them safely leaning up against their father, all thinking about their mother. The story conveys warmth and love despite the gloomy winter night and the sense of loss. It emphasizes the girls' courage and resourcefulness, an inheritance from their strong mother.

Russo, Marisabina. *Come Back, Hannah!* 2001. Hardcover: Greenwillow. Ages 2–6.

Young Hannah, clad in bright red overalls, loves to crawl. No matter what her mother is doing—writing a letter or making a phone call—Hannah can't sit still, even when she has a hammer and pegs or a cupboard of pans to play with. She crawls away, with her mother calling, "Come back, Hannah!" She crawls after balls and toward the sound of their dog's jingling collar. She's fearless as she sits on top of the large dog and heads up steep stairs. No wonder her mother chooses to read her a book about a race. But even then, Hannah races away until naptime finally arrives and she lies contentedly, at least for a moment. Her understanding mother, who herself wears sweat clothes and sneakers and tries to fit in some exercising, seems to enjoy her child's energy. Vibrant colors characterize the gouache paintings that add to the fun.

Russo, Marisabina. *When Mama Gets Home*. 1998. Hardcover: Greenwillow. Ages 3–7.

It is simply a given in this single-parent household that Mama works and the children help out around the home. The youngest of three children narrates the story, starting with a five o'clock phone call from Mama, saying she is about to leave work and catch the train. The older sister and brother begin cooking, while the younger girl sets the table. True-to-life, all three children bombard their mother with their news when she walks in the door, and she tells them to "hold their horses" until she has settled in a little. Later, Mama tucks the narrator in and reads her a story: "Finally I have Mama all to myself!" A warm picture of a working mother and a family dealing with realistic circumstances, aptly illustrated in rich gouache pictures.

Sasso, Sandy Eisenberg. *But God Remembered: Stories of Women from Creation to the Promised Land*. Illustrated by Bethanne Andersen. 1995. Hardcover: Jewish Lights. Ages 6–10.

Taken from the midrashic tradition, which extends stories in the Bible, this lovely book portrays strong women whose stories are not well known. It tells of Lilith, who came before Eve but argued with Adam when she insisted on equality. The second tale is about Serach, a harpist who knew all the ancient stories and composed music to go with the words. Bityah, also called Meroe, was a pharaoh's daughter who raised and influenced the future leader Moses. Last are the five daughters of Zelophehad, women who wandered the wilderness with their people and changed the law so that women could inherit property if a man had no sons. Graceful paintings show women who appear dignified rather than pretty, a fitting choice.

Saul, Carol P. *Someplace Else.* **Illustrated by Barry Root. 1995. Paperback: Aladdin. Ages 4–7.**

All her life Mrs. Tillby had lived in the same place and wondered what it would be like to live elsewhere. So one day she takes off in her old green truck to visit each of her grown children and see how she likes life where they live: the city, at the seashore, and in the mountains. Then she tries other places as well, including an adobe hut and a riverboat. This cardigan-clad, white-haired woman has a strong case of wanderlust. Luckily, as she heads back home pondering the fact that no place suits her, Mrs. Tillby spots a silver trailer for sale, which she buys and hooks to her truck. Evocative paintings show her tooling along in an old-fashioned truck, learning to ski, and finding the home of her dreams.

Say, Allen. *Tea with Milk.* **1999. Hardcover: Houghton. Ages 6–10.**

In this strikingly elegant picture book, a girl creates her own path in life despite traditions and opposition. May appears first in California, standing as a young child before a door and an American flag. But the second lovely watercolor shows her after high school, wearing a kimono and looking miserable because her parents moved the family back to Japan, their homeland. May finds the adjustment difficult, especially because she must attend high school again and learn to be a "proper Japanese lady." Upset that her family is trying to arrange a marriage, May breaks tradition by moving on her own to Osaka to find a job. Her first job is boring but she turns it into something much better. Exquisite, full-page illustrations face the substantial text on each double-page spread, giving the impression of a photo album belonging to the author, who reveals on the last page that the girl was his mother. An unusually beautiful picture book about a determined young woman.

Schami, Rafik. *Fatima and the Dream Thief.* **Illustrated by Els Cools and Oliver Streich. 1996. Hardcover: North-South Books. Ages 5–9.**

When their widowed mother falls sick, Fatima and her brother Hassan seek work. Hassan goes first, and finds work in the castle of a huge man. The man will pay him one gold piece for the week, unless Hassan loses his temper. In that case, he will lose his dreams and get no money. The dream thief goads Hassan into anger on the last day, and he returns home penniless and unable to sleep. His sister Fatima does better, warned by her brother. She goes to work for the dream thief, and there befriends a mute old woman. The two of them sneak into the chamber where the dreams are caged and release them. Then Fatima, who has doubled the bet by wagering the thief will lose his temper, provokes him into anger. She and the old woman, who has regained her speech, have to beat him until he agrees to pay what he owes. Whimsical, jaunty illustrations strike just the right note for this tale of a smart, brave girl.

Schuch, Steve. *A Symphony of Whales.* **Illustrated by Peter Sylvada. 1999. Hardcover: Harcourt. Ages 4–9.**

Haunting oil paintings illustrate this story about a Siberian girl named Glashka and her family, who set out one day on their dogsled to get supplies from the next village. On the way back, after Glashka's parents let her drive the dogsled, the dogs leave the trail and pull the sled to a bay where ice has trapped hundreds of beluga whales. Glashka's mother suggests contacting an ice-breaking ship, which responds but can't come quickly. The people of Glashka's village need to keep the whales alive until the ship comes. At first, the whales refuse to follow the ship through the newly made passage to the sea, but then Glashka comes up with a surprising plan.

Based loosely on a true story, this poetic tale about a resourceful girl will grip those who love whales.

Schwartz, Amy. *Bea and Mr. Jones*. 1982. Paperback: Aladdin. Ages 3–7.

Bea is tired of kindergarten and her father is tired of his job, so they change places one day, with Bea donning her father's coat and tie. Mr. Jones proves himself to be a big help at school, while Bea snags a promotion at the job with her advertising slogan for crackers. They decide to make it a permanent arrangement, and Bea quickly becomes president of toy sales. She has the brisk manner of an executive and carries herself with such confidence, despite the huge suit, that somehow the story doesn't seem as absurd as it sounds. Charming black-and-white illustrations, and fun all around.

Seibold, J. Otto, and Vivian Walsh. *Olive, the Other Reindeer*. Illustrated by J. Otto Seibold. 1997. Hardcover: Chronicle. Ages 4–8.

In this unusual Christmas story, a dog named Olive has an adventure based on a misunderstanding. She hears the song about Rudolph the reindeer, but instead of "All of the other reindeer," she hears "Olive, the other reindeer," and concludes she should be at the North Pole. Beguiling retro illustrations show her taking two buses to arrive just as Santa's about to leave. Santa decides to give Olive a chance and one of the reindeer straps her on. She hangs from the reindeer, enjoying the flight. But the other reindeer watch Olive instead of their route and crash into a tree. Olive emerges as a vital part of the team, first chewing branches to release the sleigh, then smelling gumdrops and hearing flutes that are falling from the hole the tree made in Santa's bag of presents.

Finally, caught in fog on the way home, Olive guides the sleigh because she can smell cookies baking at the North Pole.

Shaw-MacKinnon, Margaret. *Tiktala*. Illustrated by Laszlo Gál. 1996. Hardcover: Holiday House. Ages 6–9.

Set in the Far North, this story is about a girl who wants to be a soapstone carver, a traditional occupation among her people. The wisest woman of the village advises the girl to go in search of a spirit helper. Although she is afraid, Tiktala undertakes the quest, during which she turns into a harp seal. Traveling with another seal, she learns how dangerous humans are to seals, especially the pups. An act of physical courage turns Tiktala back into a human being and sends her home, ready to begin her life as a carver. Stiff paintings in subtle colors depict a cold world of snow and ice. Slightly sentimental, with a strong message about ecology, this story is noteworthy for the fact that a girl, not a boy, goes on a spiritual quest.

Sisulu, Elinor Batezat. *The Day Gogo Went to Vote: South Africa, April 1994*. Illustrated by Sharon Wilson. 1996. Hardcover: Little, Brown. Paperback: Little, Brown. Ages 6–9.

On the cover of this picture-story book is a quote from Nelson Mandela, "Inspiring and moving"—an apt description of the book's impact. Set in South Africa in April, 1994, it tells of an old South African woman from the viewpoint of her young granddaughter Thembi. Gogo, which means grandmother, has never had the opportunity to vote due to the political system of apartheid. She announces to her surprised family that she fully intends to vote, even though she never leaves the family's yard. Concerned about her health, they argue against her plan, to no avail. Someone loans her a car and driver, and Gogo insists that Thembi come, too. A spirit of celebration pervades the trip to the voting booth and the rest of the day, and Thembi becomes aware of the importance of voting. Warm pictures of a loving family and a happy event make this story and its message accessible to children.

Slawson, Michele Benoit. *Apple Picking Time.* **Illustrated by Deborah Kogan Ray. 1994. Hardcover: Crown. Paperback: Dragonfly. Ages 3–6.**

Not many children have a chance to earn money, so the narrator in this nostalgic book is excited about going to pick apples for pay. Soft-edged pictures show a young girl on a ladder with her canvas bag strapped onto her stomach. Her ambition is to fill a bin this year for the first time. She picks all day through the increasing heat, and finally hears the sound she has been waiting for, a girl's voice calling, "Full." She gets her ticket punched and rushes off to cash it in. Her parents and grandparents express their pride at her efforts and that night she dreams of filling two bins next year. A quiet story that encourages girls to work hard and be rewarded.

Smucker, Anna Egan. *No Star Nights.* **Illustrated by Steve Johnson. 1989. Paperback: Knopf. Ages 6–9.**

"When I was little, we couldn't see the stars in the nighttime sky because the furnaces of the mill turned the darkness into a red glow." So begins this beautifully illustrated book about growing up in a mill town in West Virginia. The narrator is a girl whose father works at the steel mills. She plays baseball, goes to Pittsburgh Pirates games as a special treat, and climbs the slag heaps, huge hills of glassy refuse from the mills. Set in the 1950s, the story shows girls who enjoy sports and adventures that dirty their blue jeans. These girls are as curious as any boy about the mills dominating their lives. Evocative oil paintings show both the beauty and the bleakness of life in the mill town. One of the few children's books with an industrial setting, this is all the more unusual because it focuses on girls.

Steig, William. *Brave Irene.* **1986. Hardcover: FSG. Paperback: FSG. Ages 3–7.**

This is one of Steig's few books with strong females. Irene's mother, a seamstress, has finished a beautiful ball gown for the duchess but is too sick to deliver it. Her daughter insists on braving the wintry weather, tucks her mother in bed, and sets out to deliver the dress. She battles the snow and a particularly nasty wind, and is almost buried in a snowdrift, but finally makes it to the palace by cleverly using the dress box as a sled. When things look the worst, Irene draws on her inner resources "in an explosion of fury" and triumphs. It would be preferable if Irene braved the blizzard for something other than a ball gown, but Steig's talent is such that the story rises above this limitation.

Stewart, Sarah. *The Gardener.* **Illustrated by David Small. 1997. Hardcover: FSG. Paperback: FSG. Ages 4–8.**

Because of the Depression, Lydia Grace must leave her parents, her grandmother, and her garden to live in the city with her uncle, who is a baker. Lydia writes letters home that express her feelings and reveal her character. She is a kind girl of great determination, who is a hard worker and loves beauty. Using her knowledge of gardening, Lydia Grace makes her plans and plants flowers in window boxes when spring comes. But she has a more ambitious scheme that entails carrying pails of dirt up long staircases and spending hours creating a marvelous surprise for her uncle. Meanwhile Lydia Grace learns to knead and bake bread, and keeps up her spirits despite the distance from home. The conclusion is guaranteed to make readers smile. A Caldecott Honor Book, this has captivating illustrations of Lydia Grace and her accomplishments.

Thomas, Joyce Carol. *I Have Heard of a Land.* **Illustrated by Floyd Cooper. 1998. Hardcover: Harper. Paperback: Harper. Ages 4–8.**

"I have heard of a land / Where the earth is red with promises," opens this poetic tribute to black pioneers. The speaker, a black woman, has staked a claim in the Oklahoma territory, willing to put in hard physical labor to earn her new land. Superb, soft-edged illustrations show her progress, including her sod hut with a goat on the roof, surrounded by empty prairie. The lyrical text extends from her arrival until she has prospered enough to build a log house. Although she gets help from, and gives help to, her neighbors, the narrator also makes her own fate and succeeds in difficult circumstances. The author's note discusses black settlers in the West and reveals the author's family connection to the story. Outstanding.

Thompson, Kay. *Eloise.* **Illustrated by Hilary Knight. 1955. Hardcover: Simon & Schuster. Ages 4–8.**

Eloise is one of a kind in the world of children's books. She tears around her home, the Plaza Hotel in New York, as if it were a playground. Sometimes she takes two sticks and drags them along the walls, disturbing guest after guest, or if she wants to make a "really loud and terrible racket," she "slomps" her skates along the walls. She saws her doll in half for the excitement of imagining an ambulance and surgery. She drives her tutor crazy by imitating his every word and gesture. Her room could hardly be messier. At the same time she has a loving, jolly relationship with her nanny and appears certain that everyone in the hotel is glad to see her. The hilarious text is matched by funny, apt illustrations. The incorrigible Eloise deserves her years of popularity. Other books include *Eloise in Paris*, *Eloise in Moscow*, and *Eloise at Christmastime*.

Turkle, Brinton. *Do Not Open*. 1981. Hardcover: Dutton. Paperback: Dutton. Ages 3–7.

Miss Moody and her cat live by the beach, where Miss Moody loves storms and the treasures they deposit on the sand. One day she discovers a bottle and opens the stopper, which releases a huge, fearsome creature that gets bigger and more fearsome when it realizes that Miss Moody is not afraid. To get rid of it, she tricks the creature into becoming a mouse and the cat eats it. For children who love scary books, this has a truly ugly monster and a very brave woman, a great combination.

Tyler, Anne. *Tumble Tower*. Illustrated by Mitra Modarressi. 1993. Hardcover: Orchard. Ages 3–7.

In this lighthearted tale by well-known author Anne Tyler, Princess Molly the Messy finds herself at odds with her much tidier parents and brother. Completely belying any notion that girls are naturally neat, Molly strews her clothing all over her room and leaves dishes and old food lying about. She even has an orange tree grown from an orange she never ate. Molly answers her family's complaints by insisting, "It's my own private room, and I like it just the way it is." She knows just what she likes. In the end, her family comes to appreciate Molly's habits when the rest of the castle floods. They seek refuge in her tower room, where they have no problem finding clothes and food for all. After this episode, her parents start to be a bit messier themselves. Charming pictures make the family and messiness even more vivid.

Van Allsburg, Chris. *The Widow's Broom.* **1992. Hardcover: Houghton. Ages 5–9.**

When the widow Minna Shaw aids a witch who has fallen into her cornfields, the witch leaves Minna her old broom. Soon the broom is helping merrily with the chores and even playing the piano in the evening. But her straitlaced male neighbors are scandalized and label the broom evil, although their wives point out what a big help it is around the house. Minna and the broom hatch a plot to best the interfering men, and the final scene shows the contented widow and her broom safe and cozy in their little farmhouse. The remarkable brown-and-white pencil illustrations perfectly suit the spirit of the story, set in the fall, and give the broom a jaunty personality. An enchanting book by an award-winning illustrator.

Vaughn, Marcia. *Whistling Dixie.* **Illustrated by Barry Moser. 1995. Hardcover: HarperCollins. Ages 3–7.**

Dixie Lee is a little girl with no fear and an indulgent mother. First she finds a little alligator and brings it home, saying to her mother, "I 'spect I'll keep it for a pet." Her mother objects until Dixie Lee points out it can eat the "churn turners," slimy creatures that steal buttermilk from the churn. Next Dixie Lee, who dashes around in overalls with a slingshot in her pocket, finds a snake that can scare off the bogeyman and a little owl that can keep the mist sisters from floating down the chimney. Skillful watercolors create a mischievous Dixie Lee and the scary creatures that haunt her house.

Vigna, Judith. *Boot Weather.* **1989. Hardcover: Albert Whitman. Ages 2–5.**

Snow means boot weather to Kim, and off she goes on adventures. Her real pastimes, playing in the snow and on playground equipment, are echoed by imaginary escapades. When she climbs up a slide she pictures herself mountain climbing. Zooming down the slide, she sees herself sledding down the steep mountain. She imagines herself as an astronaut, a hockey player, a construction worker, and an explorer. She gets shot from a cannon and takes off with Santa in his sleigh. A brief text and appealing watercolor pictures convey her morning of fun.

Walsh, Ellen Stoll. *Hop Jump.* **1993. Paperback: Harcourt. Ages 2–5.**

In this superb book, a frog named Betsy prefers to try something new while all the other frogs spend their time hopping and jumping. She imitates leaves she sees falling and soon she is leaping and turning and twisting—and dancing. Remarkable cut-paper collages in greens and blues capture Betsy's movements and her excitement. While at first the other frogs disdain anything new, they become so intrigued that they try dancing, too. The expansive pictures turn into a celebration of movement that practically flies off the page. Don't miss this one.

Weller, Frances Ward. *Madaket Millie.* **Illustrated by Marcia Sewall. 1997. Paperback: Paper Star. Ages 5–9.**

Legend mixes with fact in this story of Millie Jewett, a lifelong resident of Nantucket who was a hero on her own small island. Although she wasn't welcome in the Coast Guard as she had hoped, she made herself useful during the Second

World War by training dogs to patrol the beach. When the Coast Guard shut down their Madaket station near her, Millie watched the shores herself and helped save many boats from danger. Stories like the one where she used a pitchfork to force a shark out of a creek and onto the beach made her a hero and a legend. Superb prints show her island life and convey the determination and strength of this unusual woman who knew the Nantucket shores better than anyone.

Wells, Rosemary. *McDuff Comes Home*. Illustrated by Susan Jeffers. 1997. Hardcover: Hyperion. Paperback: Little, Brown. Ages 2–7.

McDuff, a small, white dog, spots a rabbit in the garden one day, and cannot resist chasing it. In flower-filled pictures, they dash through yards and gardens until the rabbit disappears down a hole too small for McDuff. He falls asleep in a vegetable garden, where an older woman picks him up and says she will drive him to the police station. Then, to the surprise of young readers, she puts McDuff in the sidecar of her big red motorcycle, and, wearing goggles and a leather helmet, she sets off. In response to McDuff's barking, she ends up at his owners' house to everyone's delight. Although McDuff's owners seem to have traditional gender roles, the sight of the older woman on the motorcycle is priceless. Illustrations with an old-fashioned charm add to the book's appeal.

Westcott, Nadine Bernard, adapter. *The Lady with an Alligator Purse*. 1988. Hardcover: Little, Brown. Paperback: Little, Brown. Ages 2–7.

This adaptation of a familiar jump-rope rhyme jumps with joy. The whimsical pictures are perfect for the upbeat text about a lady with an alligator purse who cures Tiny Tim after he eats up all the soap. Her remedy, in contrast to the medicines recommended by the (male) doctor and (female) nurse, is—to the pleasure of the children listening—pizza! Then, a perfect ending to the short rhyme shows the lady, her alligator purse, and a healthy Tiny Tim sliding merrily down the banister. Here is a woman who knows how to have fun in a way children appreciate.

Wiesner, David. *June 29, 1999*. 1992. Hardcover: Clarion. Ages 4–8.

The slight plot in this book is a vehicle for its ingenious illustrations. Holly Evans, a very capable girl, is conducting a science experiment for school, studying the effects of sending vegetable seedlings into space. She appears first at home launching her experiment, with a picture of Einstein on her bulletin board and the periodic table of elements on the wall behind her. She is sending seedlings on cardboard trays out the window, borne aloft by small helium balloons. Soon giant vegetables appear in the sky throughout the country. In one wonderful picture, people rein in giant red peppers. A gigantic broccoli plant appears in Holly's yard and she builds a treehouse in it. She is shown clipping newspaper articles about the vegetables and keeping a chart of where they've appeared. But she is baffled because some of the vegetables are not ones she sent into space, but a true scientist to the end, she is "more curious than disappointed." A final picture of some equally puzzled space aliens solves the mystery for the reader.

Willard, Nancy. *Shadow Story*. Illustrated by David Diaz. 1999. Hardcover: Harcourt. Ages 4–9.

When Holly Go Lolly is born, the shadow of a fairy godmother grants her a wish, which is that the girl will never be afraid of the dark. Alas, her father soon is eaten by a monster called the Ooboo, leaving Holly and her mother very poor.

Holly amuses herself by creating shadow figures with her hands, far beyond what most people could do. By the time she is fourteen, she can make shadow antelopes and peacocks, daffodils and tiger lilies. But one of her shadows angers the West Wind, who enlists the help of the Ooboo to get revenge. On the advice of her fairy godmother, Holly climbs to the Ooboo's mountaintop palace and schemes to defeat the Ooboo before it defeats her. Magical illustrations in delightful colors create a fairy-tale world where the brave heroine and her amazing shadows flourish.

Williams, Karen Lynn. *Painted Dreams*. Illustrated by Catherine Stock. 1998. Hardcover: Lothrop. Ages 4–8.

Ti Marie, who lives in Haiti, loves to draw pictures, but her family needs her to do chores and cannot afford to buy her paints. After passing a local artist's house, Ti Marie goes back at night and gets his discarded paint tubes. With these, she cleverly devises a way to increase her family's income. Their spot at the marketplace never attracts many customers until Ti Marie clears the white wall behind it of moss and paints a colorful, eye-catching picture. Even the island artist comes and admires it. Enjoying the crowd's admiration and the artist's interest, Ti Marie vows to practice her talent. Lovely watercolors develop the characters and setting in this story about a young painter.

Williams, Linda. *The Little Old Lady Who Was Not Afraid of Anything*. Illustrated by Megan Lloyd. 1986. Hardcover: Harper. Paperback: Trophy. Ages 3–7.

A plucky old woman goes out to gather herbs and nuts in the forest one day. On her way home in the dark, she finds herself followed by a pair of shoes that go "CLOMP, CLOMP," which are joined by a pair of pants that go "WIG-

GLE, WIGGLE" and so on. She starts running only when a scary pumpkin head yells "BOO, BOO!" Safe in her house, she plucks up her courage to answer the door, and unafraid, gives the collection of items a piece of advice. Next morning in her garden stands a scarecrow made up of all the scary items. A cumulative tale popular with children.

Williams, Sherley Anne. _Girls Together_. Illustrated by Synthia Saint James. 1999. Hardcover: Harcourt. Ages 3–8.

Striking illustrations in geometric shapes and bright colors raise this above most picture-story books. Five black girls who are good friends spend a summer day together, with their pastimes related in the narrator's conversational style: "We leave out the Project, all us girls together. Hey, hey, we say, and link arms when we walk." To avoid taking care of little brothers, the five walk past the vacant lots and empty buildings near the Project until they come to a neighborhood with small houses and large trees. One girl knows the names of the trees they climb, like sycamore, pines, and magnolias. Caught up in the mood of the summer day, they all put flowers in their hair, ending the book with a vivid picture of one girl "in a white flower hair barrette." This unusually attractive book emphasizes friendship among girls and their adventurous spirit.

Williams, Suzanne. _Library Lil_. Illustrated by Steven Kellogg. 1997. Hardcover: Dial. Paperback: Puffin. Ages 4–8.

This upbeat tale breaks all the stale stereotypes of librarians, introducing the young, strong, and outgoing Library Lil. Even as a child, Lil loved to read—and was stronger than the other children. She played soccer at age five and built tree forts at seven, consulting books for both. When she'd finished reading the fiction at her town library, she started on the encyclopedia, carrying the volume she was reading in one hand

and the other twenty-five volumes stacked in the other hand. Once grown, she became a librarian but found the people in her town were too busy watching television to read. Her chance came when the power went out for two weeks. Lil pushed the old bookmobile through town and by the end of the power outage, everyone loved to read. When Bust-'em-up Bill, a motorcycle gang leader, came through town, Lil even converted him. Steven Kellogg's funny drawings perfectly suit this tall tale about an assertive, muscular, book-loving librarian.

Williams, Vera B. *Music, Music for Everyone.* **1984. Paperback: Mulberry. Ages 3–8.**

Glowing colors fill this book about a girl and her friends who form a band. Rosa, who tells the story, wants to help earn money now that her grandmother is sick. Remembering that her other grandmother used to play music at parties and weddings for pay, Rosa forms the Oak Street Band with three friends. Rosa plays the accordion, Leora the drums, Jenny the fiddle, and Mae the flute. The four girls, encouraged by relatives, practice together and successfully perform at their first paid job. Williams's beautiful watercolors show a multicultural group of four girls in a working-class environment, banding together for fun and profit. One of the few children's books featuring an all-girl band, this is a gem. Other beautifully illustrated books about Rosa include *A Chair for My Mother* and *Something Special for Me.*

Williams, Vera B. *Three Days on a River in a Red Canoe.* **1981. Hardcover: Greenwillow. Paperback: Mulberry. Ages 3–7.**

In this original work, the narrator, her brother, her mother, and her aunt take a three-day canoe trip together. To plan it, the mother and aunt happily pore over maps of canoe trips they took before the children were born. The four camp at night, and the narrator learns about camping as well as canoeing. Her new knowledge appears in illustrations of how to tie half hitches and put up a tent. The story, which feels like a scrapbook about the trip, also includes maps, recipes, and labeled drawings of fish they see. Fun to read and look at, this outstanding book about females outdoors will have the reader longing to take a canoe trip.

Wood, Audrey. *Red Racer*. 1996. Hardcover: Simon & Schuster. Paperback: Aladdin. Ages 3–8.

Enthusiastic bicyclist Nona longs for a new bike. When she sees the Deluxe Red Racer in a shop window, she sets her heart on it, but her parents object to the price. Then Nona has a "wicked thought," which appears as a large green blob. The thought is to wreck her old bike so she'll need a new one. She tries to drop it off a cliff and then into the water, but both times a well-meaning person rescues it. Turning green herself, Nona leaves the bike on a railroad track to get run over. But when she arrives home to find her parents ready to fix up her old bike, she manages to save her old bike and the three of them fix it up together. Nona's realistic "wickedness" will appeal to children, who will relate to her enthusiasm for bikes and her desire for a new one. Wildly energetic, exaggerated pictures add to the fun of this story about a girl with a mind of her own.

Yee, Wong Herbert. *Hamburger Heaven*. 1999. Hardcover: Houghton. Ages 3–6.

After an elephant sits on Pinky Pig's clarinet, she needs to buy a new one, but she doesn't have the money. To finance her purchase, she gets a Friday after-school job at Hamburger

Heaven. As she is mopping the floor one day, she over-hears two employees talking about how slow business is and how Pinky Pig may lose her job. Heading home on her skate-board, Pinky Pig studies the problem and that night comes up with a plan to bring in more customers. Armed with a note-book, she goes out on Saturday morning to ask everyone she meets what kind of burgers they like. On Sunday, she buys art supplies and creates new menus. She distributes them all week and when Friday rolls around, Hamburger Heaven is packed with satisfied customers eating their favorite burgers. An en-joyable rhyming story about a savvy pig.

Yolen, Jane. *Owl Moon.* **Illustrated by John Schoenherr. 1987. Hardcover: Philomel. Ages 4–8.**

This exquisite book, which won the Caldecott Medal for its pictures, is about a girl who goes out owling at night with her father for the first time. It is winter and the child (who is identified as a girl in the jacket copy but not the text) is bun-dled up against the cold. She doesn't complain about the weather because her older brothers have warned her that you have to keep quiet "and make your own heat" and be brave. The persistence of child and father is finally rewarded by the sight of a great horned owl, beautifully depicted in water-colors. What a magical experience for a young girl, to be out on an adventure on a winter night—and this book fully con-veys the magic.

Young, Ed. *Seven Blind Mice.* **1992. Hardcover: Philomel. Ages 3–7.**

While this Caldecott Honor Book is most notable for its stunning design and artwork, it also features a female mouse who solves a problem six male mice couldn't. Each of the seven mice sets off on a different day to figure out what the new Something is that has appeared by their pond. Each mouse misinterprets the part of the Something he touches. The first one, for example, feels the animal's leg and reports that it's a pillar. Readers will figure out that the Something is an elephant, as the girl mouse does when she sets off last and explores the whole animal instead of just one part. A remarkably beautiful and cunningly wrought book.

2

Folktales

Fairy tales with passive female characters like Cinderella and Sleeping Beauty have become metaphors for women who believe that a Prince Charming will enter their lives and make everything perfect. Parents who want to send a different message will find the books described in this chapter invaluable. The heroines in these tales offer a welcome alternative to Disney's insipid, glamorous fairy-tale females. Even in these books, the girls and women tend toward the beautiful, but they also take the lead and have adventures, instead of waiting to be rescued.

In addition to folktales, this chapter includes fairy tales and parodies. Folktales come from an oral tradition in which they are passed down through time, changed by tellers along the way. There is no specific author for such tales, although collectors and retellers attach their names to published versions. Technically speaking, fairy tales are stories that resemble folktales but are written by an identified author who draws from traditional folklore for structure, style, and content. Katherine Paterson's *The King's Equal*, which falls into this category, is an original story that sounds like a traditional tale. In recent years, a number of books have parodied well-known folktales using a type of broad humor that appeals to many children. *Cinder Edna* and *Rumpelstiltskin's Daughter*, for example, are lighthearted spoofs of "Cinderella" and "Rumpelstiltskin."

These books are for a wide range of ages; again, the range given indicates listening level, not reading level. Many of the folktales work well for reading aloud because of the exciting plots and honed language. Many are beautifully illustrated, too. Most can also be read alone by good independent readers, although the vocabulary is usually too difficult for beginning readers.

The first section of this chapter contains illustrated versions of single tales, which resemble the picture-story books in the previous chapter. Most are thirty-two pages and can be read in one sitting. The next section lists collections of folktales, books with fifteen or more stories gathered together. These longer volumes present a valuable contrast to traditional collections of folktales in which men and boys play the leading roles.

Single Tales

Aardema, Verna. *Borreguita and the Coyote: A Tale from Ayutla, Mexico*. Illustrated by Petra Mathers. 1991. Paperback: Dragonfly. Ages 3–8.

A little female lamb named Borreguita outwits a hungry coyote again and again in this Mexican folktale. Illustrations in vivid hues show an innocent, curly-haired white lamb staring guilelessly at the evil-eyed coyote as she talks him out of eating her. First she advises waiting until she is fatter, and after he has waited, fools him with two other schemes. In the last trick, Borreguita combines cleverness and physical force in a feat that sends the coyote slinking away for good. Borreguita is young and female, and very clever indeed. Outstanding illustrations and a satisfying plot.

Aardema, Verna. *Rabbit Makes a Monkey of Lion: A Swahili Tale*. Illustrated by Jerry Pinkney. 1989. Hardcover: Dial. Paperback: Puffin. Ages 3–8.

Twice Rabbit steals honey from Lion's supply, and twice she tricks him—"makes a monkey of him"—and gets away. The second time her companion is Turtle, who escapes by tricking Lion into putting her into a pond. Thus, two smaller females triumph over a fierce male lion. The third time she considers stealing, Rabbit decides that judgment is the better part of valor and stays home. Lush pencil and watercolor illustrations in yellows, greens, and browns add humor and beauty. The rhythmic storytelling makes this Swahili tale perfect for reading aloud.

de Paola, Tomie. *Fin M'Coul: The Giant of Knockmany Hill.* **1981. Hardcover: Holiday. Paperback: Holiday. Ages 3–7.**

In de Paola's cheerful illustrations, the giants Fin M'Coul, his lovely great wife Oonagh, and the enemy Cucullin barely fit on the pages, they are so huge. Red-haired, freckled Fin learns how smart his wife is when Cucullin comes looking to fight Fin and Oonagh fools him. First she has Fin dress up as a baby and climb into the cradle, and she bakes iron pans into loaves of bread. When a bellowing Cucullin arrives, she feeds him the bread, which breaks his teeth. After two more tricks, Cucullin, the fiercest giant around, loses his strength, and Fin is safe. The comical story, the appealing illustrations with their lovely borders, and the giant heroine result in a first-class Irish tale.

Del Negro, Janice. *Lucy Dove.* **Illustrated by Leonid Gore. 1998. Hardcover: DK Ink. Paperback: DK Ink. Ages 5–9.**

This original fairy tale, with its creepy setting, clawed monster, and haunting pictures will satisfy the many children who crave scary books. "When wishes were horses and beggars could ride," it begins, a rich, superstitious laird—a man of power and wealth—offered gold to anyone who would sew him trousers by moonlight in an old graveyard. Old Lucy Dove, who has more courage than money, resolves to win the gold. In the moonlit graveyard, she encounters a fearsome monster and defeats it with her wit. Storyteller Del Negro has fashioned a rhythmic text perfect for reading aloud, accompanied by deliciously ghostly paintings.

Demi. *One Grain of Rice: A Mathematical Folktale.* **1997. Hardcover: Scholastic. Ages 6–10.**

Detailed artwork, decorated with gold, provides the perfect accompaniment to an Indian folktale. A raja makes farmers give him nearly all their rice, but promises to distribute it if a famine occurs. But when a famine comes, he fails in his promise. When a village woman named Rani sees rice falling from baskets being carried to the raja's storehouse, she gathers it and returns it to the raja. Impressed, he offers her a reward. The clever Rani asks for a grain of rice, with the amount she receives to be doubled each day for a month. The raja agrees, then is shocked as the month comes to an end and she has all his rice. A fold-out page shows 256 elephants with rice baskets carrying her reward. Rani gives the rice away, including some to the raja, who promises not to take more than he needs in the future. A wonderful combination of folklore, math, and a smart young woman.

Ernst, Lisa Campbell. *Little Red Riding Hood: A New-fangled Prairie Tale*. 1995. Hardcover: Simon & Schuster. Paperback: Aladdin. Ages 3–7.

Another modern Red Riding Hood, this one wears a red sweatshirt with a hood as she zooms around on her bicycle. On the way to deliver muffins to her grandmother, she does get taken in by the nattily dressed wolf, but her sturdy grandmother does not. Looking for an "ancient granny," the wolf finds a female farmer who is ready to crush him "like a bug, if need be." The self-possessed grandmother tames the wolf in an unexpected way, leading to a funny ending. Ernst's deft illustrations extend the clever text in this fresh version.

Forest, Heather. *The Woman Who Flummoxed the Fairies*. Illustrated by Susan Gaber. 1990. Paperback: Voyager. Ages 3–7.

Captivating, round little fairies flit through this story, decorating the initial letter on each page, hiding in flowers and flying around in their world. The king of the fairies has discovered an excellent bakerwoman and has his fairies capture her. But the bakerwoman knows that if she bakes him a cake, the king will never let her go home, because her cakes are so good. So she insists the fairies fetch a series of things she needs from her home. Humorous pictures show her husband and baby watching in astonishment as flour and eggs float out the window, followed later by the cat and dog. Knowing how fairies hate noise, she has them bring her baby, too, and the husband follows behind. When they are all gathered in the fairy's home, the bakerwoman provokes the most noise possible from the dog, cat, and baby until the king of the fairies can take no more. He settles for having her bake him a cake at home, and rewards her generously. The illustrations enhance the magic and humor of this tale about a woman who gets the best of the fairy king.

Hoffman, Mary, reteller. *Clever Katya: A Fairy Tale from Old Russia*. Illustrated by Marie Cameron. 1998. Hardcover: Barefoot Books. Ages 5–9.

Set once upon a time in Russia, this story opens with two brothers, Dimitri who is rich and Ivan who is poor, riding together to market. Ivan's mare, which Dimitri gave him, gives birth during the night and both brothers claim the foal is theirs. They take their dispute to the Tsar, who decides to get some enjoyment out of the silly situation. Even though he realizes the foal belongs to Ivan, he tells the two men that the one who solves four riddles will get the foal. Ivan's clever daughter Katya gives her father the answer to the riddles. But then the Tsar sets her another challenge, which she uses her wit to solve. Colorful detailed pictures with lovely borders make this an attractive version of a well-known tale.

Hong, Lily Toy. *The Empress and the Silkworm*. 1995. Hardcover: Albert Whitman. Ages 4–8.

Charming stylized pictures accompany this legend about Si Ling-Chi, a Chinese empress said to have discovered how to make silk. According to the story, more than four thousand years ago the empress was taking tea when a cocoon fell from a mulberry tree and began to unravel in the heat of the tea. Si Ling-Chi saw its possibilities as thread that could be woven into strong, beautiful cloth. Although the emperor's male advisors laughed at her scheme, the empress proved herself right: After months, workers under Si Ling-Chi's supervision finally produced a magnificent silk robe for the emperor. A note at the end explains the origins of the legend and gives information about the process of making silk.

Hooks, William H. *The Three Little Pigs and the Fox*. Illustrated by S. D. Schindler. 1989. Paperback: Aladdin. Ages 5–9.

"This story happened a long time ago, way back when the animals could still talk around these parts," begins this tale from the Great Smoky Mountains. As in the traditional tale, a mother pig sends her three children off into the world, only in this version her third child is a girl pig named Hamlet. Hamlet's older brothers go off, one at a time, and get caught by the "mean, tricky old drooly-mouth fox" to be eaten later. But Hamlet is brighter and braver than her brothers. She wards off the fox and builds herself a strong house. Then she tricks him into telling her where her brothers are and sends him down the river in a churn. Hamlet then sets the brothers free and they all return home happy and hungry. The story's Appalachian language has a rollicking rhythm and flavor, perfect for reading aloud.

Isaacs, Anne. *Swamp Angel*. Illustrated by Paul O. Zelinsky. 1994. Hardcover: Dutton. Paperback: Puffin. Ages 4–9.

Here is a new figure in the tradition of tall tales: Angelica Longrider, known as Swamp Angel. Born in 1914 in Tennessee, "The newborn was scarcely taller than her mother and couldn't climb a tree without help." When she was two, she built her first log cabin and when she was twelve, she rescued a whole wagon train from a swamp and earned her nickname. In the main incident, she pursues a giant bear and eventually defeats him after a series of outlandish skirmishes. Zelinsky's witty paintings, done on wood veneer, so beautifully extend the story that the book was named a Caldecott Honor Book. The last we see of the folk heroine, she is dragging the enormous bear pelt behind her on her way to more open territory. Swamp Angel is a mighty good addition to the American tall tale.

Jackson, Ellen. *Cinder Edna*. Illustrated by Kevin O'Malley. 1994. Hardcover: Lothrop. Paperback: Mulberry. Ages 4–8.

There's nothing subtle in this funny retelling of the Cinderella story. In an updated setting, the mopey Cinderella and the self-reliant Cinder Edna live next door to each other. They both have to work for their wicked stepmother and stepsisters, but Cinder Edna uses the toil as a chance to master a few tasks. She also makes money on the side working for neighbors. Unlike Cinderella, Edna is no beauty, but "she was strong and spunky and knew some good jokes." When the king announces a ball, Cinderella calls on her fairy godmother, but Cinder Edna wears a dress bought with her extra earnings. The traditional girl goes by pumpkin, Edna by city bus. Although Edna finds the prince dull as can be, his brother

Rupert, who runs a recyling plant, is just her type of man. And so, Cinderella ends up with the dull but handsome prince and Edna with an intelligent man who shares her interests and values. The last line: "Guess who lived happily ever after." Boisterous, exaggerated pictures add to the fun.

Keams, Geri. *Grandmother Spider Brings the Sun: A Cherokee Story*. Illustrated by James Bernardin. 1995. Paperback: Rising Moon. Ages 4–8.

Children enjoy reading about someone very small who saves the day, such as little Grandmother Spider who succeeds where the bigger, male Possum and Buzzard couldn't. Their task is to fetch some sun from the light side of the world to brighten up the dark side where the animals live. After Possum and Buzzard fail, the other animals scoff when Grandmother Spider volunteers, even though she has done many things in her time to help them. But she persists and sneaks by the fearsome Sun Guards to deliver the light. Witty illustrations in acrylic and colored pencil develop the personality of each animal, from sly Coyote to feisty little Spider.

Kellogg, Steven. *Sally Ann Thunder Ann Whirlwind Crockett: A Tall Tale*. 1995. Hardcover: Morrow. Paperback: Mulberry. Ages 4–9.

Tall tale heroine Sally Ann Thunder Ann Whirlwind lives up to her name from the start. Just after birth she proclaims, "I can out-talk, out-grin, out-scream, out-swim, and out-run any baby in Kentucky!" And she proves it on the spot by outrunning her nine older brothers. When she turns eight, she sets off for the frontier and new challenges such as skinning bears and wrestling alligators. Who could she marry but the most famous outdoorsman in the country, Davy Crockett? From beginning to end, the frenzied, funny pictures show Sally

Ann beating all opponents and having a good time at it. A good match to the many tall tales about frontiersmen.

Kimmel, Eric A. *The Four Gallant Sisters*. Illustrated by Tatyana Yuditskaya. 1992. Hardcover: Henry Holt. Ages 5–9.

This charming variation on a fairy tale, apparently adapted from the Grimms, features four sisters seeking their fortunes after their mother dies. Each, disguised as a man, apprentices herself to learn a trade: tailoring, hunting, sleight of hand, and star-gazing. Each sister excels at her choice and leaves after seven years with a special gift from her master. They go to serve the king, and from there go to rescue a princess and four princes captured by a dragon. Their special gifts combined with their courage save the day. Back at the castle, the princes say of their rescuers, "We never had truer friends or more valiant companions," and in the end each sister agrees to marry one of the princes. A remark by the rescued princess denigrating women mars the text, but overall, this is a fairy tale with unusually strong heroines.

Kimmel, Eric A., adapter. *Rimonah of the Flashing Sword: A North African Tale*. Illustrated by Omar Rayyan. 1995. Hardcover: Holiday. Ages 5–9.

Although this North African version of "Snow White" features the usual wicked stepmother, the heroine diverges from the usual story by being strong and fearless. After she escapes from the death ordered by her stepmother the queen, Rimonah joins a group of bedouins. As the years pass, she grows in bravery until she rides "with the reckless daring of a bedouin horseman." Excellent with both dagger and sword, she grows in fame, which eventually brings her to her stepmother's notice. No longer safe with her comrades, Rimonah takes refuge in a cave with forty thieves, honest people who had suffered under the queen. Rimonah rides with the thieves and as the boldest of all becomes known as "Rimonah of the Flashing Sword." Reverting to a passive plotline, Rimonah nearly dies and is only rescued from her glass coffin by the prince of her dreams. However, she then rescues her father, also from a coffin, and defeats her stepmother. Ornate, fanciful pictures create a setting reminiscent of the *Arabian Nights*. An unlikely version of a familiar tale with a strong, sword-wielding heroine.

Knutson, Barbara. *How the Guinea Fowl Got Her Spots: A Swahili Tale of Friendship*. **1990. Hardcover: Carolrhoda. Paperback: First Avenue. Ages 3–7.**

An unusually attractive design and illustrations of watercolors and ink on scratchboard make this tale a visual treat. The simple story tells of two female friends, Nganga the Guinea Fowl and Cow. Nganga, a glossy black bird at the beginning, saves Cow from an attack by Lion, and the next day, she saves her friend again. In thanks, Cow sprinkles milk over Nganga's shiny black feathers and gives the guinea fowl the white speckles it has today. Not only is her coloration beautiful, but it saves her a third time from Lion, who doesn't recognize her. Borders of African designs, large typeface, and lots of white space add to the outstanding visual appeal of this story about two female friends.

Le Guin, Ursula K. *A Ride on the Red Mare's Back*. **Illustrated by Julie Downing. 1992. Hardcover: Orchard. Paperback: Orchard. Ages 5–9.**

A brave girl sets off through the wintry woods to try to rescue her brother who has been stolen by trolls. When she meets her first troll, the wooden toy horse she's brought magically becomes life-size and helps her with her quest. They gallop through the darkness and snow to the troll's High House, where the brother is a prisoner. While the red mare distracts the trolls, the girl courageously saves her brother. Though the horse turns back into a toy, the girl leads her brother safely on the long journey home. Lovely watercolors, which show some truly ugly trolls, grace this beautifully designed book, making it a pleasure to read and look at. A brave girl aided by a stalwart female animal are an unusual, welcome combination.

Lowell, Susan. *Cindy Ellen: A Wild Western Cinderella.* **Illustrated by Jane Manning. 2000. Hardcover: Harper. Ages 4–9.**

When cowgirl Cindy Ellen cries because her stepsisters have gone to the rodeo without her, her gun-toting fairy grandmother bucks up her spirit with the advice, "What you need first, gal, is some gravel in your gizzard. Grit! Guts!" In this sparkling Western retelling of the old favorite, Cindy Ellen rides a bucking bronco, wins the trick-roping event, and beats Joe Prince in the horse race. When she loses her diamond spur at the square dance, Joe finds her and they get hitched. Joe appears more than happy to marry a girl who can ride better than he can, and Cindy Ellen regains her confidence and flair with her rodeo performance. Colorful exaggerated illustrations match the tall-tale tone of this fractured "Cinderella."

Lowell, Susan. *Little Red Cowboy Hat.* **Illustrated by Randy Cecil. 1996. Hardcover: Henry Holt. Paperback: Henry Holt. Ages 4–9.**

This retelling of Little Red Riding Hood concerns a red-headed girl called Little Red, who lives on a ranch in the

Southwest. One day her mother sends Little Red to take some bread and cactus jelly to her sick grandma, warning her, "Don't dillydally along the way." Angular, amusing pictures show Little Red in her red cowboy hat riding her horse across the desert, where she encounters a wolf in a vest and hat. He beats her to grandma's ranch, where grandma is usually outside "doctoring a cow or mixing cement." When the wolf is about to pounce on Little Red, grandma comes in from chopping wood, and together she and Little Red chase him down the road, with plenty of satisfying sound effects. Colorful language and apt illustrations are the keys to this appealing new version with its strong Western females.

Lunge-Larsen, Lise, and Margi Preus, retellers. *The Legend of the Lady Slipper*. Illustrated by Andrea Arroyo. 1999. Hardcover: Houghton. Ages 4–8.

This Ojibwa legend about a courageous girl tells the origin of the lady slipper, a delicate flower that grows in northern climates. A girl lives with her extended family in a village near a lake, where her favorite older brother serves as the village messenger. But when everyone falls ill except the girl, she must be the one to cross the frozen lake to fetch healing herbs from a neighboring village. She puts on her beautiful moccasins and goes out into a raging storm. Despite the wind and snow, she reaches the other village. But instead of resting, she turns back immediately with the medicine. She loses her moccasins and her feet bleed, but she arrives in time to heal her family. Tidy watercolors full of rounded shapes show her dangerous journey and its happy conclusion.

Manna, Anthony L., and Christodoula Mitakidou. *Mr. Semolina-Semolinus: A Greek Folktale*. Illustrated by Giselle Potter. 1997. Hardcover: Atheneum. Ages 4–8.

When a princess named Areti cannot find a suitor she likes, she bakes herself a man, whose name—Mr. Semolina-Semolinus—comes from the ingredients. "He was five times beautiful and ten times kind," a fact which becomes known across the world and attracts a princess who kidnaps him. Areti makes a perilous journey to rescue him, wearing out a pair of iron shoes, and seeking help from the sun, moon, and stars, and their mothers. She finally succeeds and sails home with Mr. Semolina-Semolinus, "where they lived blissfully but no better." Lyrical writing with the cadences of oral tradition and fresh, amusing illustrations create a charming combination.

Merrill, Jean. *The Girl Who Loved Caterpillars*. Illustrated by Floyd Cooper. 1992. Hardcover: Philomel. Paperback: Paper Star. Ages 5–9.

In this twelfth-century tale from Japan, the girl named Izumi becomes known as "The Girl Who Loved Caterpillars." Her aristocratic parents would prefer her to act more sedately and concentrate on more seemly pastimes, but Izumi is fascinated with creatures that squirm, crawl, or hop. She fills her room with them and befriends scruffy boys who bring her more. She defies other conventions as well, refusing to pluck her eyebrows or blacken her teeth, as the fashionable young ladies do. She takes a lot of criticism, which unfortunately comes mostly from other females. She earns the admiration of a nobleman, but romance holds no appeal for Izumi: She ignores the nobleman to ask a peasant boy for fresh leaves for the caterpillars. No fairy-tale ending for this budding scientist who clearly has a mind of her own.

Mollel, Tololwa M. *Song Bird*. Illustrated by Rosanne Litzinger. 1999. Hardcover: Clarion. Ages 4–9.

In this adaptation of a tale from southern Africa, when a

family's cattle disappear, the family decides to clear the now empty fields to farm them. But when only the daughter Mariamu is watching, a bird sings and the fields revert to their uncleared state. When questioned, the bird offers the family all the milk they want if they will leave the fields alone. Mariamu's parents cage the bird, but the girl frees it and the two embark on a journey to the land of the monster who has stolen the cattle. The bird uses her magic to defeat the monster and Mariamu brings the missing cattle back home. Although the pretty illustrations do not add much to the story, the prose incorporates repeated phrases and a song in Swahili that make it good for reading aloud.

Osborne, Mary Pope. *Kate and the Beanstalk.* **Illustrated by Giselle Potter. 2000. Hardcover: Atheneum. Ages 3–8.**
The cover of this reworked fairy tale shows a girl with a determined look climbing a beanstalk. Instead of the more famous Jack, it's Kate who trades a cow for magic beans, to her mother's disgust. A beanstalk springs up and Kate climbs to the top, where she sees a castle in the distance. She meets a sparkling old woman who tells her that the castle once belonged to a knight who was killed by a giant. The knight's wife and child survived but need someone to right their wrong. Kate agrees to help by taking the hen that lays golden eggs, a bag of gold coins, and a magical harp. In her first two tries, she succeeds. During the last attempt, the giant runs after her, but Kate chops down the beanstalk and destroys him, leading to the expected happy ending. Large delightful illustrations show the girl's brave feats and add touches of humor.

Oughton, Jerrie. *The Magic Weaver of Rugs: A Tale of the Navajo.* **Illustrated by Lisa Desimini. 1994. Hardcover: Houghton. Ages 5–8.**

When cold and hunger beset their people, two Navajo women go on a quest to seek help. Spider Woman, hearing their pleas, lassoes them with a web and lifts them to her high canyon wall. There she teaches them how to weave on a loom she constructs from four large trees. The women, under Spider Woman's directions, weave a rug from all the colors of the world. But they doubt and question her, and consequently weave an imperfect rug. Quick to anger, Spider Woman will not give the rug to them but sends them on their way, saying they have the gift they need. Returning to their people, the two women teach them how to weave beautiful rugs, which eventually they trade for food and other necessities. A haunting tale, powerfully illustrated in deep colors, this attributes the origin of Navajo rugs to two brave women and the mythological Spider Woman.

Paterson, Katherine. *The King's Equal*. Illustrated by Vladimir Vagin. 1992. Hardcover: Harper. Paperback: Trophy. Ages 5–10.

In this splendid original fairy tale, an arrogant, selfish prince receives a strange blessing from his dying father: "You will not wear my crown until the day you marry a woman who is your equal in beauty and intelligence and wealth." Since the prince thinks so highly of himself, his ministers cannot come up with a bride he will accept. When a peasant named Rosamund appears, aided by a magic wolf, the prince discovers that she is more than his equal. He must earn her hand in marriage through a year of living in the mountains that she comes from. The brave Rosamund proves to be a much more industrious, successful ruler than the absent prince, who returns a wiser man. Ornate illustrations by a Russian artist add to the fairy-tale quality of this charming book.

Paterson, Katherine. *The Wide-Awake Princess*. Illustrated by Vladimir Vagin. 2000. Hardcover: Clarion. Ages 4–9.

Princess Miranda's fairy godmother gives her the gift of being awake in all her waking hours, so the girl spends her childhood paying attention to everything, especially the world of nature. But when her parents die, powerful noblemen don't want a twelve-year-old queen. So Miranda sets off into her country to learn how to be a queen. First she must defend her animal friends against a troll. Then she works side-by-side with the poor people in the fields, listening carefully to her new friends who are discouraged and heavily taxed. Angry at their conditions, she forms a plan that leads to a splendid unexpected ending. The many illustrations add color and touches of humor to this original fairy tale about a girl who becomes her country's leader.

San Souci, Robert D. *Brave Margaret: An Irish Adventure*. Illustrated by Sally Wern Comport. 1999. Hardcover: Simon & Schuster. Ages 5–9.

Dramatic paintings convey the adventurous nature of this folktale. As it opens, Margaret lives alone tending her cattle and fishing. But when Simon, a handsome prince, appears looking for meat for his sailors, she insists on going with him to see the world. They are soon parted by a sea serpent and by the time Margaret defeats the monster, Simon's ship has been thrust out of sight by the serpent's tail. Margaret takes refuge with an old woman, who is a sorcerer, and Margaret has to defeat a giant to save her own life and rescue Simon. Returning with Simon's crew to his father's kingdom, the two are married and "their happiness lasted a lifetime." Drawn from Irish folktales, this fast-paced story packs a lot of adventure into its thirty-two pages, with Margaret as the central, bravest figure.

San Souci, Robert D. *Fa Mulan: The Story of a Woman Warrior*. **Illustrated by Jean and Mou-Sien Tseng. 1998. Hardcover: Hyperion. Paperback: Hyperion. Ages 4–9.**

As many now know from the Disney movie, Fa Mulan was a legendary Chinese girl who fought in the khan's army. When this version of the story opens, the Tartars have invaded and are burning towns. Mulan, knowing her father is too old and weak to fight, volunteers to go in his place, disguised as a man. Expansive pages, designed to look like part of a scroll, paint pictures of Mulan changing her appearance, leaving her family, and fighting in the beautiful, mountainous countryside. She soon excels at soldiering and leading her companions in battle, until finally she is made a general. The khan offers her a reward for defeating the enemy in a key skirmish, and Mulan asks to return home, where her close fighting companions are shocked to learn she is a woman. Stunning artwork adds greatly to the story's effect.

San Souci, Robert D. *The Samurai's Daughter*. **Illustrated by Stephen T. Johnson. 1992. Paperback: Puffin. Ages 5–10.**

Set in medieval Japan, this tale revolves around Tokoyo, the daughter of a samurai warrior. Her father schools Tokoyo, his only child, in the arts of the samurai, such as shooting a bow and riding a horse. He also instills in her the samurai's sense of honor. When she gets older, she dives with the amas, women divers who are better than men at harvesting abalone and oysters. One day, at the command of their lord, soldiers seize her father to imprison him on an island. Tokoyo arms herself with a dagger and follows, disguised as a peasant. After a dangerous journey she reaches the island. There she takes the place of a young woman about to be sacrificed to a sea serpent and succeeds in killing the serpent and by chance also freeing her father from exile. Powerful paintings show her diving with the dagger in her teeth and attacking the huge white monster. A tale of courage and strength, not to be missed.

San Souci, Robert D., reteller. *A Weave of Words: An Armenian Folktale.* Illustrated by Raúl Colón. 1998. Hardcover: Orchard. Ages 4–9.

Prince Vachagan is a warm-hearted, handsome young man who loves to ride and hunt. Used to getting his own way, he hasn't learned to read or write, much less mastered a craft. He is confident when he offers his hand to a weaver's accomplished daughter, but she objects to marrying a man who can't read or write, as she can, and who cannot earn a living by his own hands. Chastened, the prince vows to better himself and when he succeeds, sends her a beautiful carpet that he wove. Happily married, tragedy enters their lives when the prince gets enslaved by a three-headed demon. He buys time with his ability to weave and cleverly manages to get a message to his wife, who fights the demon to rescue her husband. Beautifully textured illustrations fashion a fairy-tale world of long ago for this story of love and courage.

Schroeder, Alan, reteller. *The Tale of Willie Monroe.* Illustrated by Andrew Glass. 1999. Hardcover: Clarion. Ages 5–10.

In this adaptation of a Japanese folktale, a muscular young man in the American South learns a lesson in strength from a young woman and her grandmother. As the tale opens, Willie Monroe is described as having "arms as big as stovepipes and a chest as broad as a barn door." The exaggerated pictures show him with muscles popping out everywhere. When he sees a notice about an arm-wrestling contest, Willie decides to enter and heads off to Carolina for it. On the way, he meets Delilah carrying a bucket on her head and decides to tease her by dumping it over. To his surprise, she traps his hand and he can't get it back because she is stronger than he is. She takes him home, where they see her grandmother carrying a full-grown horse on her back. Delilah and her granny offer to train Willie so he will win the contest and, though they have to go easy at first, they succeed. Tall-tale expressions and funny, homespun pictures make this an amusing new version of a traditional story about very strong women.

Shepard, Aaron. *Savitri: A Tale of Ancient India.* Illustrated by Vera Rosenberry. 1992. Hardcover: Albert Whitman. Ages 5–8.

This legend drawn from the Mahabharata, a classical Sanskrit epic of India, tells of the princess Savitri. Beautiful and intelligent, Savitri intimidates the local men, so she leaves home to find a husband worthy of her. But the man she chooses, Prince Satyavan, has only one year to live, according to a prediction. Firm in her love, Savitri marries him anyway. When Yama, the god of death, comes to take the sleeping Satyavan, Savitri follows them. Yama is impressed with her courage and endurance, and grants her three favors, anything but Satyavan's life. On the third favor, Savitri tricks Yama and the god returns her husband to her. Delicately colored illustrations decorate this tale.

Sierra, Judy. *Tasty Baby Belly Buttons.* Illustrated by Meilo So. 1999. Hardcover: Knopf. Paperback: Dragonfly. Ages 3–7.

In this Japanese folktale, a man and woman who wish they had a child find a watermelon with a baby in it. Delighted, they take the baby as their own and name her Uriko-hime, "melon princess." Uriko, who grows faster than other children, is taught how to to cook dumplings by her mother and studies sword fighting with her father; so she is prepared when the terrible monsters known as oni steal the village's babies in order to eat their "tasty baby belly buttons." Uriko, who has no belly button herself, sets out to save the children. With three helpful companions, a sword, and some millet dumplings, she succeeds. The lively prose, which incorporates rhythmic phrases like "*tontoko, tontoko*," makes this perfect for reading aloud. Lovely watercolors that evoke Japanese artwork show a determined Uriko defeating the enormous oni. A splendid rendition of a folktale about a heroic girl.

Stanley, Diane. *Rumpelstiltskin's Daughter*. 1997. Hardcover: Morrow. Ages 5–10.

The traditional story of Rumpelstiltskin is turned on its head in this clever, fractured fairy tale. When the little man arrives to help the miller's daughter, whose name is Meredith, turn straw into gold, he proves to be a conscientious, friendly, family-oriented man who wins Meredith's heart in some very funny dialogue. Then he spins a golden ladder, they escape, and live happily ever after. But, wait . . . they have a daughter who attracts the greedy king's interest as her mother did in the original folktale. This time, though, Rumpelstiltskin's daughter gets the best of the king, while she also helps the impoverished people of the kingdom. Large illustrations full of humorous details and expressions add to the fun of this outstanding story that will amuse adults as well as children.

Stewig, John Warren. *Clever Gretchen*. Illustrated by Patricia Wittmann. 2000. Hardcover: Marshall Cavendish. Ages 5–9.

This folktale, retold in many collections, concerns a smart

young woman and the husband she chooses. The mayor's daughter Gretchen is ready to marry but no one meets her father's standards. One day Gretchen talks with a pleasant young man named Hans, and he resolves to ask for her hand in marriage. On his way to this hopeless task, he meets a round little stranger with goat feet. The stranger offers to make Hans the greatest marksman in the world to meet the mayor's requirement. In exchange Hans must become the stranger's servant in seven years unless Hans can pose a question the stranger can't answer. With Gretchen's support, Hans does some crack shooting and the mayor accepts him as a son-in-law. Seven years later, Gretchen cleverly outwits the stranger, who turns out to be a dwarf, and saves her husband. Large, congenial watercolors show the action and add personality to the happy couple.

Wisniewski, David. *The Wave of the Sea-Wolf*. 1994. Hardcover: Clarion. Paperback: Houghton. Ages 4–8.

Wisniewski's remarkable cut-paper illustrations draw from the motifs of Pacific Northwest native peoples for this original tale. Tlingit princess Kchokeen resolves to see Gonakadet, the Sea-Wolf, because anyone who sees him receives wealth and honor. Disobeying her mother's warning not to go near the mouth of the bay, Kchokeen falls into the hollow trunk of a great tree. While her friends are going for help, a great sea wave lifts her out and she sees the marvelous vision of Gonakadet, which no girl had ever seen before. As a result of her vision, Kchokeen can predict the coming of destructive waves and advise fishermen when the water will be safe. Thanks to her, her village prospers. When a French ship threatens the village, Kchokeen saves her people by leading a party of warriors in a war canoe and luring the French ship into a fatal sea wave. The distinctive illustrations convey the power of the sea wave and the expansive beauty of the Northwest. Well worth seeking out.

Xiong, Blia. Adapted by Cathy Spagnoli. *Nine-in-One, Grr! Grr!* Illustrated by Nancy Hom. 1989. Hardcover: Children's Book Press. Paperback: Children's Book Press. Ages 2–6.

In this entertaining Hmong tale from Laos, a tiger goes to a male god and asks how many cubs she will have. Rather carelessly, the god replies, "Nine each year," but tells the tiger that she must remember that number for it to happen. So the tiger makes up a rhyme and recites it: "Nine-in-one, Grr! Grr!" She is overheard by the clever Eu bird, another female, who asks the tiger what her rhyme means. The answer dismays the bird who realizes the island will soon be overrun with dangerous tigers. She goes to the god, but he admits that fate cannot be changed as long as the tiger remembers. So the bird distracts the tiger, who forgets her rhyme. The bird teaches it back to her as "One-in-nine, Grr! Grr!" thus saving the island's animals from being crowded out by tigers. Colorful silk-screened artwork that draws from Hmong stitchery enhances the tale.

Yolen, Jane. *The Emperor and the Kite.* Illustrated by Ed Young. 1988. Hardcover: Philomel. Paperback: Paper Star. Ages 4–8.

Exquisite illustrations, made to resemble Chinese cut-paper art, extend this story of a young girl who rescues her father, the emperor. Tiny Djeow Seow, as the youngest of the emperor's eight children, has long been ignored and learns to entertain herself flying her kite. One day, sitting by unnoticed, she sees villains steal away her father and hide him in a tower. While her siblings weep and sigh, Djeow cleverly supplies her father with food using her kite and comes up with a way to save him. In return, she gets the attention and love she has longed for, sits by his side while he rules, and succeeds him as ruler. A delightful story about someone small who accomplishes something big. A Caldecott Honor Book.

Yolen, Jane. *Tam Lin.* **Illustrated by Charles Mikolaycak. 1990. Paperback: Voyager. Ages 7–10.**

Accompanied by graceful, romantic illustrations, this story based on an old ballad tells of Jennet MacKenzie, who saved a man from death. Jennet, a headstrong girl known for saying what she thought, is determined to reclaim the castle that belonged to her ancestors. Ignoring her parents' protest, she sets off to the castle on her sixteenth birthday. There she encounters Tam Lin, a young man from the past who is to be sacrificed that night by the fairies unless someone is caring enough and strong enough to save him. Although it means wrestling with dangerous beasts, Jennet succeeds. Here is a tale in which a female does the rescuing and the fighting. It is she, not the man she saves and marries, who later restores the castle for their descendants. She is a true heroine, depicted as more resolute than beautiful.

Young, Ed. *Lon Po Po: A Red-Riding Hood Story from China.* **1989. Hardcover: Philomel. Paperback: Paper Star. Ages 4–8.**

Watercolor and pastel illustrations arranged in panels that echo Chinese art create an atmosphere of drama in this version of the Red Riding Hood story. A mother leaves her three children home, warning them not to let anyone in, but the younger children let in a wolf who claims to be their grand-mother. Fortunately the eldest and cleverest child, a girl named Shang, sees through the disguise. She outwits the wolf by luring him up a tree to eat gingko nuts and dropping him in a basket to the ground, where his heart breaks to pieces. A Caldecott Medal winner for its striking, powerful pictures.

Collections

Hamilton, Virginia. *Her Stories: African American Folktales, Fairy Tales, and True Tales*. Illustrated by Leo and Diane Dillon. 1995. Hardcover: Scholastic/Blue Sky Press. Ages 8–14.

This beautifully made book combines elegant design with outstanding illustrations. The carefully chosen details—dust jacket, quality of paper, graceful typeface—make it a pleasure just to hold. Hamilton also does a masterful job at retelling the folktales and legends she has brought together, all of which feature African-American women. Her intent, however, is not to concentrate on strong heroines, so only a few of the stories provide role models. Of those that do, the lighthearted "Malindy and Little Devil" offers a sassy, happy girl who sells her soul to the devil but tricks him when he comes to collect it. In another, "Woman and Man Started Even," the first man tries to get the upper hand by appealing to God, but the first woman outsmarts him. The legend of Annie Christmas describes her as the biggest woman in the state of Louisiana, a keelboat operator on the Mississippi who could outfight any other boatman. Some powerful characters in other stories are evil, such as the her-vampire and the bog hag. Still other tales are about more ordinary women who deal with mistakes, jealousy, and sometimes, magic. This is a groundbreaking collection, the first book to gather together stories about African-American girls and women.

Krishnaswami, Uma, reteller. *Shower of Gold: Girls and Women in the Stories of India*. Illustrated by Maniam Selven. 1999. Hardcover: Linnet Books. Ages 9–13.

A warrior queen who defends her people, a princess skilled

in hunting and swordplay, and goddesses who destroy demons are among the strong females in this fine collection. Some of the eighteen stories focus on women rewarded for their kindness, but most have girls and women who stand out for their self-reliance, intelligence, courage, and physical skills. The reteller heard some of the stories as a girl, and documents those personal experiences as well as written sources after each story, along with some explanatory notes about each tale. A glossary, pronunciation guide, and list of characters appear at the back. Black-and-white drawings by an Indian artist accompany each of the skillfully retold tales.

Lansky, Bruce, editor. *Girls to the Rescue: Tales of Clever, Courageous Girls from Around the World*. 1995. Paperback: Meadowbrook. Ages 5–10.

To offset the many fairy tales about helpless maidens, this collection of ten stories focuses on fairy-tale heroines. Five are adaptations of traditional tales, the other five original stories. Perhaps the most unusual is "Savannah's Piglets," about a black pioneer girl who manages a farm on her own, relying on her many outdoor skills, when her father leaves. "The Royal Joust" features a girl who competes in a jousting tournament disguised as her brother. The few princes who appear are either pleasant but ineffectual, or more selfish than attractive. The girls use their wits and sometimes their physical strength to gain what they want. Although fairy tales written today don't have the timeworn smoothness of traditional tales, these provide a useful alternative to most of the folklore children hear. The first in a series of *Girls to the Rescue* collections.

Minard, Rosemary. *Womenfolk and Fairy Tales*. Illustrated by Suzanna Klein. 1975. Hardcover: Houghton. Ages 5–12.

As one of the earlier collections of folktales about heroines, this has more stories of female strength than most among its twenty-two tales. The succinct retellings read aloud well and many are accompanied by a stylized black-and-white drawing. They come from all over the world, including Japan, China, Persia, and Africa, although information about the origin of each story is scant. The heroines are ordinary people and princesses who draw on their wits and courage. Many marry at the end of the stories, but always to men who respect them. A solid group of stories that break fairy-tale stereotypes.

Phelps, Ethel Johnston. *The Maid of the North: Feminist Folk Tales from Around the World.* **Illustrated by Lloyd Bloom. 1982. Hardcover: Holt. Paperback: Holt. Ages 6–13.**

This second collection by Ethel Johnston Phelps offers twenty-one tales with female heroes, including three told by Native American peoples. It is a nicely designed volume, although its small typeface makes it less accessible to young readers than other collections. Familiar tales include "East of the Sun, West of the Moon" and "The Husband Who Stayed at Home," but many of the others will be new to readers. In one particularly good story from West Pakistan, "The Tiger and the Jackal," a farmer's wife disguises herself as a man and frightens away a fierce tiger who had thoroughly scared her husband. "The Twelve Huntsmen," a German tale, features twelve young women disguised as men. Their disguises fool a king, who observes, "They handle their bows as well as any huntsmen." Their leader, Katrine, uses logic to get the king to keep his promise to her. Dramatic black-and-white illustrations are scattered throughout the book.

Phelps, Ethel Johnston. *Tatterhood and Other Tales.* **Illustrated by Pamela Baldwin Ford. 1978. Paperback: Feminist Press. Ages 6–13.**

"Tatterhood," the first story in this collection of twenty-five tales, is outstanding. Wild Tatterhood loves adventures and doesn't care what others think of her. "She was strong, raucous, and careless, and was always racing about on her goat." When a troll puts a calf's head on her twin sister, Tatterhood sails off with her sister to remedy it. She succeeds and also finds a man who admires her insistence on making her own choices. Another particularly good tale is "Kupti and Imani," in which a king's daughter insists she can make her own fortune and builds up a business until she is as rich as her father. This is an impressive collection with well-chosen stories, a thoughtful introduction, and useful endnotes.

San Souci, Robert D. *Cut from the Same Cloth: American Women of Myth, Legend, and Tall Tale.* Illustrated by Brian Pinkney. 1993. Hardcover: Philomel. Paperback: Puffin. Ages 8–14.

American legends and tall tales about men are easy to find, but those about women are scarce. This collection introduces fifteen hardy, strong-willed women from American folklore. Grouped according to geographical region, the stories include a range of ethnic groups. Some of the tales revolve around exciting adventures, while others offer a mishmash of details without a plot. The vigorous black-and-white scratchboard illustrations have an appropriate folkloric feel in this appropriately large volume. Well documented, this volume is a good start toward filling a gap in children's books about American folklore.

Tchana, Katrin. *The Serpent Slayer and Other Stories of Strong Women.* Illustrated by Trina Schart Hyman. 2000. Hardcover: Little, Brown. Ages 5 and up.

The full-page color illustrations that accompany each story, along with a smaller illustration on each title page, are the highlights of this folktale collection. Caldecott Medal winner Trina Schart Hyman gives a magical quality to her lively pictures, perfect for folktales. While the retellings by the author's daughter, many of which are drawn from other collections of feminist folktales, are not as strong as the illustrations, the stories all feature strong girls and women who determine their own fates. The heroines outwit their opponents, which include dragons, devils, and unfair fathers. A handsome collection drawn from countries around the world.

Yolen, Jane, collector and reteller. *Not One Damsel in Distress: World Folktales for Strong Girls.* **Illustrated by Susan Guevara. 2000. Hardcover: Harcourt. Ages 8–12.**

Here is a collection of traditional stories about "sword-wielding, spear-throwing, villain-stomping, rescuing-type heroes who also happen to be female," as the introduction describes them. They come from all parts of the globe: Greece, Niger, Germany, Argentina, China, and many more places. Some, like Molly Whuppie, may be familiar to readers, but many will not. The collection includes tales about a pirate princess, a samurai's brave daughter, and a dragon-slayer, among other brave females. The prose flows well and lends itself to reading aloud. Full page black-and-white pictures accompany each story. Yolen gives careful notes in the back about where she found the stories and how she has altered them. Another welcome collection to balance the many better known tales about brave males.

3

Books for Beginning Readers

These books for children who are beginning to read independently (typically ages six to eight) are divided into three categories. The first is Easy Readers, specifically geared toward the early stages of reading. These books use a controlled vocabulary with many words that children can sound out. They also feature illustrations that closely follow the story, providing clues to words the reader doesn't know. Many of these are also suitable for reading aloud to children who do not read yet, which is reflected in the age guidelines.

The second category, Short Novels, offers fare for children ready to try chapter books, but who need guidance in finding stories at an accessible level. Educators call these shorter novels "transitional" books, moving children from the first stages of reading to longer novels. They tend to have large print, an open design, and frequent illustrations. It can be difficult to find transitional books; most children's novels are geared toward slightly more advanced readers who are comfortable with longer books, smaller print, and no pictures. For the children at the upper end of this reading stage, check the chapter titled, "Books for Middle Readers," which lists other possibilities for this group.

The final category is Biographies. Most of these books also have large print and lots of pictures. They cover a wide spectrum of women and a few girls: rulers, pirates, scientists, artists, and more. Some are famous, others are little-known historical figures. A few of the biographies have been fictionalized and could have been listed as picture-story books. Since readers interested in famous people are more likely to look in this section, I have included the fictionalized biographies here and noted in the annotation which ones fall into that category.

Don't limit your choices to this chapter alone. All children at this stage should also be listening to books read aloud, including picture-story books and folktales, most of which are still too difficult for them to read alone. Also check "Books for Middle Readers" for longer books to read aloud, such as the fantasy books about animals, popular with all ages.

Easy Readers

Albee, Sarah. *The Dragon's Scales*. Illustrated by John Manders. 1998. Hardcover: Random House. Paperback: Random House. Ages 6–9.

This simple story tells about a small town where everyone loves berries. The townspeople cross a bridge to plant fields of all different kinds of berries that they harvest after a big parade. One year, though, when the parade reaches the bridge, a dragon awaits them and claims the berries. A young girl saves the day by challenging the dragon to a contest of simple math questions: Which weighs more, one apple or two peas? The girl immediately bests the dragon, whose logic is faulty. But she gives him a chance to think hard, answer one question, and become her friend. The cartoonlike pictures add little, but the heroine's courage and math ability are appealing in this entry in the "Step Into Reading Plus Math" series.

Amstel, Marsha. *Sybil Ludington's Midnight Ride*. Illustrated by Ellen Beier. 2000. Hardcover: Carolrhoda. Paperback: First Avenue. Ages 6–9.

In this exciting book based on a true story, a teenage girl rides through a rainy Connecticut night to alert soldiers to a British invasion. On April 26, 1777, a messenger rides up to the Ludingtons' house to tell Colonel Ludington that two thousand British have attacked Danbury, Connecticut. The colonel needs to gather together his soldiers, who live on farms in the surrounding countryside. His sixteen-year-old daughter Sybil, who loved to ride, volunteers for the job and sets out into the cold, moonless evening. She gallops dozens of miles through the woods, pounding on doors with a stick to awaken the soldiers. She carefully avoids a group of outlaws who would steal her horse, and completes her mission successfully. Color paintings on every page illustrate the difficult journey, and the final picture shows a statue of Sybil Ludington and her horse erected in Carmel, New York.

Avi. *Abigail Takes the Wheel*. Illustrated by Don Bolognese. 1999. Hardcover: Harper. Paperback: Trophy. Ages 6–9.

Abigail and her younger brother Tom ride on their father's freight boat from New Jersey to school in New York City, late in the 1800s. One morning, the boat's fate is thrust into Abigail's hands. Her father goes to pilot a damaged ship, leaving his assistant to tow it through the harbor and into the pier. But the assistant becomes too ill to steer and Abigail has to guide in both ships. The harbor is crowded with large and small boats, some of which she must avoid to land her charges safely. With the help of Tom, she succeeds and gains the new nickname "Captain Abigail." With more text than many easy readers, and informative pictures on every page as well as a map, this is an enjoyable historical story about a capable girl.

Bang, Molly Garrett. *Tye May and the Magic Brush*. 1981. Paperback: Mulberry. Ages 4–7.

Orphaned Tye May wants to learn to paint when she sees a man teaching male pupils. When she asks the loan of a brush, the teacher scoffs at the idea of a beggar girl painting. "But Tye May had an iron will." She uses sticks and reeds to develop her skills, and one night in a dream a woman brings her a magic brush. When Tye May paints with it, whatever she draws comes to life, so she kindly creates tools for the poor. But a wicked landlord locks her up to make her paint what he wants. She escapes and tricks her strong male pursuers by drawing a net to capture them. Next she outwits the greedy emperor with her art. This adaptation of a Chinese folktale is illustrated in black and white, with touches of red, in a style reminiscent of Chinese art. Delightful.

Bonsall, Crosby. *The Case of the Double Cross.* **1980. Hardcover: Harper. Paperback: Trophy. Ages 5–8.**

Marigold and her two friends are tired of seeing the sign "No Girls" on Wizard's private-eye clubhouse, which he shares with three other boys. The girls would like to join, but only on their terms. Thanks to Marigold's plan, they get what they want. Marigold writes a letter in code and, disguised as a little man with a beard, delivers it to the youngest of the boys. The code baffles the boy detectives, so Wizard finally concedes that he has been fooled and offers to let them join his club. Only when they all agree it's their club, not his, and the "No Girls" sign is down do they join forces to solve future puzzles. Funny, expressive pictures capture the spirit of the story.

Buck, Nola. *Sid and Sam.* **Illustrated by G. Brian Karas. 1996. Hardcover: Harper. Paperback: Trophy. Ages 4–8.**

In this book for beginning readers, a girl named Sid meets her friend Sam and they sing together. Sid is an exuberant character dressed in a bright shirt, shorts, and red cowboy boots, with binoculars hung around her neck. Sam finds Sid's singing overwhelming and tries to tone her down to no avail. Full of alliteration and wordplay, the simple text rises above most easy-to-read stories in its cleverness and appeal. Whimsical illustrations convey Sid's bounciness and the friendship between her and the more sedate Sam.

Coerr, Eleanor. *The Big Balloon Race.* **Illustrated by Carolyn Croll. 1981. Hardcover: Harper & Row. Paperback: Trophy. Ages 4–7.**

Based on real people, this easy reader describes a balloon race entered by Carlotta Myers, a leading aeronaut in the 1880s. In the story, Ariel, daughter of Carlotta and balloon maker Carl Myers, falls asleep in her mother's balloon just before a race. Unnoticed by her mother, she only awakens once the balloon is in the air. Ariel's added weight makes it more difficult to win, and so does landing in a lake, but the mother-and-daughter team prevail thanks to quick thinking, and they defeat the male aeronaut they are racing. Delightful illustrations show Carlotta the Great formally dressed for her flight but clearly in command as she reads her compass and maneuvers her bright-colored balloon. An outstanding book about a skilled woman.

Cristaldi, Kathryn. *Baseball Ballerina.* **Illustrated by Abby Carter. 1992. Hardcover: Random House. Paperback: Random House. Ages 4–7.**

In this beginning reader, a gender stereotype is turned on its head. The girl who narrates it loves baseball and worries that her teammates will laugh at her if they find out about her ballet lessons. Her mother thinks that baseball is for boys and that her daughter should be doing more "girl things." The narrator hates pink; her mother thinks it's a good color for girls. At ballet class, when they practice positions, the narrator in her baseball cap announces that the only position for her is shortstop. But at their dance recital, she combines ballet and baseball as she leaps to recover a crown that flies off her friend's head. Her male and female teammates in the audience cheer, and she realizes ballet can be fun—although not as good as baseball. Although the mother leaves something to be desired, the narrator is an appealing modern girl who slaps high fives and makes the best of a situation she hasn't chosen.

Cushman, Doug. *Aunt Eater's Mystery Vacation.* **1992. Paperback: Trophy. Ages 4–7.**

Aunt Eater the anteater loves to read mystery novels and to solve real mysteries. In four short chapters, she encounters four mysteries while on vacation. The puzzles are simple enough that the reader might solve them. Humorous pictures depicting different types of animals as characters show a dowdy Aunt Eater who divides her time between reading and action. Mystery stories are popular with beginning readers, and few at this level feature female detectives. Other books featuring the anteater sleuth are *Aunt Eater Loves a Mystery* and *Aunt Eater's Mystery Christmas.*

Levinson, Nancy Smiler. *Clara and the Bookwagon.* **Illustrated by Carolyn Croll. 1988. Hardcover: Harper. Paperback: Trophy. Ages 5–8.**

In a story set in Maryland in 1905, young Clara, who works alongside her father in the fields, wants to learn to read, but there are no schools for farm children where she lives. When she wants to borrow a book for free from a store that serves as a book station, her father won't let her. Books, he says, are for rich people, not for farmers. But a determined woman, Miss Mary Titcomb, drives to their farm in the country's first bookmobile. She persuades Clara's father that reading is important, and Clara checks out her first books. Based on facts about the first bookmobile, the four chapters have crisp illustrations that show a friendly, dignified woman driving a horse-drawn carriage alone through the countryside, a pioneer in her profession.

Lewis, Thomas P. *Clipper Ship*. **Illustrated by Joan Sandin. 1978. Paperback: Trophy. Ages 5–8.**

This beginning history book describes a voyage around Cape Horn from New York to San Francisco. Although the captain of the clipper ship *Rainbird* is a man, his wife charts the course using her chronometer and sextant. When Captain Murdock gets sick, his wife declares, "I will sail the ship" and she does. She gives orders and negotiates the journey through an icy Cape Horn and into San Francisco. Her daughter and son help her, and one picture shows the girl steering the ship with her mother. The children climb one of the masts together, although while sitting at the top the daughter spends her time rolling her hair into curls. On the whole, however, this is an unusually positive portrayal of a woman in the last century, based on true stories about various women who went to sea with their husbands.

Maccarone, Grace. *Soccer Game!* **Illustrated by Meredith Johnson. 1994. Paperback: Scholastic. Ages 3–7.**

This simple story about girls and boys playing soccer together is written for the very beginning reader. Many pages have only two or three words on them, such as "We run," and "We pass." In the cartoonlike pictures, as many girls as boys participate energetically in the game. To add humor, two dogs clad in uniforms join in the game, one of which wears a hair ribbon. A girl seems to make the goal that wins the game and she is shown celebrating with one of her male teammates. The pictures clearly show girls enjoying a team sport and boys treating them as full-fledged teammates and opponents.

McDonald, Megan. *Beezy at Bat*. **Illustrated by Nancy Poydar. 1998. Hardcover: Orchard. Paperback: Orchard. Ages 6–9.**

In the first of three chapters, Beezy is spending a

comfortable evening on the porch with her grandmother, cracking nuts. When their neighbor Mr. Gumm drops by, he starts cracking jokes instead of nuts. The three of them trade riddles as evening sets in, shown in small, congenial watercolor pictures on each page. The second chapter, titled "Trouble," starts with Beezy and her friend Merlin setting off to pick blackberries. But Merlin is afraid of snakes, so he spends his time trying to get Beezy to leave. When a snake does appear, Beezy picks it up and takes it home, planning to surprise her grandmother with it. Finally, in "Jaws," Beezy and her friends want to play baseball but need another player. They enlist Sarafina, who has nicknamed her baseball mitt Jaws and who has a few surprises up her sleeve. This book is one in a series about Beezy, a modern girl who likes snakes and baseball, whose friends are boys as well as girls.

Mozelle, Shirley. *Zack's Alligator.* **Illustrated by James Watts. 1989. Paperback: Harper. Ages 4–8.**

Although the main human character in this book is a boy named Zack, the star is a talking female alligator. When Bridget, a present from the boy's uncle in Florida, arrives, she is the size of a key chain, but she becomes full grown when Zack pours water on her. She exudes energy and enthusiasm in the upbeat, colorful pictures. Don't miss the one of her stretched out on the couch, hollering to Zack to bring her some food. She devours a huge plate of food, wrestles with the snakelike garden hose, and plays on all the equipment at the park. When the park policeman tells Zack that Bridget needs a leash and adds, "Keep him under control," Bridget's reaction is an incensed "Him? Well, I beg your pardon. How rude! Hasn't he ever seen a girl gator before?" Any reader will be glad to have met this original girl gator. In the sequel *Zack's Alligator Goes to School*, Zack brings Bridget on a chaos-producing visit to school.

O'Connor, Jane. *Molly the Brave and Me.* **Illustrated by Sheila Hamanaka. 1990. Paperback: Random House. Ages 5–8.**

Beth greatly admires her friend Molly, who isn't afraid of anything, it seems. Beth herself is afraid of many things but does her best to hide it. She finds that pretending she's brave sometimes results in having an unexpectedly good time. Visiting Molly's country house, Beth has a chance to be the braver of the two and ends up feeling great: "Maybe I really am a kid with guts!" An added plus is that Molly and her parents have dark skin and Beth has light skin, although race doesn't enter into the story.

Pomerantz, Charlotte. *The Outside Dog.* **Illustrated by Jennifer Plecas. 1993. Hardcover: Harper. Paperback: Trophy. Ages 5–8.**

Marisol is a model of persistence. She lives with her *abuelito*, her grandfather, in a little house in Puerto Rico. She would love to have one of the stray dogs in the neighborhood as a pet, but her grandfather objects. She befriends one of the dogs and names it Pancho. Slowly and cleverly Marisol convinces her grandfather that a pet dog is a good idea. Endearing pictures extend the personalities of the people and the dog. Marisol is an active girl who sometimes goes fishing with a neighbor. Another neighbor is a friendly woman who owns a little grocery store. With four short chapters and a sprinkling of Spanish words that are defined in the front, this is an outstanding book for young readers.

Rappaport, Doreen. *The Boston Coffee Party*. Illustrated by Emily Arnold McCully. 1988. Paperback: Trophy. Ages 5–8.

This history book is based on a true event recorded by Abigail Adams in the 1760s. During the Revolutionary War, women whose husbands were fighting asked local merchants to keep down their prices for sugar and coffee to support the war effort. In this fictionalized version, Sarah Homans and her younger sister Emma go from store to store in Boston trying to buy sugar. The one merchant who has sugar sells it to someone else who will pay the highest price. When Mrs. Homans and her friends realize that same merchant has hidden away barrels of coffee to sell when the price rises, they rebel. Sarah and Emma march along with the women to demand the key to the merchant's warehouse, where they take the hoarded coffee. Charming illustrations by award-winning artist Emily McCully show how people lived and dressed at the time, and capture the spirit of the group of angry women, an unusual sight in children's books.

Wyeth, Sharon Dennis. *Tomboy Trouble*. Illustrated by Lynne Woodcock Cravath. 1998. Paperback: Random House. Ages 6–9.

A girl named Georgia decides to cut her long hair because it is hot when she plays baseball, but when she enters a new school, dressed in jeans, sneakers, a T-shirt, and a baseball cap, other children mistake her for a boy. She explains that she's a girl, but a boy named Jerry protests that she is wearing a boy's hat and sneakers, and has a boy's haircut. He teases her so often that she writes a note to his teacher, on the advice of her own teacher. Then she makes two friends, a long-haired girl who gets her hair cut to imitate Georgia, and a boy with long hair who gets teased for looking like a girl. As

Georgia says at the end, when asked if she's a tomboy, "I'm *no* kind of boy . . . I'm just my own kind of girl." Cheerful illustrations show how easily these questions can arise in a time when boys and girls dress alike and wear their hair all different lengths. An unusual, welcome exploration of a contemporary issue.

Short Novels

Ackerman, Karen. *The Night Crossing*. **Illustrated by Elizabeth Sayles. 1994. Hardcover: Knopf. Paperback: Random House. Ages 7–9.**

This is the simple story of a courageous Jewish family who tramp through the night and bitter cold to escape the Nazis. Young Clara, who knows the pain of wearing a yellow star and being taunted by her old friends, overhears her parents making plans to leave Austria. Soon she, her older sister Marta, and their parents set off on foot, leaving behind almost all they own. When Clara's family is nearly discovered by some soldiers, she realizes how dangerous the journey really is. At the last minute, it is up to Clara to think quickly and save the family. This approachable story for young readers captures the point of view of a child who suffers but is lucky enough to escape. Clara's small act of bravery is at the level a child can understand without knowing more about the Holocaust, which is described in more detail in the epilogue.

Adler, David A. *Cam Jansen and the Mystery at the Haunted House*. **Illustrated by Susanna Natti. 1992. Hardcover: Viking. Paperback: Puffin. Ages 6–9.**

The girl detective in this series earned her nickname "Cam" from her photographic memory. She can memorize any scene she sees and recall it later in detail. When her aunt's wallet is stolen at an amusement park, Cam and her friend Eric try to solve the mystery. They eliminate various suspects by combining Cam's talents with some close observation. In the end, Cam solves the mystery and recovers wallets stolen from several people in the park. The park owner, a woman, rewards her with free passes to the park. Short chapters, large print, and frequent illustrations make this an excellent series for readers new to chapter books. Among the many titles in this series are *Cam Jansen and the Mystery of the Dinosaur Bones* and *Cam Jansen and the Mystery of the Stolen Diamonds*.

Berleth, Richard. *Mary Patten's Voyage*. Illustrated by Ben Otero. 1994. Hardcover: Albert Whitman. Ages 7–10.

This short novel is based on a true story about the clipper ship *Neptune's Car*, which raced two other ships from New York City to San Francisco in 1856. When the ship's captain fell ill with tuberculosis, his eighteen-year-old wife Mary Patten took over as captain. Due to her skills as a navigator, she took the ship safely around Cape Horn through terrible storms. Some of the male sailors considered a woman, especially a pregnant one, incapable of leading the ship and bad luck as well. But Mary Patten persisted and proved herself a talented and knowledgeable sailor. Although the ship came in second in the race, as the sailor who narrates the story proclaims, "She had proven for all time what a woman could achieve against the sea." The U.S. Merchant Marine Academy hospital in New York is named in Mary Patten's honor. An exciting adventure based on true life, amply illustrated with color paintings.

Bulla, Clyde Robert. *Shoeshine Girl*. Illustrated by Leigh Grant. 1975. Hardcover: Harper. Paperback: Trophy. Ages 6–9.

Ten-year-old Sarah Ida, sent to spend the summer with her Aunt Claudia, feels unwanted and angry. Fiercely independent, she insists on carrying her own luggage and wants the sense of freedom money gives her. When Aunt Claudia won't give her money, Sarah Ida decides to earn her own. She gets a job helping a shoeshine man named Al, who overcomes his initial skepticism about having a girl do the job. Sarah Ida half hopes her aunt will forbid her to do such messy work, but when she doesn't, Sarah Ida works hard and learns a lot. She even manages the stand alone when Al spends a few days in the hospital. A terrific short novel about a girl who earns money and grows in responsibility.

Cleary, Beverly. *Ramona the Pest.* **Illustrated by Louis Darling. 1968. Hardcover: Morrow. Paperback: Avon. Ages 7–10.**

Ramona's great popularity has endured for more than twenty-five years. She represents the kind of girl who has not been subdued by adults or the world in general. When Ramona has a question, such as where the storybook character Mike Mulligan goes to the bathroom, she asks it, to the admiration of her fellow kindergarteners. She careens fiercely around on her tricycle, converted to a bicycle by removing one wheel. She loses her temper and can't be swayed when she has stubbornly made up her mind to something. When she's happy she sings it out and twirls with joy. True, her greatest wish is to please her teacher, but even that is easily forgotten when she is tempted to pull another girl's curls. Ramona has some clear notions about differences between girls and boys—boys are not supposed to want ribbons—but she doesn't seem to limit herself to certain roles. She stomps in the mud with the best of them, a thoroughly likable and strong-minded child. A popular read-aloud for younger children, too. Other books about the irrepressible Ramona and her escapades include *Ramona the Brave*, *Ramona and Her Father*, and more.

Duffey, Betsy. *The Gadget War.* **Illustrated by Janet Wilson. 1991. Paperback: Puffin. Ages 7–9.**

Kelly Sparks likes to invent things. Her desk at school is full of tools and gadgets, and her career goal is to be a "Gadget Wiz." The walls of her bedroom hold pegboards covered with every kind of tool. The first black-and-white drawing shows her smiling as she hammers a nail into a small board, surrounded by a pliers, a screwdriver, a ruler, and wire. But when a new boy enters the third grade wearing an inventor's camp T-shirt, Kelly has a rival for the first time. The new boy, Albert Einstein Jones, quickly challenges her and they each use their inventions to annoy the other. To her mother's dismay, Kelly invents a food-fight catapult, carefully writing down each test result as she tries it out in their increasingly messy kitchen. The gadget war escalates until Kelly inadvertently hits the principal with an orange half. Kelly and Albert both get into trouble, but it also spells the end of their rivalry and the beginning of their friendship. A slight but lively story about an uncommon girl who likes tools and solving problems with them.

Fowler, Susi Gregg. *Albertina the Practically Perfect.* **Illustrated by Jim Fowler. 1998. Hardcover: Greenwillow. Ages 7–9.**

Two girls smile out from the cover of this short novel, one with a saw in her hand and the other with a hammer. Molly has just moved to a new neighborhood where she immediately becomes friends with her cheerful neighbor Albertina. The two of them embark on an ambitious project to build a tree house like the one Molly's grandfather had built at her old house. Grandpa helps out with building the floor, then the two girls are on their own to build the walls. It's hot, hard work, but their enthusiasm for the project keeps them going.

Meanwhile Molly clashes with another girl, who is—as Albertina describes her—strong, smart, and tough, like Molly. Attractive drawings appear every few pages, ending with a final picture of a toolbox and a can of nails.

Gauch, Patricia Lee. *This Time, Tempe Wick?* Illustrated by Margot Tomes. 1974. Hardcover: Putnam. Ages 6–10.

This short novel is based on a legend set during the time of the Revolution. Temperance Wick was known for her strength and her courage even as a child. She could stay at the plow as long as her father and beat him in a horse race. When ten thousand American soldiers occupied Jockey Hollow in Pennsylvania where she lived, Tempe and her family pitched in to help the troops, sewing and cooking and sharing their farm produce. But after most of the army had left, two disgruntled soldiers who stayed behind tried to steal the family horse. Tempe fooled them for days, even taking the musket from one, and saved her horse. Tomes's homespun illustrations suit the story perfectly, giving a lively sense of time and place.

Giff, Patricia Reilly. *Kidnap at the Catfish Cafe.* Illustrated by Lynne Cravath. 1998. Hardcover: Viking. Paperback: Puffin. Ages 7–10.

In this first book of "The Adventures of Minnie and Max," sixth grader Minnie starts on her life as a detective and acquires Max as a pet. Orphaned Minnie lives with her adult brother Orlando, who runs the largely unsuccessful Catfish Cafe on the Florida waterfront. Minnie is lounging around on the dock one summer day when she sees a cat jump off a truck, followed by an amber ring. When she tries to find the truck to return the ring, she loses the ring and finds herself locked in a shack. She's rescued by a female police officer, and the two of them join forces to find the neighborhood purse-snatcher and solve the mystery of the amber ring. Black-and-white illustrations add to this enjoyable read, which is followed by *Mary Moon Is Missing*.

Griffin, Judith Berry. *Phoebe the Spy*. **Illustrated by Margot Tomes. 1977. Paperback: Scholastic. Ages 6–9.**

A short historical novel set in the time of the Revolutionary War, this is based on a true story about an African-American girl. Phoebe Fraunces, whose father ran the most popular tavern in New York City, finds herself working as a housekeeper for George Washington, then commander of the American army. Her father has gotten her the job so she can help prevent an unidentified enemy from possibly killing Washington. She listens to guests and officers, trying to overhear clues. At the last minute, she figures out who the killer is and prevents him from poisoning the future president. Charming illustrations add to this simple story.

Haas, Jessie. *Beware the Mare*. **Illustrated by Martha Haas. 1993. Paperback: Beech Tree. Ages 7–10.**

This short novel introduces Lily, a girl who loves horses, and Beware, a mare that Lily's grandfather has just bought. Lily has learned a lot from her grandfather about caring for horses and riding them. Gramp buys Beware, hoping she will be the perfect horse for Lily, but the horse's name worries Gramp. Beware seems well behaved and compliant, and Lily starts to ride her regularly. But the whole family still wonders if something will go wrong. The same day that Gramp learns what's behind Beware's name, Lily figures it out herself. The girl handles a difficult situation intelligently and bravely, leading to a happy ending. The first book in a popular series, this offers strong writing and a competent, horse-loving girl.

Hesse, Karen. *Sable.* **Illustrated by Marcia Sewall. 1994. Paperback: Henry Holt. Ages 6–10.**

Tate, who is always wearing overalls, would rather help her father with his furniture-building work than work with her mother around the house. Although her mother is against it, Tate wants more than anything to keep the stray dog that shows up at their mountain home one day. Sable, a loving but wandering dog, gets in so much trouble with the neighbors that she must be sent away. Tate resolutely constructs a sturdy fence that proves to her parents she is responsible enough to keep Sable. After being lost, the dog finally returns and is welcomed even by Tate's mother.

Johnson, Angela. *When Mules Flew on Magnolia Street.* **Illustrated by John Ward. 2000. Hardcover: Knopf. Ages 7–9.**

Charlene, known as Charlie, loves living on Magnolia Street. She loves going fishing with her friends Lump and Billy, even when they have to swim after their lost fishing poles. Charlie climbs a trellis when the three of them investigate the mystery of a family who disappeared overnight, and finds out she likes dirt when she joins a new girl in creating a garden. When she meets a family in which the father and his daughters are adept at magic tricks, Charlie decides to practice magic in addition to practicing her trumpet. She is enthusiastic about life and even willing to join forces with her annoying older brother in a good cause. The occasional black-and-white pictures and unusually large print will attract readers to these episodic chapters about a vibrant African-American girl, who also appears in *Maniac Monkeys on Magnolia Street.*

Keller, Holly. *Angela's Top-Secret Computer Club.* **1998. Hardcover: Greenwillow. Ages 7–10.**

Who has infiltrated the computer system at Angela's

school and messed up the report cards? It's the last day of school, and Angela vows that she and her computer club friends will solve the mystery before the summer is over. When her friend Albert starts getting mysterious e-mail messages, the club realizes they are clues, and Angela suspects a girl who is working in the school biology lab for the summer. But it is hard to find evidence and right before school starts, disaster strikes again. This time, with the help of the librarian Mrs. Carver, Angela puts together the pieces of the puzzle and saves the school from further computer sabotage. The large typeface and occasional pictures make this accessible to younger readers. A lively mystery about a girl who's at home with computers.

King-Smith, Dick. *Sophie's Snail.* Illustrated by David Parkins. 1991. Paperback: Candlewick. Ages 7–9.

Sophie, who lives with her family on a farm in England, announces that she plans to be a farmer and lists the animals she will have. Though only four, she immediately starts saving money for her farm, with some help from her great-great-aunt. While planning for the future, she has to settle for small pets like a snail, wood lice, centipedes, earthworms, earwigs, and a slug. Her single-mindedness gets Sophie into trouble, but it doesn't stop her from doing just what she wants. She also keeps up with her fast-moving, mischievous twin brothers, who are six. The first book in a fine series, all of which involve plenty of pets, this is good for reading aloud to younger children.

Krensky, Stephen. *Louise, Soccer Star?* Illustrated by Susanna Natti. 2000. Hardcover: Dial. Ages 7–9.

A poster of the Women's U.S.A. World Cup champions has a place of honor on the walls of Louise's bedroom. No surprise then that Louise is excited about her first soccer practice of the season. But when she gets there, a new British girl named Trelawney has taken the uniform with Louise's favorite number. That's just the beginning of Louise's annoyance at Trelawney, who turns out to be an excellent soccer player, far better than Louise. Louise's daydreams about being a star prove unrealistic, even though she adopts a new program for conditioning. Slowly Louise comes to like Trelawney and realizes that her best bet for succeeding on the team is to practice with the other girl, which she does with great success. Lots of black-and-white illustrations add to the enjoyment of this satisfying sports story, one in a series of short books about Louise.

Landon, Lucinda. *Meg Mackintosh and the Mystery at the Medieval Castle: A Solve-It-Yourself Mystery*. 1989. Paperback: Secret Passage Press. Ages 6–9.

In this popular series, the reader can search for clues in the pictures in order to solve the mystery along with Meg Mackintosh. Meg, the rest of the History Club, and their teacher Mrs. Spencer are on a field trip to a castle when a valuable chalice is stolen. Meg immediately starts taking notes and snapping instant photographs; when the police arrive she is ready to help solve the mystery. Despite her teacher's admonition to let the police take care of the problem, Meg and her friend Liddy go down into the dungeons and conclude that the police are arresting the wrong person. With her usual cleverness, Meg schemes to trick the real criminals into confessing. She is a girl who likes adventure even if it's dangerous, and loves to figure things out. This short mystery, with its many drawings, involves readers in a way appealing to many children. Other equally strong titles in the series include *Meg Mackintosh and the Mystery at Camp Creepy* and *Meg Mackintosh and the Mystery in the Locked Library*.

MacLachlan, Patricia. *Sarah, Plain and Tall.* **Illustrated by Marcia Sewall. 1985. Hardcover: Harper. Paperback: Trophy. Ages 6–10.**

"I am strong and I work hard and I am willing to travel. But I am not mild mannered." So writes Sarah Wheaton to Anna's father Jacob, who has advertised for a wife. Anna, her younger brother Caleb, and their father wait anxiously in their prairie frontier home for Sarah to visit them. When she does, she proves to be all she had said and more. She is kind and sings; she slides down haystacks, learns to plow, and helps fix the roof. She insists on learning to drive the wagon, then drives it into town one day. Caleb and Anna worry she won't come back, but she does—for always. It is hard to imagine a more beautifully written story. The simple words convey warmth and humor and, most of all, love. Each small incident conveys a lot about the characters. When Sarah dons a pair of Jacob's overalls, Caleb protests, "Women don't wear overalls," to which Sarah "crisply" replies, "This woman does." Anna, who narrates the story, is a strong girl who cares for her brother and works the farm. This Newbery Medal winner is truly a gem, wonderful for reading aloud. The sequels are *Skylark* and *Caleb's Story.*

Mathis, Sharon Bell. *Sidewalk Story.* **Illustrated by Leo Carty. 1971. Paperback: Puffin. Ages 7–10.**

The news that her best friend Tanya is being evicted from her apartment stuns nine-year-old Lilly Etta Allen. Tanya's mother, who has a hard time caring for her six children while holding down a job, has missed a few rent payments. She is evicted and her furniture is piled up on the sidewalk. Knowing that an old woman on the street had been saved from eviction by publicity, Lilly Etta forms a plan. She and Tanya contact a reporter who is impressed by Lilly Etta's initiative. Ultimately, and to everyone's surprise, Lilly Etta's determination pays off for her and her friend. The handful of black-and-white paintings show that the girls are African-American, a fact mentioned only briefly in the text. Lilly Etta, as the reporter says, is "quite a girl"—a loyal friend who is not afraid to speak up.

Park, Linda Sue. *Seesaw Girl.* **Illustrated by Jean and Mousien Tseng. 1999. Hardcover: Clarion. Paperback: Young Yearling. Ages 7–10.**

Twelve-year-old Jade Blossom has always lived within the walls of her wealthy family's compound in seventeenth-century Korea. Her slightly older cousin, Graceful Willow, has been her closest friend. Together they've played practical jokes on their brothers, and also shared the traditional pastimes of embroidery and household tasks. But Graceful Willow gets married and leaves forever. Breaking all tradition, Jade sneaks out of the compound to try to visit her cousin, but realizes afterward that she must find other ways to deal with her fate as a sheltered female. She turns to art, then ingeniously assembles a seesaw that allows her to jump high enough to see the magnificent mountains in the distance, which she hopes to paint. This charming book acknowledges the reality of Jade's restricted life, but also gives credit to her independence and ingenuity. A graceful design and full-page black-and-white pictures add to the reader's pleasure.

Porter, Connie. *Meet Addy: An American Girl.* **Illustrated by Melodye Rosales. 1993. Hardcover: Pleasant Company. Paperback: Pleasant Company. Ages 8–10.**

In this entry in the popular American Girls series, life is grim for ten-year-old Addy, a slave during the Civil War. When her father and brother are sold, Addy and her mother try to escape. Although thoroughly frightened, Addy saves her mother from drowning in a creek they must ford. Later she tricks Confederate soldiers into thinking she is a boy and so avoids getting caught. The suspenseful escape by this brave mother and daughter leads them to a safe house where an old woman helps them. The story closes as they head for Philadelphia having, as Addy puts it, "taken their freedom," an expression that emphasizes the role runaway slaves took in changing their own fate. Eight pages at the end give a short history of slavery and the Civil War, heavily illustrated with photographs. The story itself has occasional full-page paintings as well as smaller decorations. Although some adults will be put off by the commercial nature of the series, which exists in part to sell dolls and clothing, the girls do have brave adventures. The writing and pictures tend to be stiff, but that doesn't seem to discourage young readers. The first in a series of books about Addy's adventures.

Roop, Peter and Connie. *Keep the Lights Burning, Abbie.* **Illustrated by Peter E. Hanson. 1985. Hardcover: Carolrhoda. Paperback: Carolrhoda. Ages 6–9.**

This fictionalized account of a real person focuses on the courage and determination of a lighthouse keeper's daughter in 1856. When Captain Burgess has to leave their Maine island to fetch his wife's medicine, he leaves his daughter Abbie in charge of the lights that keep ships from being wrecked on the rocky coastline. A huge storm prevents the captain from returning, and for four weeks Abbie has to keep the lights burning in two lighthouses and, with the help of her sisters, care for her sick mother. She gets up at night to scrape ice off the windows so the light could get through. The storm grows so fierce that the family moves into one of the lighthouses and subsists on eggs from the chickens Abbie has rescued from the rain. An easy-to-read account of a girl who proves brave in discouraging circumstances and saves the lives of those at sea.

Ross, Pat. *Hannah's Fancy Notions: A Story of Industrial New England.* **Illustrated by Bert Dodson. 1988. Paperback: Puffin. Ages 7–9.**

Hannah is tired of being capable. Ever since her mother died and her father stopped working steadily as a wallpaper hanger, Hannah has had to take care of her three younger siblings and do the housework. Fifteen-year-old Rebecca spends the week in Lowell, doing mill work and living in a boardinghouse. One day, wanting to replace Rebecca's ragged traveling sack, Hannah experiments with cardboard and scraps of wallpaper to make a colorful bandbox like the hatboxes she has seen. When her father helps her construct the box, the final product is so attractive that Rebecca's friends want to order their own. Hannah and her father concentrate on making the boxes, while Rebecca takes orders and keeps the books. Into each box Hannah fixes a card that reads "Made and sold by Hannah the Bandbox Maker." An enterprising nineteenth-century girl, Hannah makes the most of her talents and improves the lot of her family.

Ruepp, Krista. *Midnight Rider.* **Illustrated by Ulrike Heyne. 1995. Hardcover: North-South Books. Paperback: North-South Books. Ages 7–9.**

More than anything, Charlie wants to ride her neighbor's beautiful horse Starlight along the beach. But unfriendly Mr. Grimm won't even consider her request. So Charlie coolly leaves her house one night and goes through the dark to make her dream happen. By chance, Grimm wakes up and sees her wild ride on the beach, which calls forth his grudging admiration: "That was one brave little girl! And she rode like the devil." Charlie's venture leads to mishap, but all ends well. Her act of defiance is rewarded, a rare event for fictional girls. Expressive watercolors show a disheveled, red-headed girl exulting in her magnificent ride on the beach. Followed by *Horses in the Fog.*

Stevens, Carla. *Lily and Miss Liberty.* **Illustrated by Deborah Kogan Ray. 1992. Paperback: Scholastic. Ages 6–9.**

When France gave the United States the Statue of Liberty in 1885, the children of New York were among those who helped raise money for its pedestal. In this short novel, eight-year-old Lily comes up with a creative scheme to make money for this project. She and her grandmother use paper to construct crowns like the statue wears, and Lily and her friend Rachel sell them on the street. When a newspaper carries a picture of the crowns, business takes off. Lily's mother is not enthusiastic about the statue, but Lily is free to disagree with her, for her family believes that freedom of belief is an American tenet. As was common at the time, Lily's grandmother works in a shop sewing garments, as does one of Lily's young female classmates. An appendix gives detailed directions for making your own Liberty crown. A strong early chapter book.

Tripp, Valerie. *Meet Josephina: An American Girl.* **Illustrated by Jean-Paul Tibbles. 1997. Hardcover: Pleasant Company. Paperback: Pleasant Company. Ages 8–10.**

This entry in the popular American Girls series introduces Josephina Montoya, a nine-year-old who lives on a New Mexico ranch in 1824. Although her father owns the ranch and the family is prosperous, Josephina and her three older sisters work hard, doing laundry by hand, cooking, gardening, and more. They are still coping with their mother's death a year earlier and taking on more duties because of it. Josephina overcomes her fear of a mean goat at one point in the short novel and surprises herself with her newfound courage. Because Josephina speaks Spanish, Spanish words are woven into the text, with a glossary at the back. An appendix supplies information and a few photographs about New Mexico history. Despite the commercial tie-ins, this is especially welcome because so few short novels feature Latinas.

West, Tracey. *Fire in the Valley.* **1993. Hardcover: Silver Moon Press. Ages 7–10.**

Eleven-year-old Sarah lives on a California farm with her twin brother, her parents and her uncle in 1905. She is constantly struggling against her father's view of how a young lady should act. She wants to be riding horses, not sewing. Despite her father's disapproval, she is interested in a local political controversy over an aqueduct that would divert their water to Los Angeles. The issue gives Sarah several chances to test her moral and physical courage. She speaks out against the aqueduct to the highest authority she can think of. She also risks injury by riding bareback at night in an emergency. Sarah has an "independent streak," as her mother calls it, a trait that proves important to the whole family.

Biographies

Adler, David A. *America's Champion Swimmer: Gertrude Ederle.* Illustrated by Terry Widener. 2000. Hardcover: Harcourt. Ages 6–10.

Gertrude Ederle was a phenomenal athlete. She won three medals at the 1924 Olympics when she was seventeen, and by the time she was nineteen, she had set twenty-nine U.S. and world records. She then resolved to swim the English Channel, a twenty-one mile distance previously conquered by only five swimmers, all men. In her first attempt, she swam for nine hours and was seven miles from shore when her trainer insisted she get out. The next year, with a new trainer, she not only crossed the channel, but set a time record despite stormy conditions. "All the women of the world will celebrate," she said afterward, and two million people celebrated her feat in a New York City parade. Striking sculptural illustrations convey Ederle's sturdiness, strength, and optimism. An excellent combination of text, pictures, and an inspiring subject.

Adler, David A. *A Picture Book of Florence Nightingale.* Illustrated by John and Alexandra Wallner. 1992. Hardcover: Holiday House. Paperback: Holiday House. Ages 5–8.

This simple biography of an important woman in medicine looks like a picture-story book, with attractive line-and-watercolor illustrations on every page. Nightingale rejected the privileged life of her family and insisted on studying nursing, not then considered a respectable profession in England. Her role organizing nurses for the British soldiers in the Crimean War won her great honor but also resulted in lifelong ill-health.

Back in England, Nightingale dedicated herself to improving nursing and hospital conditions. She was the first woman to receive the Order of Merit from the king of England. A fine introduction to Nightingale and her accomplishments.

Blos, Joan W. *The Heroine of the Titanic: A Tale Both True and Otherwise of the Life of Molly Brown.* **Illustrated by Tennessee Dixon. 1991. Hardcover: Morrow. Ages 6–8.**
Legend mixes with fact in this story of Molly Brown, a flamboyant woman who survived the sinking of the *Titanic*. Loose, sometimes rhyming verse follows her from her birth, during a big storm in Missouri in 1867, through her exciting life in the West. She moved to the mining boomtown of Leadville, Colorado, when she was eighteen, hoping to get rich. She made her living singing for miners until she married J. J. Brown and began to raise a family. J. J. struck it rich and the family moved in style to Denver. But after Molly and her husband separated, she decided to see the world, traveling to Hawaii, China, Siam, Tibet, and all through Europe. At the end of a trip to Europe, including a stopover in Switzerland to learn to yodel, she embarked on the *Titanic* for its maiden voyage. When it began to sink, she boarded a lifeboat and kept up the spirits of the others all through the night until they were rescued. She rowed and got others to take their turns; she sang, yodeled, and told stories. Back in America, she was proclaimed a heroine. Large, sweeping illustrations convey the larger-than-life story of Molly Brown, who proved brave in the face of great danger.

Blos, Joan W. *Nellie Bly's Monkey: His Remarkable Story in His Own Words.* **Illustrated by Catherine Stock. 1996. Hardcover: Morrow. Ages 5–10.**
In 1889, journalist Nellie Bly started from New York and

traveled around the world in seventy-two days. She broke stereotypes about women travelers by traveling light and beating her original goal of seventy-five days. The bestseller she wrote about the trip mentions a monkey she bought in Singapore, the monkey who tells his version of her travels in this unusual biographical picture book. Each double-page spread features a charming watercolor-and-ink illustration of Nellie Bly and McGinty, as she named the monkey. They travel by ship and train through Asia, to San Francisco, and across the United States. As McGinty tells the story, he takes note of the excitement that greets Nellie Bly at every stop. Once in New York, McGinty goes to live at the New York Menagerie while Nellie Bly resumes her work as a writer. A two-page note entitled "For Those Who Wish to Know More" supplies details about Nellie Bly's life and career. An original approach to a venturesome woman's exciting race against time.

Blumberg, Rhoda. *Bloomers!* Illustrated by Mary Morgan. 1993. Paperback: Aladdin. Ages 5–9.

Imagine wearing a dress so heavy it drags through mud and trips you on the stairs. Imagine wearing a corset that makes it hard to breathe freely. Such were fashionable women's clothes in the 1850s. Wearing comfortable clothes, such as the bloomers popularized by editor Amelia Bloomer, was viewed as controversial and even scandalous. Bloomers were loose pants worn under a knee-length dress. They not only provided freer movement than conventional dresses, but were a symbol of the freedom for women. Political leaders Elizabeth Stanton and Susan B. Anthony, who were striving to win the vote for women, were among those who wore bloomers. Humorous, cheerful pictures illustrate the new fashion and show the disadvantages of the old one in this intriguing episode from women's history.

Brown, Don. *Alice Ramsey's Grand Adventure.* **1997. Hardcover: Houghton. Paperback: Houghton. Ages 5–10.**

"On June 9, 1909, Alice Ramsey drove out of New York City and into a grand adventure." That adventure was to be the first woman, and the third person, to drive a car across the United States. As the appealing watercolor illustrations show, the few roads that existed were in poor shape, and Ramsey had to care for her car herself. No good maps existed to guide her. The text conveys the excitement as well as the constant hardships and obstacles, while the pictures provide a sense of the vastness of the country and its varying terrain in a less populated age. This picture-book biography effectively opens children's eyes to a time when cars were new and introduces a woman who broke stereotypes and had a grand time doing it. "Over the next seventy years," the book concludes, "Alice Ramsey drove across America more than thirty times." Highly recommended.

Brown, Don. *Rare Treasure: Mary Anning and Her Remarkable Discoveries.* **1999. Hardcover: Houghton. Ages 4–9.**

Mary Anning, who lived from 1799 to 1847, grew up hunting fossils with her father on the beaches and cliffs of England. They used shovels and picks to uncover remains of different plants and animals from the past. When her father died, she carried on the work, selling her finds to support her mother and brother. Although Anning had little schooling, she taught herself geology and related sciences. Her discoveries were so impressive that she became internationally known among geologists. Among her finds were an ichthyosaur skeleton, the first complete fossil of a plesiosaur, and the rare fossil of a pterodactyl. Evocative watercolors show Anning at work, mostly on the beach, in this fine short biography.

Brown, Don. *Ruth Law Thrills a Nation.* **1993. Hardcover: Ticknor & Fields. Paperback: Houghton. Ages 4–8.**

In simple language and attractive watercolor-and-pen pictures, this book tells the story of Ruth Law, a pilot who tried to fly from Chicago to New York City in one day. On November 19, 1916, she took off alone through the freezing air and flew 590 miles nonstop to Hornell, New York. After an emergency landing when she ran out of gas, Ruth Law took off again but stopped short of New York City when darkness set in and she could no longer read her instruments to fly safely. Although she did not meet her original goal, she set a record and was hailed as a hero when she reached the city the next day. This charming picture book conveys the fascinating details of her memorable story. A gem.

Brown, Don. *Uncommon Traveler: Mary Kingsley in Africa.* **2000. Hardcover: Houghton. Ages 5–8.**

Mary Kingsley endured a dreary childhood in Victorian England, taking care of her sick mother while her father traveled. Never sent to school, she nevertheless became a great reader and escaped through books. After her parents' deaths, thirty-year-old Kingsley ignored all advice and set off in 1893 to explore Africa. She encountered hippos and fought off crocodiles, rode canoes up dangerous rivers, and trekked through lush forests. Words from Kingsley's own writings lace the text, describing her narrow escapes in a dry British voice. A note at the end tells more about her life, followed by a short bibliography. Expressive watercolors contrast her grim early years with her adventures in West Africa in this well-crafted introduction to a daring woman.

Coles, Robert. *The Story of Ruby Bridges.* **Illustrated by George Ford. 1995. Hardcover: Scholastic. Ages 5–9.**

In 1960, six-year-old Ruby Bridges was the first African-American child to attend William Frantz Elementary School in New Orleans. Feelings ran so strongly against integration that each morning for months armed federal marshals guarded Ruby on her walk to school. She and her teacher were alone in the classroom because parents were keeping their children home in protest. Ruby's calm courage in the face of threatening, yelling crowds of adults was extraordinary. Her family's strong support and religious beliefs kept her going. A final scene shows Ruby praying in front of the angry mob for God to forgive them. An afterword explains that later in the year white children began to return to school and tells a little about Ruby's later life. An inspiring story of a young moral leader.

Fritz, Jean. *Surprising Myself.* **1992. Paperback: Richard C. Owen. Ages 7–9.**

Children's book writer Jean Fritz considers herself an explorer. She likes to travel and explore new places, and to do research and explore the past. Color photographs show her in Alaska, China, Ireland, and the Caribbean, gathering information for her work. She also appears at home, writing and enjoying her family. Charming illustrations from some of her books are scattered through the slim volume. In the short text, Fritz gives a sense of her life and how she approaches writing. She chooses apt details to entertain the reader, like the fact that when she goes away, she leaves her manuscript in the refrigerator to protect it from fire. Fritz's fans will enjoy learning more about her, and those who don't know her books will want to seek them out after reading about this lively author.

Gilliland, Judith Heide. *Steamboat! The Story of Captain Blanche Leathers.* **Illustrated by Holly Meade. 2000. Hardcover: DK Ink. Ages 6–10.**

Vibrant illustrations that combine painting and cut paper draw the reader into this surprising story about a woman who became a steamboat captain on the Mississippi River. The picture-book biography not only introduces the remarkable Blanche Leathers, it conveys fascinating information about steamboats, how they were piloted, and their place on the great river. Blanche grew up on the shores of the Mississippi and by age twelve knew she wanted to become a steamboat pilot. She married Bowling Leathers, captain of the steamboat *Natchez*, and studied piloting with him, learning to read the river and steer the boat. She impressed the examiners in New Orleans with her knowledge and demonstrated her navigational skill in a test on the river to gain her official license in 1894. An outstanding combination of picture, text, and a terrific subject—don't miss this one.

Joseph, Lynn. *Fly, Bessie, Fly.* **Illustrated by Yvonne Buchanan. 1998. Hardcover: Simon & Schuster. Ages 5–10.**

This picture-book biography introduces the courageous aviation pioneer Bessie Coleman to young readers. It opens with nine-year-old Bessie picking cotton in Texas in 1901, where she encounters racial prejudice but also learns pride from her mother. Next, it is 1915 and Bessie moves to Chicago, where she becomes enamored of flying. But people tell her, "Colored women are cooks and maids, not pilots," and she realizes she must go abroad to learn. She saves her money, learns French, and in 1920 sets sail for France, where she becomes the first black woman to earn a pilot's license. The book ends in 1922, four years before her death in a crash, with a final scene of her performing in her plane. Stylized watercolors add a sense of the times and of Bessie's indomitable spirit.

Krull, Kathleen. *Wilma Unlimited: How Wilma Rudolph Became the World's Fastest Woman.* **Illustrated by David Diaz. 1996. Hardcover: Harcourt. Paperback: Voyager. Ages 5–8.**

Striking collage illustrations suit the drama of Wilma Rudolph's life. The winner of three Olympic gold medals in track in 1960, Rudolph had an unlikely childhood for a future Olympian. She was born prematurely, weighing only four pounds, and she was crippled from polio as a child. Through relentless hard work and exercise, she regained the full use of her legs and went on to be a high school basketball star. Her college track career led her to the Olympics where, despite a swollen ankle, she won two individual events and a team relay race. Pictures of her African-American family and community show the support Rudolph had while she overcame her incredible obstacles. A powerful story beautifully conveyed.

Lasky, Kathryn. *Vision of Beauty: The Story of Sarah Breedlove Walker.* **Illustrated by Nneka Bennett. 2000. Hardcover: Candlewick. Ages 5–9.**

Madam C. J. Walker, born Sarah Breedlove, was the first black woman millionaire in the United States. This attractive picture-book biography follows her life, from her childhood in the 1870s as the child of poor sharecroppers who were former slaves, to her triumph as a woman addressing mostly men at a business convention. Despite the obstacles she faced, Walker turned her impressive energy and ingenuity to inventing hair products for black women and enlisted her customers as salespeople. She expanded the business and, once successful, gave generously to her community. Spacious pencil-and-watercolor illustrations convey emotions and details about the time. One of the few books for younger readers about a woman who excelled in business.

McCully, Emily Arnold. *The Pirate Queen.* **1995. Hardcover: Putnam. Ages 5–8.**

According to the book jacket, Emily McCully "loved to draw 'rip-roaring action pictures' " as a child. This tale of Irish pirate queen Grania O'Malley gave her the perfect opportunity for action-filled paintings. In one picture, dark-haired Grania leaps into a crowd of fighting pirates to save her father from being killed. In others, she is commanding a fleet of ships, fighting along with her crew. She ruled over a part of the waters off the coast of Ireland and extracted money from ships that sailed those waters. At the height of her power, Grania O'Malley held five castles and married into a sixth. Stirring pictures of the pirate queen and the ocean she sailed dominate the book, leaving a powerful impression of a strong and memorable woman.

McGill, Alice. *Molly Bannaky.* **Illustrated by Chris K. Soentpiet. 1999. Hardcover: Houghton. Ages 7–11.**

In 1683, seventeen-year-old Molly Bannaky, a servant to an English lord, spilled a pail of milk and was punished by exile to the British colonies, although she could have been put to death for the offense. She served seven years as an indentured servant, planting and plowing her new master's tobacco fields. When her service ended, he gave her the required ox, cart, plow, hoes, seeds, and a gun, and Molly Bannaky went four miles into the wilderness and staked a claim. Few women staked claims alone, but she was determined and got a start with the help of her neighbors. Realizing she needed another worker, she purchased a slave, vowing to set him free when her land was cleared. As it turned out, she and the man got married and had four children, working the land together. As the last page reveals, their grandchild was the renowned Benjamin Bannaker, a scientist and mathematician, known for his almanacs. Striking watercolor illustrations on oversized pages take the reader back to the past for this splendid book based on a true story.

McGovern, Ann. _The Secret Soldier: The Story of Deborah Sampson_. Illustrated by Ann Grifalconi. 1987. Paperback: Scholastic. Ages 7–10.

This presents a fictionalized account of the life of Deborah Sampson, a Revolutionary soldier. Separated from her parents, Sampson had a hard childhood, spent mostly working for other families. She did housework, cared for younger children, helped with the plowing, and learned how to make household items like stools and baskets. She became a teacher, and deliberately taught her female students more academic subjects than most girls studied then. Although old enough to settle down and marry, Sampson wanted to travel before she entered the restrictive life of marriage, and she decided to enlist in the army as a means of adventure and travel. She disguised herself as a man and served for one and a half years. She once pried a bullet from her own leg to avoid detection, but during another illness a doctor discovered her secret. After leaving the army, Sampson married and had children but still had an urge to travel. She became the first woman in the United States to go on the lecture circuit, where she talked about her experiences in the army. Later she received a pension like other wounded soldiers did, and after her death a warship was named for her. This lively story, with its apt illustrations, portrays a brave and adventurous woman who made her own fate.

Moss, Marissa. *Brave Harriet: The First Woman to Fly the English Channel.* Illustrated by C. F. Payne. 2001. Hardcover: Harcourt. Ages 5–9.

In 1912, Harriet Quimby became the first woman to fly across the English Channel. Earlier she had been the first woman to get a pilot's license in the United States, after which she performed in air shows. She was a journalist by profession and wrote about her own exploits. This picture-book biography focuses on her dangerous flight across the English Channel, shown in expansive paintings. Her fellow aviators advised her against the exploit because fog made navigation so difficult that pilots had died trying. But Quimby was determined. Her flight in an open cockpit airplane proved very cold and as dangerous as predicted. Nevertheless, she landed safely in France. The author's note, which includes a black-and-white photograph of Quimby on a French beach, de-emphasizes the fact that she died later the same year while flying, but gives other information about this ground-breaking pilot.

Parks, Rosa, with Jim Haskins. *I Am Rosa Parks.* Illustrated by Wil Clay. 1997. Hardcover: Dial. Paperback: Puffin. Ages 6–9.

In four chapters, Rosa Parks introduces children to her part in the civil rights movement and, through looking at her own life, gives them a sense of why the movement came about. She starts with her arrest for not giving up her seat on the bus to a white person, and corrects the misunderstanding that she was just tired: "Some people think I kept my seat because I'd had a hard day, but that is not true. I was just tired of giving in." As this example shows, her words are simple, clear, and accessible to fairly new readers. Parks looks back at her childhood growing up in Alabama, where she attended a poor segregated school and experienced racial bias. Paintings on most pages add information about the time and emotion to the scenes. The last two chapters describe the Montgomery Bus Boycott and its aftermath. Although short, this book does an excellent job of conveying Rosa Parks's sincerity and strength, and increasing readers' understanding of our country's history.

Patrick, Jean L. S. *The Girl Who Struck Out Babe Ruth.* **Illustrated by Jeni Reeves. 2000. Hardcover: Carolrhoda. Paperback: First Avenue. Ages 6–9.**

In a 1931 preseason game of the minor league Chattanooga Lookouts against the New York Yankees, seventeen-year-old Jackie Mitchell struck out Babe Ruth and then Lou Gehrig. Soon after, the baseball commissioner made the Lookouts break their contract with Mitchell, and she was banned from playing professional ball, with the explanation that the game was "too tough" for women. But Mitchell had already proven the commissioner wrong. She had been pitching for years and trained with future major-league players. As the author's note explains, women had been playing baseball since the 1860s, when Vassar College formed a women's team. Other women such as Babe Didriksen had played in major-league exhibition games, too. This piece of baseball history makes a good story, illustrated with colored-pencil drawings on every page.

Quackenbush, Robert. *Daughter of Liberty: A True Story of the American Revolution.* **1999. Hardcover: Hyperion. Paperback: Hyperion. Ages 7–9.**

This story about a courageous woman during the American Revolution comes from the author's family, handed down over generations and verified in library research. One evening

BIOGRAPHIES

in November of 1776, Wyn Mabie was galloping to her home in Tappan, a town twenty miles north of New York City. She halted when a man walking near a tavern startled her horse, and discovered the man was General George Washington, commander of the Continental Army. Stopping to talk, she learned that Washington had lost his headquarters that morning to the British and left behind important papers. Mabie volunteered to try to recover the papers, reasoning that the British would be more likely to ignore a woman than a man. She persuaded Washington to let her help, rode to the Hudson, rowed across to the headquarters, disguised herself as a laundry maid, and succeeded in her mission. Although the conversations tend to be stiff, Mabie's dangerous true adventure will grip young readers.

Ringgold, Faith. *Aunt Harriet's Underground Railroad in the Sky*. 1993. Hardcover: Crown. Paperback: Crown. Ages 5–8.

Artist Ringgold has created a dreamlike account of a modern girl and boy who meet Harriet Tubman and travel the Underground Railroad. Powerful paintings, reminiscent of folk art, show the girl's strenuous imaginary trip from slavery to freedom. At each dangerous stop on the Underground Railroad, bounty hunters lurk in the background ready to pounce on her. But a variety of stouthearted railroad conductors help her through. Finally she flies over Niagara Falls and is reunited with her little brother. In a surrealistic ending, the children and Harriet Tubman are surrounded by freed slaves and a huge circle of women dressed in white. Two pages at the end give facts about Harriet Tubman and the Underground Railroad. This is an effective introduction to Harriet Tubman and the evils of slavery, although young children may find it frightening.

Rockwell, Anne. *Only Passing Through: The Story of Sojourner Truth.* **Illustrated by R. Gregory Christie. 2000. Hardcover: Knopf. Ages 7–10.**

Dramatic stylized paintings draw the eye again and again to the figure of Sojourner Truth in this picture-book biography about the great African-American orator. The full page illustrations in saturated colors show figures with enlarged heads and hands, and elongated limbs, giving the viewer a powerful sense of Sojourner Truth's dignity, religious faith, pain, and, most of all, her compelling personality. The substantial text describes her life from childhood, with grim facts about her life as a slave and how she earned her freedom. It tells of her lawsuit that saved her son from being sold illegally, and her emergence as an influential speaker. Winner of a Coretta Scott King Illustrator Honor Book Award, this is a striking introduction to an important woman.

Schroeder, Alan. *Minty: A Story of Young Harriet Tubman.* **Illustrated by Jerry Pinkney. 1996. Hardcover: Dial. Paperback: Puffin. Ages 6–9.**

This large, handsome book gives a fictionalized version of the childhood of Harriet Tubman, whose nickname was Minty. It portrays her as a young slave eager for her rights and understandably resentful of her servitude. Her mistress and the overseer are particularly cruel, as they destroy her only doll and whip her for freeing a trapped animal. Her father encourages her to learn about nature in ways that will help her run away, something she dreams about doing. He teaches her swimming and such outdoor survival skills as how to recognize the North Star. In the outstanding watercolor-and-pencil illustrations, Minty's red bandanna provides a bright spot against a muted background, like a beacon of hope. The back cover shows a much older Harriet Tubman, with a walking stick and a red bandanna under a shawl. The author's note at the end gives more details about this courageous woman. A beautiful blend of text and picture.

Spinner, Stephanie. *Little Sure Shot: The Story of Annie Oakley.* **Illustrated by Jose Miralles. 1993. Hardcover: Random House. Paperback: Random House. Ages 6–8.**

This biography introduces the fascinating character known as Annie Oakley. The short chapters, with their bright illustrations, follow her through her childhood when she learned to shoot and sold game to support her family. Sent to live with her older sister in Cincinnati, she frequented shooting galleries and one day competed against a sharpshooter named Frank Butler for a hundred dollars. Although he was older and more experienced, she won. She ended up marrying him and they traveled around the country and later to Europe giving exhibitions of trick shooting. Annie Oakley, as she called herself on stage, would shoot a coin out of her husband's hand and the end off a cigarette in his mouth. She was extraordinarily talented and she perfected her talent with practice. Annie Oakley was unique in an era when women rarely competed with men in public, especially not for money. A simple biography with well-chosen anecdotes about a remarkable woman.

Stanley, Diane and Peter Vennema. *Cleopatra.* **Illustrated by Diane Stanley. 1994. Hardcover: Morrow. Ages 7–12.**

Cleopatra was far more than a beautiful woman, as this slim biography makes clear. She ruled Egypt for twenty-one years, beginning when she was eighteen. When driven out two years later, she raised an army to fight for her throne. Her two well-known relationships, one with Julius Caesar and the other with Mark Antony, were political alliances as well as romantic ones. According to the historian Plutarch, the men were drawn to her, not by her beauty, but by her great intelligence and force of character. This attractive "storybook biography" emphasizes Cleopatra's struggles for power and her ability to recover from defeats. In a time when women rarely wielded direct power, Cleopatra was a fascinating exception. The beautiful ornate paintings reflect Egyptian artwork.

Stanley, Diane and Peter Vennema. *Good Queen Bess: The Story of Elizabeth I of England.* **Illustrated by Diane Stanley. 1990. Hardcover: Harper. Ages 7–11.**

This beautifully illustrated short biography introduces one of the most important queens in history. Elizabeth I ruled England for more than forty-four years, and presided over the cultural flowering in which Shakespeare wrote and performed. She became queen at age twenty-five and quickly learned to deal shrewdly with her own advisors and with foreign powers. She never married or shared the power of her throne. When Spain sent the Spanish Armada to try to conquer England and convert it to Catholicism, Elizabeth thrilled her defending soldiers by riding through their ranks in steel armor; ultimately England prevailed over Spain. One of the exquisite gouache illustrations shows Elizabeth on horseback brandishing a sword among her troops. The jewel-like tones and intricate details of the pictures convey a sense of Elizabeth's glamorous court and the times in general.

Swoopes, Sheryl, with Greg Brown. *Bounce Back.* **Illustrated by Doug Keith. 1996. Hardcover: Taylor. Ages 7–10.**

"My name is Sheryl Swoopes, and I've been playing basketball since I was seven years old," opens this photo-autobiography, with a smiling snapshot of a young Sheryl Swoopes next to the words. The conversational tone continues throughout the book as Swoopes shares her life story and her thoughts with readers, returning often to her underlying theme that, "No matter how far life pushes you down, no matter how much you hurt, you can always bounce back." She describes her childhood, her games as a high school student, and her college career, which culminated in a stellar performance that helped her team win the NCAA championship. The final pages focus on her experiences on the winning Olympic basketball team, ending before she began playing professional ball. A number of family photographs fit in with the personal tone, and basketball fans will enjoy the color photographs of Swoopes on the court, although the colored-pencil illustrations add little. Another welcome addition to the growing number of books about female athletes.

Tallchief, Maria, with Rosemary Wells. *Tallchief: America's Prima Ballerina.* Illustrated by Gary Kelley. 1999. Hardcover: Viking. Paperback: Puffin. Ages 7–10.

In this autobiography, Maria Tallchief explores how she ended up as one of the great American ballerinas. She describes her childhood and her strong attachment to music and dance, crediting her mother with encouraging Maria and her sister to take dance and piano lessons. To give the girls more opportunities, the family moved to Los Angeles, where the future ballerina's father, an Osage Indian, advised her to make a choice between ballet and piano. She chose ballet, knowing it would incorporate music as well, and studied with a talented Russian teacher. The striking full-page illustrations, which echo the poster art of the twenties and thirties, include many pictures of Maria and others dancing, with a final round-framed picture of a train as she leaves California to pursue her art in New York. An evocative, inspiring story of a girl who found her path early in life and made her dream come true.

Venezia, Mike. *Georgia O'Keeffe.* **1993. Hardcover: Children's Press. Paperback: Children's Press. Ages 7–9.**

This heavily illustrated, short biography in the Getting to Know the World's Greatest Artists series introduces Georgia O'Keeffe in a way that appeals to young readers. The large print makes it easy to read, and the humorous drawings include funny conversation in cartoon balloons. The text itself is straightforward, combining details from the artist's childhood and life with observations about her art. Seventeen paintings from throughout her career appear, along with three photographs of O'Keeffe and small reproductions of a few works that influenced her.

Venezia, Mike. *Mary Cassatt.* **1989. Hardcover: Children's Press. Paperback: Children's Press. Ages 7–9.**

Another book in the Getting to Know the World's Greatest Artists series, this slim biography of American artist Mary Cassatt emphasizes her role as a pioneer. She became a painter in the late 1800s when it was unusual for women to be artists. As a painter, she chose to paint scenes from everyday life rather than the grand subjects most artists painted. She joined the Impressionists who were using some revolutionary new techniques. Her intimate paintings of mothers and children were another innovation. The brief, simple text describes Cassatt's life and career, using many examples of her paintings. Several colorful cartoons add humor that will attract some children who don't usually choose to read about art. An approachable way to begin appreciating art and an important artist.

Wallner, Alexandra. *Abigail Adams.* **2001. Hardcover: Holiday House. Ages 7–10.**

Born in a later time, Abigail Adams might have been a

leader herself instead of only married to one. As it was, she did her best to influence her husband, John Adams, a leader in the Revolution and later president of the United States. Because they were often separated for months at a time, Abigail Adams wrote numerous letters that have preserved her strong opinions, including her firm belief in the equality of women. She also ran their farm and large household and raised their children with efficiency and generosity. Illustrations on every page use a folk-art style to show her surroundings in her Massachusetts childhood, the farm and Boston home in which she raised her family, and in the White House. This simple biography introduces readers to the beginning years of our country as well as an important woman of the time.

Wallner, Alexandra. *Beatrix Potter*. 1995. Hardcover: Holiday House. Paperback: Holiday House. Ages 5–9.

Ornate illustrations full of intriguing details are a fitting element of this short biography of Beatrix Potter, well known for her small children's books. The story explains how she escaped from the loneliness of her strict upbringing through art and her love of animals. At thirty-five she turned her energies to writing and illustrating a book for children, and had it printed herself when several publishers rejected it. The result was the very successful book *The Tale of Peter Rabbit*. With her earnings, Potter bought a farm, which she filled with animals. She died in 1943, the author of more than twenty-five books, many of them known to children throughout the world.

Wells, Rosemary. *Streets of Gold*. Illustrated by Dan Andreasen. 1999. Hardcover: Dial. Ages 7–10.

When Mary Antin was twelve, her family immigrated to Boston from Russia, where they had lost nearly everything because of prejudice against Jews. As an adult, Mary Antin wrote extensively about her experiences. Rosemary Wells has condensed those writings into a picture-book biography, with direct quotations from Antin on every page. Emotionally powerful oil paintings fill the pages opposite the extensive text, showing how Mary and her family suffered in Russia. A map of their journey fills two pages, with their train route across Europe and their ship route to Boston. Although their poverty kept Boston from being perfect, the family worked together and the children studied hard. The remarkable highlight of Mary's school days was a thirty-five-stanza poem she wrote in English about George Washington, read in front of her school, and had published in a Boston newspaper just six months after arriving in the United States. A moving story about a brave, talented girl.

Yolen, Jane. *The Ballad of the Pirate Queens*. Illustrated by David Shannon. 1995. Hardcover: Harcourt. Paperback: Voyager. Ages 5–9.

The distinguishing feature of this book is that it is about two female pirates, a topic of interest to children. Told in verse, the story is based on sketchy facts about Anne Bonney and Mary Reade, who sailed on the *Calico Jack* and were tried for piracy. Anne and Mary avoided a death sentence because they were pregnant. Melodramatic paintings accompany the uninspired verse. A note at the end gives further information about the two pirates.

4

Books for
Middle Readers

At this stage, most readers really come into their own. A wealth of wonderful books are written for this general age group (around nine to eleven), making it an exciting time for children who like to read. At this point, certain children become voracious readers and consume books by the dozens. Others tend to be interested in only one genre or series. It is not unusual for children to reread favorite books over and over again for pleasure and security.

I have divided the books in this chapter into two main categories: Fiction, and Biographies and Nonfiction. Fiction is further divided into six genres: adventure and survival stories; contemporary life; sports stories; mysteries and ghost stories; historical fiction; and fantasy and science fiction. The historical fiction, and fantasy and science fiction sections contain noticeably more books than the other sections, while adventure, mystery, and sports stories contain the least.

Biographies and Nonfiction is divided into six smaller

groups: leaders and activists; professionals and businesswomen; scientists and inventors; women in the arts; sports biographies and nonfiction; and more dynamic girls and women, a catch-all area of interesting titles including books on the women's suffrage movement.

As always, do not limit your choices to this one chapter. Novels and biographies in the preceding and following chapters will suit some middle readers, depending on their reading skill and interests. Like many adults, children this age still enjoy heavily illustrated books. Check the first and second chapters for picture-story books and folktales that sound appealing. Note that the folktale collections at the end of chapter 2 are particularly suited to middle readers.

Fiction

Adventure and Survival Stories

Aiken, Joan. *The Wolves of Willoughby Chase.* **Illustrated by Pat Marriott. 1962. Hardcover: Delacorte. Paperback: Dell. Ages 10–13.**

For those who like books filled with heroes and villains, this adventurous melodrama is perfect. A cruel governess and a heartless orphanage director try to make life miserable for Bonnie, a plucky rich girl deprived of her wealth, and Sophie, her kind, poor cousin. A bleak landscape of snow and snarling wolves accompanies the opening events when Bonnie's parents leave her and Sophie in the hands of the scheming Miss Slighcarp. Sent to a wretched orphanage, the girls—with the help of Simon, an orphan who lives in a cave and raises geese—head to London to seek justice. One suspenseful scene follows another, with emotions running high and danger everywhere. The first in a series, this is great fun.

Alexander, Lloyd. *Gypsy Rizka.* **1999. Hardcover: Dutton. Paperback: Puffin. Ages 10–13.**

Rizka, who lives on her own in a caravan, spends her leisurely days outwitting the pompous men who run the nearby small town. When her cat steals a roast chicken from Rizka's worst enemy, and the cat is put on trial, Rizka flamboyantly defends the cat and wins her case. When two sweethearts are kept apart by their feuding fathers, Rizka tricks the men into giving permission for the marriage. The townspeople appreciate the clever girl, while the men in power, especially the Chief Councilor, do their best to run her out of town. But Rizka can match wits with anyone and come out on top. Lloyd Alexander, who excels at creating imaginary countries populated by colorful characters, has done so again in an entertaining story about a clever girl.

Bledsoe, Lucy Jane. *Tracks in the Snow*. 1997. Hardcover: Holiday House. Paperback: Avon. Ages 8–11.

Erin, this survival story's ten-year-old narrator, believes that something has happened to her baby-sitter, Amy. Although usually reliable, sixteen-year-old Amy didn't show up one evening to baby-sit, and everyone else assumes Amy left town with her mother who has moved away. But based on things Amy said in the past, Erin thinks the teenager has run away to an old miner's cabin in nearby hills. Erin and Tiffany, her new science partner, go into the woods on Saturday morning to document animal tracks, but Erin really has in mind finding Amy. She tries to get Tiffany to go home, but Tiffany refuses. They have gone deep into the woods without finding the cabin, when a snowstorm sets in. Since they can't get out before dark, the two draw on every survival skill they have to make it through a winter night in the woods. A suspenseful story about two brave, smart girls who refuse to give up when the going gets tough.

Booth, Martin. *Panther*. 2001. Hardcover: McElderry. Ages 10–13.

British teenager Pati is fascinated with big cats. She has read all about them and watched television specials, preparing herself for a future job working with wildlife. So when she hears that a panther has been spotted in the English countryside, she is determined to see it. She and her friend Simon go camping with their parents near where the panther was seen, and spend each day out looking for it. Between the two of them, they know a great deal about tracking and identifying wild animals. Soon they spot the panther and start to follow it, leading to the most exciting experience in Pati's life. This straightforward story focuses entirely on their adventure, which makes it unusually accessible to reluctant or less strong readers, who will get caught up in the chase.

Cohen, Barbara, and Bahija Lovejoy. *Seven Daughters and Seven Sons*. 1982. Paperback: Beech Tree. Ages 10–14.

Set in the Middle East long in the past, this story tells of Buran, the fourth daughter of a poor man who has seven daughters. Whereas sons can help earn money, daughters cost money for their dowries, to the family's despair. Their uncle, in contrast, is a rich man with seven sons who disdain Buran's family. Buran, whom her father has educated like a son, decides to disguise herself as a man and try her hand at trade. She travels by caravan from Baghdad to Tyre and uses her wits and hard work to try to make a fortune. Buran befriends and then falls in love with Mahmoud, son of Tyre's ruler. In their hours of talk, Mahmoud professes the common wisdom that women are inferior to men. He realizes his mistake only after Buran has left Tyre to seek revenge on her disdainful cousins. A delightful tale about a smart, ambitious woman who succeeds against all odds.

Cottonwood, Joe. *Quake!* 1995. Paperback: Scholastic. Ages 10–12.

This realistic novel is based on a powerful earthquake that shook northern California in 1989. The narrator, fourteen-year-old Franny, and her friend Jennie are baby-sitting her brother while their parents go to the World Series. Their rickety home in the mountains near Santa Cruz is hard hit by the 5:00 P.M. quake. Franny finds courage she didn't know she had as she risks turning off dangerous gas mains in her house and others nearby. The three children roll a Volkswagen off an injured neighbor and find a nurse to help take him to the emergency center. Franny, who wants to be a geologist, meets a female geologist who is analyzing the effects of the quake and who encourages Franny in her ambition. The aftershocks, the uncertain fate of their parents, and the continuing dangers provide constant suspense.

George, Jean Craighead. *The Talking Earth*. 1983. Hardcover: Harper. Paperback: Trophy. Ages 10–12.

Because thirteen-year-old Seminole Billie Wind doubts the legends of her tribe, her uncle sends her off for a night in the Everglades. But the night turns into many weeks, starting when a fire sweeps over the island she is on and Billie must hide in a cave for days. When she emerges, she builds herself a new dugout canoe, but decides not to return home immediately. With a young otter she has saved, she journeys through the Everglades, learning more about the world around her and about herself. She draws on her knowledge of nature to survive by fishing, hunting, and harvesting plants. She turns her dugout into a houseboat and makes her way away from her home toward the ocean. Near the end of the journey, her life is endangered by a hurricane, and she must rely again on her ingenuity and good sense to survive. She is a brave, thoughtful, self-reliant girl on a serious quest. Her mother is head of the Wind Clan, and Billie shows the leadership qualities she needs to follow in her mother's footsteps. Although the message about the relationship between humans and their environment gets heavy-handed at times, all in all, this is a good adventure with a serious theme.

George, Twig C. *Swimming with Sharks*. Illustrated by Yong Chen. 1999. Hardcover: Harper. Ages 8–11.

At the beginning of her summer visit to her grandparents, ten-year-old Sarah wants nothing to do with her marine biologist grandfather's interest in sharks. But as she starts snorkeling in the Florida waters, she too becomes enthusiastic about sharks, helps her grandfather catch them temporarily for study, and learns from him about their biological traits. At the same time, she learns how to handle a boat. Drawing on her courage and prompted by her curiosity, she gets used to slipping off the side of the boat to swim with sharks, which she is surprised to hear that her mother and grandmother have also done. In the second half of the book, Sarah joins forces with other shark advocates to trap people who are killing sharks for their fins. An enjoyable story full of details about sharks and a girl who grows to loves them.

Lindgren, Astrid. Translated by Patricia Crompton. *Ronia, the Robber's Daughter*. 1983. Hardcover: Viking. Paperback: Viking. Ages 10–12.

In this unusual story translated from Swedish, Ronia lives in a fortress with her father, Matt, her mother, Lovis, and her father's gang of robbers. One day in the woods she meets Birk, son of Matt's greatest rival, Borka, and they forge such a close friendship they feel as though they are sister and brother. Her father disowns Ronia when he hears about the friendship, and she runs away to live in a cave with Birk. Lyrical descriptions capture the joy they take in living outdoors, where they are equals in energy and courage. Both tame wild horses after many tumbles and revel in swimming dangerously near a waterfall. Lovis, a strong and levelheaded mother, supplies them with bread and, though she would like Ronia back, understands her anger at Matt. In the end Ronia and Birk are reconciled with their parents but assert their independence by vowing never to be robbers themselves. Lindgren, author of *Pippi Longstocking*, which is described in the fantasy and science fiction section, has created another indomitable girl who leads a free, exciting life.

Myers, Edward. *Climb or Die*. 1994. Hardcover: Hyperion. Paperback: Hyperion. Ages 10–13.

Fourteen-year-old Danielle and her family are driving through a snowstorm in the Rockies when they have an accident on a deserted mining road. Danielle's parents are both hurt, so it is up to her and her thirteen-year-old brother Jake to go for help. Danielle's strengths are her fine athletic ability—Jake calls her a jock—and the skills she learned at a mountaineering school. Jake, on the other hand, excels at problem solving but is weak on athletic ability. At first his skills dominate, as he insists they try to climb a mountain to a weather station he believes is at the top. He has brought tools from the car and rigs up a compass. Soon Danielle's strengths come into play as they get higher and she has to teach Jake mountaineering skills. Each of them develops new abilities along the way: Jake challenges himself physically, while Danielle improvises with tools to make climbing equipment. The climb is perilous and the end uncertain, adding to the suspense. A gripping story of physical challenge in which a girl tests her limits.

O'Dell, Scott. *Island of the Blue Dolphins*. 1960. Hardcover: Houghton. Paperback: Dell. Ages 9–12.

Set on a small island off the coast of California, this survival story concerns a twelve-year-old Native American named Karana. When her tribe is leaving the island for more prosperous lands, Karana jumps off the ship and swims back to her island to get her brother, who was accidentally left behind. She expects the ship to return for them soon, but her brother dies immediately and many years pass before a ship arrives. The mesmerizing story details her survival as she builds shelters and gathers food. Going against the laws of her tribe for women, she learns to fashion spears and a bow and arrows. She kills wild dogs who endanger her, but befriends a dog left behind by Aleut hunters. Excitement enters her everyday life as she restores a canoe, hoping to leave the island on her own, and when she fights to survive a tsunami and an earthquake. The exquisite writing conveys the beauty of her surroundings and draws readers into her daily life. A modern classic based on a true story, this Newbery Award winner has been a popular book for more than thirty years. The sequel, *Zia*, recounts the story of Karana's niece.

Roberts, Willo Davis. *Baby-Sitting Is a Dangerous Job.* 1985. Paperback: Aladdin. Ages 10–12.
Thirteen-year-old Darcy wants to earn enough money to buy her own tape deck, so she takes on a baby-sitting job for the wealthy Foster family. She finds spending afternoons with the three children a challenge, but she persists. Meanwhile, she and her friend Irene are helping out a classmate who has run away from a father who beats her. Darcy finds herself in serious trouble, too, when she and the Foster children are kidnapped. Darcy tries to reassure the children while figuring out a way to outwit the kidnappers. Her courage and cleverness convincingly save Darcy and her charges in this suspenseful story.

Contemporary Life

Anderson, Laurie Halse. *Fight for Life*. 2000. Hardcover: Pleasant Company. Ages 8–12.

Fifth grader Maggie lives with her grandmother, who is a veterinarian, and helps out at Gran's animal clinic. Together they care for dogs, cats, birds, and other pets. But when Maggie's grades fall too low, Gran brings in other kids as volunteers, two girls and a boy. Then Maggie's cousin Zoe comes to stay for a few months. Despite a little jealousy, Maggie adjusts to working with a group and enlists them in her campaign against a local puppy mill, an illegal business that mistreats dogs. In the process, Maggie learns about laws concerning animals and teaches the other kids about working at the clinic. Gran is a hard-working, brisk but friendly vet who welcomes the kids and encourages the two girls who are interested in becoming vets. An engaging story, the first in a series, full of strong females.

Bawden, Nina. *Granny the Pag*. 1996. Hardcover: Clarion. Paperback: Puffin. Ages 9–12.

Catriona's grandmother defies all stereotypes. She is an eminent retired psychiatrist who still gives lectures and treats a few sad patients. She wears jeans or, when she rides her motorcycle, leather clothes. And to Cat's chagrin, she smokes cigarettes. Granny the Pag, as Cat calls her, has taken care of her granddaughter since she was young and her actor parents could no longer take her on the road. Their life together has been eccentric but loving. Now that Cat is eleven, her life has become more complicated. A bully in her class is giving her a bad time because she refuses to be picked on. Worse still, her parents have bought a house in London and want her to live with them. But Cat is unwilling to let her life be decided by others, and she draws on all she has learned from Granny the Pag to prevail. Two strong females, one young and one old, make a formidable team in this engaging British novel.

Bonners, Susan. *Edwina Victorious.* **2000. Hardcover: FSG. Ages 8–10.**

When Eddy helps her mother clear out her great-aunt's attic, she finds a stash of old letters that Aunt Edwina wrote to town officials. The letters urge improvements in the town's parks, library, train station, and more. Inspired, Eddy decides to write to the mayor about some broken swings. But she realizes that a letter from an adult would carry more weight, so she signs it with her full name, which is the same as her great-aunt's name, and puts her great-aunt's return address. The mayor, knowing that Eddy's aunt is wealthy, promptly has the swings fixed. Eddy's next letters suggest improving an overgrown empty lot owned by the city, and fixing the town clock. Eventually Eddy's aunt realizes that her activist grand-niece is using her name and the two join forces to effect the next big change. A lighthearted story about social activism by two females, illustrated with occasional black-and-white pictures.

Chocolate, Debbi. *NEATE to the Rescue.* **1992. Paperback: Just Us Books. Ages 9–11.**

Naimah Gordon's mother is struggling to keep her seat on the city council after a nasty, bigoted opponent has succeeded in having electoral districts redrawn. Thirteen-year-old Naimah and four of her friends resolve to help Ms. Gordon win. These five personable and responsible African-American adolescents know how to succeed when they put their minds to it. They print up flyers and distribute them. Naimah wins the election to be student council president at her junior high.

Then the five organize a rally of junior and senior high students, during which Naimah urges them to get their parents to vote. A happy ending ensues. The five friends, elated by their victories, decide to call themselves NEATE from the initial letters of their first names.

Clements, Andrew. *The Landry News.* **Illutstrated by Salvatore Murdocca. 1999. Hardcover: Simon & Schuster. Paperback: Aladdin. Ages 8–12.**

Fifth grader Cara Landry, who has a history of being outspoken, channels her energy into a student newspaper at her new school, partly as a way to make friends. Her scheme works, but her teacher Mr. Larson finds himself in trouble for the newspaper. An unusually laid-back teacher—if not downright lazy—Mr. Larson gets invigorated thanks to *The Landry News*, but school administrators have been waiting for their chance to get rid of him. Only when Cara and her classmates rally to defend Mr. Larson does it look like he might keep his job. Large print and occasional pictures make this accessible to younger readers while the subject will also interest slightly older ones. A highly readable, moving, and thought-provoking book with a strong girl at the center.

Clements, Andrew. *The School Story.* **Illustrated by Brian Selznick. 2001. Hardcover: Simon & Schuster. Ages 8–12.**

Rarely does a novel portray a girl so intent on business and so obviously bound for success as Zoe, best friend to Natalie Nelson, the main character in this light novel about publishing. When Natalie writes a book-length school story, she keeps it a secret from her mother, who is an editor. But Zoe insists that it should be published and that she should act as Natalie's literary agent. The two consult with an English teacher and get legal advice from Zoe's attorney father, but they do the real work themselves. They send the manuscript under a pen name to Natalie's mother, who loves it. After a series of calls and some serious negotiating, Zoe persuades Natalie's mother to buy the novel and edit it herself, fending off the abrasive boss who wants to get credit for the book. Black-and-white drawings show the characters and a few of their actions in this dream-come-true story about a young writer.

Fenner, Carol. *Yolonda's Genius.* **1995. Hardcover: McElderry. Paperback: Aladdin. Ages 10–13.**

Yolonda is a big, strong African-American fifth grader who has just moved from Chicago to a smaller city in Michigan with her mother and her younger brother Andrew. She knows her own power and in one gripping scene uses it to punish some drug-pushing bullies who have ruined Andrew's harmonica. Yolonda believes her brother, who is slow learning to read, is a musical genius. She uses her own genius at thinking, planning, and asserting herself to convince others of Andrew's abilities. Andrew returns the love and admiration by playing music that conveys how large and powerful Yolonda is, "great like a queen." This is just one of the times that Yolonda's size is viewed as an asset. She takes after her Aunt Tiny, a huge woman who owns several immensely successful hairdressing salons. Yolonda's mother, a paralegal, wants her to do well in school and to become a doctor or lawyer. But Yolonda, who takes after her dead father, a police officer, aspires to become Chicago's chief of police someday, which seems possible for a girl of her abilities. This Newbery Honor Book is a gem: a beautifully written story of a queen-sized girl who is cherished by her family and justly confident of herself.

Fitzhugh, Louise. *Harriet the Spy.* **1964. Hardcover: Harper. Paperback: Harper Trophy. Ages 10–13.**

This nearly three-hundred-page novel, a modern classic,

follows the ups and downs of sixth-grader Harriet Welsch. Harriet, who attends a private school in Manhattan, practices to be a writer by keeping extensive notes in a series of notebooks. She follows a route to observe and write about her neighbors, even hiding in a dumbwaiter to spy on one wealthy woman. She also comments on her friends, who eventually find the book and ostracize her for her brutally honest criticisms. Harriet especially misses her friends Janie, who loves science, and Sport, a gentle boy who takes care of his father. With her parents' help and a bright idea of her own, Harriet restores her two important friendships. Harriet and Janie, who are dedicated to their hobbies, are not interested in being popular. Unlike many fictional girls in contemporary novels, they are unconventional and will likely stay that way.

Gray, Dianne E. *Holding Up the Earth*. 2000. Hardcover: Houghton. Ages 9–13.

Fourteen-year-old Hope has never quit looking for her mother, who died when Hope was six. She's endured a string of foster homes, and turned to art for consolation. Her newest foster mother, Sarah, seems better than the rest but upsets Hope by taking her from Minnesota to Nebraska for the summer, where they live with Sarah's mother, Anna, who wins Hope over with her strength and friendliness. Hope reads letters written by a fourteen-year-old girl who lived on the farm in 1869, the journal of Anna's mother in 1900, hears Anna's own story, and finally reads Sarah's diary about trying to stop a military installation near her house in the 1960s. As Hope reads about the strong women who lived on the same land, she herself becomes part of the place. Well written and thoughtful, with sympathetic characters, this book about the past and present is a pleasure to read.

Haas, Jessie. *Will You, Won't You?* 2000. Hardcover: Greenwillow. Ages 10–13.

Although Madeleine, known as Mad, descends from a strong mother and grandmother, middle school has entirely subdued her. After her best friend transferred schools, Mad survived eighth grade by rarely talking and instead spending her energy on her horse Cloud. But even then, she is too scared to ride him in shows. When Mad's mother becomes aware of her daughter's withdrawal, she enlists Mad's grandmother's aid. Mad is to spend the summer with her grandmother, the Powerful Chair of the Senate Finance Committee in her state legislature, known as P. C. for short. P. C. believes that her own hobby of Scottish dancing will give Mad the social skills she needs. Mad hates the idea, but P. C. is right. The dancing, which is torture at first, but later becomes a pleasure, gives Mad confidence, while observing her grandmother's political prowess and convictions brings out a side of Mad she didn't know she had. An engaging novel with fully developed characters that the reader will miss when the book ends.

Hesse, Karen. *Just Juice*. Illustrated by Robert Andrew Parker. 1998. Hardcover: Scholastic. Paperback: Scholastic. Ages 8–12.

Hesse, winner of the 1998 Newbery Medal for *Out of the Dust*, again writes about a family struggling with poverty and pain, relying on their love and courage for survival. This short novel concerns nine-year-old Justus Faulstich, the third of five sisters. Embarrassed because she can't read, Juice, as she is known, skips school most days and tries to cheer up her unemployed father, whose depression deepens when their run-down house is threatened with foreclosure. Juice may not be good at school, but, like her dad, she excels at anything that requires mechanical skills. With Juice's enthusiasm and help, her father starts a small business and begins to assume his responsibilities as a father again. Despite their problems, which begin to be resolved in a realistic way, the family radiates an appealing warmth more often found in old-fashioned children's books.

Hyppolite, Joanne. *Ola Shakes It Up*. Illustrated by Warren Chang. 1998. Hardcover: Delacorte. Ages 9–13.

Nine-year-old Ola doesn't want to move from her urban home, in a mostly black neighborhood, to a mostly white suburb. Worse yet, the Bensons' new house is in a cooperative development with many rules, including an early curfew for kids. Her older brother and sister adjust fairly quickly, but Ola continues to plot ways to leave the suburbs and return to her former home. She has strong planning skills, but they don't do her much good until she sets a new goal: loosening up the rules of the cooperative. Ola allies herself with Maria, whose mother is the mayor, as was her grandmother. Between Ola's planning and Maria's knowledge of town politics, the two young activists are bound to succeed. The author concocts an entertaining plot while also incorporating serious issues about racial bias and adjusting to difficult changes.

Konigsburg, E. L. *From the Mixed-up Files of Mrs. Basil E. Frankweiler*. 1967. Hardcover: Atheneum. Paperback: Dell. Ages 10–12.

This charming story of two children running away to the Metropolitan Museum of Art won the Newbery Medal for its excellent writing. Eleven-year-old Claudia finds life in her suburban Connecticut home unfair because as the oldest child and the only girl she has more than her share of responsibilities. When she decides to run away, her originality and ability to plan come to the fore. She chooses the museum because it will be comfortable and elegant, and she enlists one of her brothers, Jamie, because he is rich for his age and knows how to keep quiet. They pull off the escapade without a hitch, thanks to Claudia's leadership and Jamie's funds. Living secretly in the museum, they become fascinated with a statue of an angel that might have been created by Michelangelo, and they try to solve the mystery of its origin. This leads them to Mrs. Basil E. Frankweiler, the narrator of the story, who is a self-confident, opinionated, interesting, and very wealthy old woman who presents them with a further challenge and a wonderful reward. This book has remained popular for many years thanks to its humor, suspense, and fast-moving plot.

McKay, Hilary. *The Exiles*. 1992. Hardcover: McElderry. Paperback: Aladdin. Ages 9–12.
The exiles are the four Conroy sisters, ages six, eight, eleven, and thirteen, strong-willed girls who try any outrageous thing they want without worrying about the consequences. This gets them into a lot of trouble but keeps their lives exciting. Under protest, they are sent by their long-suffering parents to spend the summer with their grandmother. Since she is just as insistent on having her way as the girls are, the visit is a funny series of conflicts that mellows eventually into affectionate exasperation on both sides. The only male character, a practical boy from a nearby farm, is torn between admiration for the girls' daring and shock at their recklessness. Certain readers will laugh out loud at the funny, understated dialogue and the unexpected approach that the exiles take to life. The sisters continue their entertaining adventures in *The Exiles at Home* and *The Exiles in Love*. Highly recommended.

Smith, Cynthia Leitich. *Rain Is Not My Indian Name.* **2001. Hardcover: Harper. Ages 10–13.**

Fourteen-year-old Rain is one of the few Native Americans in her small Kansas town, just as her second-best friend Queenie is one of the few blacks. Rain's mother died years ago, and her military father is stationed in Asia, so Rain lives with her grandfather and older brother. After her best friend dies, Rain isolates herself and only starts to emerge from her pain slowly. Rather than attending the summer Indian Camp started by her aunt, a science teacher, Rain returns to her hobby of photography and gets a newspaper assignment to photograph the camp. Doing so draws her into a small-town political battle and reconnects her with her friends. Adept at photography and creating Web sites, Rain is smart and capable, and faces her problems with a realistic blend of reluctance and courage.

Taylor, Theodore. *The Trouble with Tuck.* **1981. Paperback: Avon. Ages 8–11.**

When Helen's parents give her a dog for her birthday, they hope to increase her confidence, teach her responsibility, and give her something special in her life. The younger sister of two handsome, athletic brothers, Helen is shy and awkward. But she loves Tuck and works hard to train him, gaining confidence as she does. When Helen turns thirteen, Tuck starts to lose his eyesight. Unwilling to tie him up all day, Helen schemes to get a Seeing Eye dog for Tuck. When her persistence finally pays off, Helen takes on the daunting responsibility of making her two dogs into a team. Despite discouraging setbacks, she succeeds through sheer grit and extraordinary love. Based on a true story, this short novel will have readers cheering for Helen and her dogs.

Williams, Vera B. *Scooter*. 1993. Hardcover: Greenwillow. Paperback: Trophy. Ages 8–11.

Artist Vera Williams has created a unique novel by incorporating artwork into the text. Elana and her mother have just moved to a housing project far from their last home. Elana, who loves to perform tricks on her scooter, quickly makes new friends. The children she meets band together into a team to enter a field day in a local park. Acrostics decorated with pictures describe some of her teammates: Beryl is the team captain, Adrienne is strong, and her visiting cousin Nanette is an "especially fast runner." Elana's mother, a working woman who cares about politics and women's rights, encourages Elana's independence. The field day, illustrated with pictures and a wonderful chart, highlights Elana's energy and persistence. An unusually lively book, this is a good read-aloud for younger children, too.

Sports Stories

Alvord, Douglas. *Sarah's Boat: A Young Girl Learns the Art of Sailing*. 1994. Hardcover: Tilbury House. Ages 9–12.

This small book combines instruction about sailing with the fictional story of twelve-year-old Sarah Miller. Shy Sarah overcomes more of her nervousness about sailing every time she masters an aspect of it. Black-and-white drawings supply details about boats and how to maneuver them, as do diagrams about tacking, jibing, and navigating. After practicing and getting tips from her grandfather, Sarah enters a race and skillfully defeats a boy who has poked fun at her boat. A glossary at the back lists parts of boats as well as sailing terms. This is one of the few books available about a girl and her boat; sailors and future sailors won't want to miss it.

Christopher, Matt. *Spike It!* 1998. Hardcover: Little, Brown. Paperback: Little, Brown. Ages 9–12.

Jamie, an intense volleyball player, takes the attitude, "Go for the kill and spike it down their throats!" Her middle school team will make the state play-offs if they can win their next few games, but Jamie's personal life starts distracting her. Her father's sudden remarriage brings not only a stepmother, but a lively, personable stepsister named Michaela. To Jamie's dismay, her friends respond warmly to Michaela. Even worse, Michaela is a natural at volleyball, just the player the team needs. Jamie struggles with the changes in her life and rejects Michaela, not noticing that Michaela is struggling, too. Despite some clichés about girls not getting along, this is a fast-paced sports novel with lots of action on the court and a group of girls who take their sport seriously.

Costello, Emily. *Foul Play.* 1998. Paperback: Skylark. Ages 9–12.

An action photograph on this book's cover shows a girl heading a soccer ball, her arms back and her face intense. The novel opens with the season's first practice for the Stars. Tess, an ambitious, talented player, can't understand why no one, including the coach, cares as much about winning as she does. She's especially upset because three of the new team members have never played soccer before. For a while, Tess tries to undermine the new players to keep them off the field, in order to improve the team's record. But as the season progresses, with many detailed descriptions of games, Tess comes to appreciate that hers isn't the only way to approach sports. A light, fast read about a girls' team with plenty of soccer action, this is the first in a series.

Holohan, Maureen. *Friday Nights.* **1998. Paperback: Pocket. Ages 9–13.**

Told from the viewpoint of Molly O'Malley, this novel has sports action on almost every page. Molly and her friends love any kind of ball games. They get together whenever they can at the local park to shoot hoops, toss around a football, play some soccer, or hit baseballs. As the story opens, the Park District has finally organized a basketball league for middle-school girls. Molly and her friends form a team coached by Molly's father and the father of her best friend, Penny. Penny, who excels at all sports, is their best player, but all of them play with intensity. Molly has to work hard to control her temper when the team rumored to be best hassles her in the park. As the story progresses, she learns not to judge other girls by how they act on the court, and as a result she makes some new friends. The first in a series that has different sports and different narrators for each book, this is an entertaining novel with a cast of personable characters.

Lord, Bette Bao. *In the Year of the Boar and Jackie Robinson.* **Illustrated by Marc Simont. 1986. Hardcover: Harper. Paperback: Trophy. Ages 9–12.**

It is 1947, and Shirley Temple Wong has just moved to New York from China. Everything is strange and worrisome, from the language to the food, from school to the stickball game that other children play. Shirley flounders until the day she walks proudly through the school yard "like an emperor" and interrupts a stickball game. She emerges with two black eyes and one good friend, Mabel, the strongest, scariest girl in the fifth grade. Mabel teaches Shirley how to play stickball and how to appreciate baseball, especially the Brooklyn Dodgers. During summer vacation, Shirley helps her father fix things in their apartment building and becomes adept with tools and repair jobs. One of her dreams for the future is to be an engineer like her father, or maybe a surgeon. For Shirley, these dreams are connected to her admiration for Jackie Robinson, the first black to play in the major leagues and a symbol of opportunity in America. Shirley's dedication to the Dodgers reflects the devotion many girls feel to a sports team. Marc Simont's sprightly black-and-white illustrations perfectly suit this optimistic story.

Mackel, Kathy. *A Season of Comebacks*. 1997. Hardcover: Putnam. Paperback: Paper Star. Ages 9–13.

The Burrows household revolves around twelve-year-old Allie, the best young softball pitcher in California, whose talent is increasingly attracting media attention. Mr. Burrows coaches the Blazers, Allie's team, and spends little time with ten-year-old Molly. Although badly disappointed when she doesn't get chosen for the Blazers, Molly has a good time playing shortstop for another team, relieved to be out of Allie's shadow. But when the Blazers lose their catcher, Mr. Burrows insists on Molly taking the position, and softball ceases to be fun for her. Their father puts pressure on both girls, not seeing the problems he is causing, although their mother tries to tell him. In the end, Allie makes a surprising choice and Molly's father rethinks his approach. Filled with softball action, this is an absorbing sports novel about two strong girls.

Mathis, Sharon Bell. *Running Girl: The Diary of Ebonee Rose*. 1997. Hardcover: Harcourt. Ages 9–12.

Eleven-year-old Ebonee Rose loves to run. Her parents encourage her, and she also finds inspiration in the stories of famous black women athletes. Ebonee Rose writes in her diary, recording her training and other details of daily life. She is gearing up for the All-City Track Meet in twenty days, where she and her team will compete in four events. An injury looks like it might set her back, but even that can't hold her down. Ebonee Rose is also dealing with a new girl on the team, Queenie, who may become a friend in time. The unusual format, which has sixty pages of the diary entries and information about athletes, looks at first glance like a picture book with a glowing girl on the cover. Athletes will enjoy the training aspects, while other readers will just enjoy getting to know the upbeat Ebonee Rose, her family, and her team.

Nelson, Vaunda Micheaux. *Mayfield Crossing*. Illustrated by Leonard Jenkins. 1993. Hardcover: Putnam. Paperback: Avon. Ages 8–10.

In the small town of Mayfield Crossing, four black children and four white children have been friends for years, sharing baseball games and attending the same small school. Now they must switch to Parkview, a new, larger school in a nearby town, where they find the other students unfriendly and in some cases racist. Narrator Meg, who is entering fourth grade, feels the pain of racism, which she had barely encountered before. She also comes to appreciate the strength of her friendships. The friends decide to use baseball to establish their place in the unfriendly school, knowing that they risk public rejection. The main girls in this thoughtful novel—Meg; Mo; hot-tempered Alice, who is known for stealing bases; and one brave Parkview girl— are at home on the baseball field, which becomes a metaphor for bigger issues they must face. Followed by *Beyond Mayfield*.

Mysteries and Ghost Stories

Bailey, Linda. *How Come the Best Clues Are Always in the Garbage?* **1996. Hardcover: Albert Whitman. Paperback: Albert Whitman. Ages 8–12.**

The first of the Stevie Diamond mysteries, this fast-moving story centers around environmental issues. Sixth grader Stevie's first case starts when a thousand dollars is stolen from her mother, who had collected it for the Garbage Busters recycling group she works for. The group has been targeting the nearby Fabulous Red Burger Barn because it produces so much unnecessary litter and garbage. When rubber chicken heads, cut from the restaurant's disposable serving tray, are stuffed along with garbage into Stevie's mail slot, she realizes the stolen-money mystery might be connected with the Red Barn. With her male sidekick, Jesse, Stevie follows clues no matter how messy and dangerous, and pinpoints the villain all too close to home. A fast read with a courageous main character and a lot of action.

Byars, Betsy. *The Dark Stairs: A Herculeah Jones Mystery.* **1994. Hardcover: Viking. Paperback: Puffin. Ages 10–13.**

Herculeah Jones's mother is a private detective and her father is a police officer, so solving mysteries comes naturally to her. She is as big and strong as her name suggests, and has an iron will. Sure of herself, she plans to be a lawyer who helps children when she grows up. She and her male friend Meat, who is big but not as brave as Herculeah, get involved in a mystery concerning an old house and a strange client of her mother's. When she breaks into the house, she gets locked in but forces her way out. During her second trip to the house, Herculeah tumbles upon a long-lost body and helps her mother solve an old mystery. Although the conclusion is not as scary as the beginning promises, the story has plenty of action and a truly strong heroine. Meat's mother, who arms herself with a frying pan to rescue Herculeah, and Herculeah's mother are strong characters as well. Herculeah continues her detecting in *Tarot Says Beware* and other sequels.

Dowell, Frances O'Roark. *Dovey Coe*. 2000. Hardcover: Atheneum. Paperback: Aladdin. Ages 10–13.

"I hated Parnell Caraway as much as the next person, but I didn't kill him," narrator Dovey Coe explains, then goes back in time to describe the events that led to Dovey's trial for the murder. Twelve-year-old Dovey lives with her parents, her older sister Caroline, and Andy, who is deaf, in the mountains of North Carolina. Dovey loves the outdoors, prefers to wear pants—not a ladylike trait in 1928—and speaks her mind. She is annoyed that her sister Caroline is letting Parnell, the richest boy in town, court her, especially since Caroline plans to go away to college soon. But when Parnell is found dead, Dovey is unconscious beside him. Readers may figure out who really killed Parnell before Dovey does, but they will still enjoy meeting such a personable, forthright narrator.

George, Jean Craighead. *The Missing 'Gator of Gumbo Limbo: An Ecological Mystery*. 1992. Hardcover: Harper. Paperback: Trophy. Ages 10–12.

Lisa K. lives outdoors with her mother in Gumbo Limbo Hammock, an undisturbed spot in the Everglades. She fishes expertly, climbs trees, and studies the wildlife around her. One day a hunter hired by the Pest Control Department comes to try to shoot one of her favorite creatures, an alligator she calls Dajun, that the department considers dangerous. Dajun seems to have disappeared, which saves him from the official, but puzzles Lisa K. She proceeds to solve the mystery of where he is, while also scheming with her friends to thwart the official. Lisa K.'s mother, who has taken Lisa away from an abusive father, is working at a diner and studying for a business degree in order to better support the two of them. Readers will learn a lot of ecological information as they unravel the mystery.

Hart, Alison. *Shadow Horse.* **1999. Hardcover: Random House. Paperback: Random House. Ages 10–13.**

Thirteen-year-old Jasmine has gone overnight from having a secure life with her grandfather on a horse farm to being a foster kid known for attacking a man. When she and her grandfather found Whirlwind, Jasmine's favorite horse, dead, her grandfather had a stroke and Jasmine struck the farm owner, Hugh. Jasmine's grandfather is in the hospital, and Jasmine is staying with a foster parent, Miss Hahn. Jasmine has reason to believe that Hugh killed Whirlwind for the insurance, and now she suspects Miss Hahn of conspiring with Hugh. Determined to prove her theory, Jasmine starts to collect evidence and stumbles on another crime from the past. Horse lovers and mystery fans will enjoy this fast-paced story and Jasmine's courage and acumen.

Keene, Carolyn. *Nancy Drew: The E-Mail Mystery.* **1998. Paperback: Simon & Schuster. Ages 8–12.**

The ace detective Nancy Drew has endured over many years, with new books updating her character and mysteries, and avoiding the ethnic stereotypes in many of the earlier books. Although the writing is formulaic, Nancy herself still stands out as a confident risk-taker who never gives up. In this case, she has volunteered to help her attorney father around his office, to solve the puzzle of why several clients have settled their lawsuits quickly and for little money rather than go to court. Early on, Nancy suspects she will find the answer in the law firm computers. When a list of e-mail transactions provides an important clue, Nancy calls in her friend Bess, who has recently learned a lot about computers. Together they run into some physical danger, but ultimately they solve the mystery in time to go on a sailing vacation with George, the other girl in their trio of friends.

Kehret, Peg. *Don't Tell Anyone*. 2000. Hardcover: Dutton. Paperback: Puffin. Ages 9–12.

When twelve-year-old Megan finds feral cats in a field near her house, she starts bringing them food and water. Soon a sign goes up on the empty lot announcing an apartment development and Megan resolves to delay the project until the cats can be moved. Little does she know that a criminal who works at the construction company is depending on the project going ahead. Learning of her hope to save the cats, he lies to reassure her. But when it's clear that she will thwart his plans to commit a crime, it puts her life in danger. A tense scene follows where she eludes him and has to drive a car to safety. A subplot concerns Megan's witnessing a hit-and-run driver. Although the writing lacks finesse, readers will enjoy the fast-paced story with its brave, resolute heroine

Kehret, Peg. *Screaming Eagles*. 1996. Paperback: Pocket. Ages 9–11.

Two twelve-year-old friends have formed a "Care Club" dedicated to caring for animals. When they take a hike in a remote area and see a man taking a baby eaglet from a nest, Rosie and Kayo follow him. They get lost in the woods and even encounter a grizzly bear, which they frighten off. Then they succeed in finding his cabin, where they discover he is a taxidermist who specializes in birds, including endangered species. When the strange man spies them, the two realize their lives might be in danger. The tension mounts as they escape once but are almost caught again, then find themselves fighting a fire. The athletic Kayo, who loves baseball and lifts weights, and the studious Rosie, who is full of useful facts, make a good team. Although this book is part of a series called Frightmares, the plot is more exciting than frightening. A quick read full of cliff-hangers, this is the kind of adventure book usually written about boys.

Morpurgo, Michael. *The Ghost of Grania O'Malley.* **1996. Hardcover: Viking. Ages 10–13.**

Set on a small Irish island, this story combines issues of modern life with ghosts from Ireland's past. Ten-year-old Jessie has always wanted to climb Big Hill on her own, but her cerebral palsy makes it difficult. Finally she succeeds, and at the top she encounters the ghost of the Irish pirate queen Grania O'Malley. But Big Hill stands for more than Jessie's personal challenge. It is a divisive subject on the island, because gold has been discovered in the hill and its owner plans to bulldoze the top and mine the gold. Jessie's mother opposes the development, but she stands almost alone in her concern for the hill's beauty and its ecology. When Jessie's cousin Jack visits from America, Jessie and Jack join in her mother's fight, with surprising help from the pirate queen. Grania and Jessie's mother are strong role models for the girl, who deals courageously with her physical problems and acts on her political convictions in this engaging modern ghost story.

Raskin, Ellen. *The Westing Game.* **1978. Hardcover: Dutton. Paperback: Puffin. Ages 9–12.**

This intricate mystery abounds in increasingly strong females. All the characters have just moved into an apartment complex called Sunset Towers and find themselves potential heirs to millions of dollars. Millionare Sam Westing's will leaves his fortune to whoever can figure out who killed him. The will designates pairs who must work together, and Westing's lawyer doles out the clues. The central character is Turtle, a strong-willed, smart ten-year-old who follows the stock market and bets that she can stay in the haunted Westing mansion, at two dollars per minute. Another resident, J. J. Ford, is the first black and first woman elected as a judge in the state, and an intelligent and generous neighbor. Turtle's sister Angela starts out too compliant, but changes as she tries to solve the mystery. Turtle's mother, a pushy social climber, also changes as she finds an outlet for her energy in a business venture. The alert reader gets all the clues she needs, as the players collect information about one another in this intriguing mystery. A Newbery Medal winner.

Stolz, Mary. *Casebook of a Private (Cat's) Eye*. Illustrated by Pamela R. Levy. 1999. Hardcover: Front Street/Cricket Books. Ages 8–11.

It's 1912 in Boston, where Eileen O'Kelly sets up shop as the first female cat detective in town. An elegantly dressed cat, she decides to record her cases in the hope of producing a book. Some cases take only a chapter to solve, while others are intertwined with one another over several chapters. She finds a home-run baseball for Smokey Jack Slattery, a feline pitcher for the Furway Bobcats. She follows an errant husband whose wife refuses to believe the detective's report about his many girlfriends. In O'Kelly's biggest case, she finds out who killed a famous chef and stole her cookbook. She gets romantically involved with another chef as she travels to Baltimore to find the criminal. Full of detail about clothing and lifestyles of the time and place, this is a light, entertaining mystery.

Van Draanen, Wendelin. *Sammy Keyes and the Hotel Thief.* **1998. Hardcover: Knopf. Paperback: Random House. Ages 9–12.**

Sammy Keyes is insatiably curious. Bored in the apartment she shares with her grandmother, Sammy starts watching the neighborhood through binoculars. She sees a man in the hotel across the street who is wearing black gloves and digging through a purse. Worse than that, he sees her. Not wanting to worry her grandmother by calling the police, Sammy sets out to solve the mystery on her own. Meanwhile, Sammy's having problems at her new junior high, which she first addresses with her fists but ultimately solves with her brains. With many likable characters, young and old, this is the first book in a lively mystery series.

Yep, Laurence. *The Case of the Goblin Pearls.* **1997. Hardcover: Harper. Paperback: Harper. Ages 9–12.**

Lily's Auntie Tiger Lil has come to San Francisco to organize a float and marching unit for the Chinese New Year's parade. Famous when she was younger for a series of adventure movies, Tiger Lil jumps right into a mystery in Chinatown, with her niece at her side. A young woman on the float is to wear a famous ancient necklace called the Goblin Pearls, but a thief makes off with it, with Tiger Lil running at his heels. He gets away, but Tiger Lil and Lilly do some keen detective work to trap the thief. Issues about bias against Asian-Americans and about garment sweat shops add substance to this light, fast-moving story with two female amateur detectives.

Historical Fiction

Brady, Esther Wood. *Toliver's Secret.* **1993. Paperback: Random House. Ages 9–11.**

Before Ellen Toliver's dangerous journey to deliver a secret message to George Washington, her grandfather tells her, "We get over fear by doing things we think we cannot do." From the start, Ellen fears the adventure in which she must disguise herself as a boy, beg a boat ride across a wide bay, and deliver a loaf of bread with the secret message baked into it. Every step along the way she encounters trouble: boys who take the bread, a boat ride to the wrong city, a ten-mile journey through dark woods. Each time she finds the courage to proceed. She whacks the boys with a broom handed to her by a feisty old woman, defies the soldier who wants her bread, fights a pig, and completes her journey in the dark. Proud of her accomplishments, Ellen feels like a new person, ready to face the bully who has scared her for weeks. A good adventure with an important message about taking risks and overcoming fear.

Brink, Carol Ryrie. *Caddie Woodlawn.* **1935. Hardcover: Macmillan. Paperback: Aladdin. Ages 9–12.**

"In 1864 Caddie Woodlawn was eleven, and as wild a little tomboy as ever ran the woods of western Wisconsin." To the despair of her mother, Caddie spends as much time as she can with her brothers, climbing trees, canoeing, and visiting their neighboring Indians. Her courage and friendship send her out on a dark, cold night to warn those Indians of an imminent attack. As the book nears its ends, Caddie's parents appear intent on reining her in. Yet at the same time her sedate mother confirms her own allegiance to frontier life, choosing it over England. Caddie, it is clear, will become, not a passive lady, but a strong pioneer woman. An enduring American story that won the Newbery Award.

Durrant, Lynda. *Betsy Zane, The Rose of Fort Henry.* 2000. Hardcover: Clarion. Ages 10–13.

Based on a true story, this historical novel centers around Betsy Zane, a girl whose family homesteaded near Fort Henry in what is now West Virginia. When the story opens, the twelve-year-old orphan Betsy has been living with her great aunt in Philadelphia. She longs to be back in the wilderness with her older brothers, and fate decrees that she will be. Finding herself on her own, she joins a family that is heading West and endures the journey to Pittsburgh mostly on foot. There she finds a guide to take her down the Ohio until she reaches her old home. But despite her vigor and accomplishments, her oldest brother, who heads the family, treats Betsy like she is fragile and needs protection. In a final dramatic episode, she proves once and for all that she is as brave as anyone else in her strong wilderness family. An enjoyable read filled with adventure, history, and romance.

Erdrich, Louise. *The Birchbark House.* 1999. Hardcover: Hyperion. Ages 8–12.

Seven-year-old Omakayas lives with her family on an island in Lake Superior in the year 1847. This novel, full of descriptions of the traditional Ojibwa life, follows Omakayas through a year of learning and heartbreak. Omakayas's life revolves around her annoying little brother Pinch, her baby brother, her older sister, her mother, and her grandmother, Nokomis. As a fur trader, her father Deydey is often gone, dealing with the white people who are increasingly a part of their lives. The family builds their summer birchbark house, plants and harvests corn, gathers wild rice, and moves to town for a tragic winter. Black-and-white drawings add details and personalities, and the endpapers show a map of the family's journey. A slow-paced but satisfying long novel.

Fisher, Dorothy Canfield. *Understood Betsy*. 1917. Hardcover: Holt. Paperback: University Press of New England. Ages 8–11.

Nine-year-old Betsy has been raised by her timid, overprotective aunt Frances, who has taught her to be afraid of dogs and dirt and hard work. When Aunt Frances must devote herself to her sick mother, Betsy is sent from the city to the country to stay with the Putneys, relatives she has never met. The Putneys—Aunt Abigail, Uncle Henry, and Cousin Ann—believe that children can be helpful and enjoy learning new things. Although doubtful of her abilities, Betsy quickly learns household tasks and overcomes her fear of dogs. Every time she accomplishes something new, she feels a glow of pride. The test of her new competence comes when she and a younger friend are stranded at a country fair, and Betsy earns enough money to get them home. Written in 1917, the story does show boys enjoying more vigorous recess activities than girls, and it has some overly sentimental moments. But overall this warm novel advocates the philosophy of many modern educators: Children learn by doing and feel good about themselves when they conquer a challenge.

Goodman, Joan Elizabeth. *Hope's Crossing*. 1998. Hardcover: Houghton. Paperback: Puffin. Ages 9–13.

Hope Wakeman, who has had a comfortable life in the

American colony of Connecticut, suddenly faces danger and dreary conditions when Tory raiders kidnap her and take her to the Tory stronghold of Long Island. One of the raiders puts her to work as servant to his petulant wife, working long painful hours with little hope. Only the raider's mother cares about Hope's fate and, despite the old woman's own Tory leanings, helps the girl escape. The two of them reach New York City, but find it impossible to journey on to Connecticut. Worse yet, they contract smallpox. Hope must rely on her own wits to survive and try to reach her family again. She grows in capability and courage and meets the challenges of her changed life.

Hahn, Mary Downing. *The Gentleman Outlaw and Me— Eli: A Story of the Old West*. 1996. Hardcover: Clarion. Paperback: Camelot. Ages 9–12.

When Eliza Yates's uncle takes his belt to her once again, she takes her dog Caesar, and heads west to Tinville, Colorado, to find her father. Eliza quickly discovers she is safer disguised as a boy, and adopts the name Elijah Bates. After she rescues a wounded young man named Calvin Featherstone, a self-proclaimed "gentleman outlaw" who is also on his way to Tinville, the two join forces. Eliza finds life as a boy considerably more enjoyable than her previous life, even when it means pulling Calvin out of dangerous situations. Tinville holds several surprises for Eliza, including a new friend, Miss Jenny Hausmann, a photographer who believes girls have more options than catching a husband. Being a girl doesn't look so bad when Miss Jenny offers to teach Eliza about photography. In Tinville, Eliza also rescues Calvin one last time, an act of defiance and bravery for which she is willing to take the consequences. An action-packed, quick-moving story about a gutsy girl who shapes her own fate.

Hesse, Karen. *Letters from Rifka.* **1992. Hardcover: Holt. Paperback: Puffin. Ages 9–12.**

After Rifka's family flees Russia in 1919 and endures a grueling journey to Warsaw, they find that Rifka cannot board the steamship to America. The twelve-year-old has a case of ringworm, which causes her hair to fall out, so she cannot leave Europe until it is cured. Rifka musters all her courage to stay behind when her parents and two brothers depart. Far from her family on her thirteenth birthday, she makes herself a Star of David and recites Hebrew prayers to celebrate becoming a woman. Even when the ringworm disappears, her troubles are far from over. Her compassion, her ability to learn quickly, especially languages, and her articulate voice save Rifka from having to return to Russia. Told in the form of letters to a beloved cousin, this novel will touch the reader's heart and also make her cheer.

Hill, Pamela Smith. *Ghost Horses.* **1996. Hardcover: Holiday House. Paperback: Avon. Ages 10–13.**

Sixteen-year-old Tabitha is fascinated by the dinosaur bones in the Black Hills near her South Dakota home. But in 1899, young ladies are discouraged from studying science. Tabitha's father, a fire-and-brimstone preacher, loathes all mention of Darwin, dinosaurs, and women's rights. Nevertheless, Tabitha resolves to work for a dinosaur hunter from Yale who is coming to dig for bones. The famous paleontologist declares he has no use for women at his site. So Tabitha comes up with a plan and, despite obstacles, starts to follow her dream and even meets a female scientist to emulate. While Tabitha is challenging the norm, her mother is also questioning her limited role in life. An exciting story about the early days of paleontology and females breaking gender barriers in science and in their homes.

Holm, Jennifer L. *Our Only May Amelia*. 1999. Hardcover: Harper. Paperback: Trophy. Ages 9–13.

May Amelia lives with her parents and seven older brothers on an Oregon farm in the late 1800s. The twelve-year-old girl loves being outdoors and having adventures with her brothers, and she chafes at her stern father's insistence that she act like more of a lady. But her real problems start when her grandmother moves in with the family and criticizes everything May Amelia does. She blames May Amelia unfairly for a tragic incident, and the girl takes refuge with her aunt and uncle in the nearby town of Astoria. Despite her troubles, May Amelia throws herself into life in Astoria, still unwilling to give up her fun for ladylike behavior. The old-fashioned photograph on the dust jacket shows a girl in overalls, holding a fishing pole—a hint to readers of the girl they will meet and enjoy in this lively Newbery Honor Book.

Howard, Ellen. *The Gate in the Wall*. 1999. Hardcover: Atheneum. Ages 9–12.

Emma has worked long hours in a bleak factory for the past three years, since she was seven. When she is late for work one morning, due to her sister's violent husband, Emma goes through a gate in a wall and ends up at a canal. She spies a sprightly canal boat and, because she never has enough to eat, steals a potato from it. But she is caught and the boat's owner, Mrs. Minshull, insists Emma help her, as repayment. Emma spends the day walking behind the canal boat's horse, then realizes she cannot easily return home. As the days go by, she learns the skills of a crew member and comes to enjoy the open air and abundant food of her new life. Even crusty old Mrs. Minshull warms to Emma, who is a hard worker. But Emma worries about her sister, and Mrs. Minshull worries about not making enough money. After a crisis, they combine their strengths to plan a better future. A delightful historical novel about a stalwart heroine, full of information about life on canal boats in Victorian England.

Hyatt, Patricia Rusch. *Coast to Coast with Alice.* **1995. Hardcover: Carolrhoda. Paperback: Carolrhoda. Ages 9–11.**

In 1909, sixteen-year-old Hermine Jahns accompanied Alice Ramsey on the first coast-to-coast automobile trip by a female driver. Ramsey, twenty-one years old, had already established herself in contests as a skillful driver when a car manufacturer offered to sponsor her in a cross-country trip. Hermine and two older women went along, although Ramsey did all the driving. This is a fictionalized account of that fifty-nine-day trip, faster than the only two previous cross-country trips, both by men. The book, which takes the form of Hermine's journal, describes the places they passed and the hazards the women faced along the way. In the 3,800 miles, Ramsey had to change eleven flat tires and have the axle replaced three times, due to mud, potholes, and generally poor roads. One well-chosen photograph shows her changing a tire, a skill which she taught to male journalists unfamiliar with cars. In another episode, Ramsey temporarily wires the broken axle together with baling wire and extra hairpins. The photographs of the four women on the road are a wonderful addition, although the other illustrations add little. This is a fascinating slice of history about a pioneer doing something we now take for granted.

Jones, Elizabeth McDavid. *Secrets on 26th Street.* **1999. Hardcover: Pleasant Company. Paperback: Pleasant Company. Ages 8–11.**

Eleven-year-old Susan lives with her mother and two younger sisters in a New York City tenement in 1914. Her mother struggles to make a living working twelve-hour days, six days a week, while Susan helps out taking care of her sisters. When they fall behind on rent money, Susan disguises herself as a boy and makes good tips shining shoes. Bea Rutherford, a British suffragette, joins the household as a boarder, and life becomes easier and more upbeat. Susan and her friends, hearing about a national women's suffrage rally in their city, sneak away to watch, and they witness brutal police treatment of the women. After the rally, when Susan's mother, who said she was going to visit a relative, doesn't return, Susan must figure out what has happened. Full of details about what life was like for females in the early 1900s and facts about the suffrage movement, this short book effectively combines mystery, history, and a likable cast of characters.

Kanefield, Teri. *Rivka's Way*. 2001. Hardcover: Front Street/Cricket Books. Ages 9–13.

Rivka lives with her family in the walled Jewish quarter of Prague in 1778. Although she is fifteen, she doesn't remember ever being outside the walls. She worries a bit about her future marriage to a medical student but generally likes her life. Yet she also longs to see more of the world. Her physician father takes Rivka with him once into the rest of Prague, and the taste of freedom prompts her to disguise herself as a boy and go again. She quickly becomes friends with a Christian boy, and when he gets into financial trouble, she wants to help despite the danger. A sympathetic character, Rivka struggles with questions about what is right and with her role as a female and a Jew in this short, quick-moving historical novel.

Klass, Sheila Solomon. *A Shooting Star: A Novel about Annie Oakley*. 1996. Hardcover: Holiday House. Paperback: Bantam. Ages 10–13.

The childhood and teenage years of Annie Oakley make a

dramatic story, as told in this novel based on true events. Born in 1860 on an Ohio farm, Annie began hunting with her deceased father's gun when she was eight, to get desperately needed food for the family. Her extraordinary aim was obvious right away. Poverty caused Annie's mother to send the girl to the poorhouse. Then she worked for a farming couple who were so cruel that she escaped and made her way home. There she eventually paid off the farm's mortgage by selling game and pelts, struggling to use her talent despite strong disapproval of females shooting. She persisted, and on a visit to her sister in Cincinnati, found her career as a performing sharpshooter, a pursuit that led her around the world.

Lowry, Lois. *Number the Stars.* **1989. Hardcover: Houghton. Paperback: Dell. Ages 9–12.**

During World War II, the small country of Denmark protected its Jewish citizens and helped smuggle nearly all seven thousand of them to Sweden. Based on a true story, this novel tells of ten-year-old Annemarie Johansen and her family, who helps her Jewish friend Ellen Rosen in such an escape. Annemarie and Ellen do not understand the danger the Nazis in Copenhagen pose until one night when Nazi soldiers come searching for Jews and find Ellen sleeping over at Annemarie's. Thanks to the bravery of both girls, Ellen escapes detection. With Annemarie's mother and her younger sister, they travel to the Danish coast across from Sweden. Again, Annemarie encounters soldiers and faces the dangerous challenge of convincing them she is innocent, even though she is carrying a valuable package to help Ellen and her family escape. Told from a child's point of view, this novel alludes to the atrocities of the war but focuses more on the courage of the Danish people, both Jewish and Christian. A moving story of friendship and strength that won the Newbery Medal.

Lunn, Janet. *The Root Cellar.* **1983. Hardcover: Atheneum. Paperback: Puffin. Ages 10–13.**

Twelve-year-old orphan Rose, lonely in her new home in Canada with her aunt's family, travels through time in an old root cellar. She finds herself back in the time of the Civil War and embarks with a girl from the past named Susan on a dangerous journey to Washington, D.C., where they hope to find Susan's friend Will. Rose disguises herself as a boy and takes charge of their travels, a role she finds she enjoys. She does strenuous work for a blacksmith when they need money and gets them through the confusion of New York City. Although the girls do find Will, who has been fighting for the North, his painful descriptions of war temper their joy. Rose's developing sense of leadership comes into play again on the journey back to Canada. An outstanding time-travel story, this novel won the Canadian award for best children's book of 1982.

Moore, Robin. *The Bread Sister of Sinking Creek.* **1990. Paperback: HarperCollins. Ages 10–13.**

When fourteen-year-old Maggie Callahan reaches the end of her journey in 1776, she finds that her only living relative has moved on from Pennsylvania to Ohio. Maggie's plans to live with her aunt and uncle in the wilderness fall apart. She agrees to serve as a bound servant for the McGrews, who run the local mill. But after a winter of ceaseless work, she moves to Aunt Franny's deserted cabin to live on her own and sell her bread, using the sourdough starter passed down through the generations by her female relatives. Her business is successful until fate cruelly intervenes, and Maggie must choose between independence and a conventional female role. The first of a trilogy, this is a compelling story about a strong teenage girl who makes a life of her own.

Nixon, Joan Lowery. A *Family Apart*. 1987. Paperback: Bantam. Ages 10–12.

In this first book in the Orphan Train Quartet, Frances Mary Kelly and her five younger siblings are living with their widowed mother in New York City in 1860. Although Mrs. Kelly and Frances clean buildings and sew piecework, poverty forces Mrs. Kelly to send her children west on the Orphan Train to find other families to live with. The Children's Aid Society takes them to Missouri, where the children are chosen by different families. Frances, determined to stay with six-year-old Petey, disguises herself as a boy so she'll be more likely to attract a farm family. Strong from her work scrubbing floors, she performs as well as a boy could at farmwork for the kind Cummings family, who chose them. Frankie, as she calls herself, takes pride in her work but worries about her disguise being discovered. Everything she does, including her aid to escaped slaves, she approaches with courage, strength, and hard work in this gripping story.

Osborne, Mary Pope. *Adaline Falling Star*. 2000. Hardcover: Scholastic. Ages 10–13.

History tells us that frontier scout Kit Carson had a daughter with Singing Wind, an Arapaho woman. This historical adventure imagines what that daughter would have been like and how she might have dealt with the world when her father was away, after her mother died. The story opens with Adaline Falling Star living with Kit's relatives in St. Louis while her father is off guiding an expedition. Her bigoted relatives treat her like a servant and assume she is uncivilized, not realizing she can read well. When Adaline's father doesn't return as promised, she sets off on her own for Colorado, where she grew up. Her adventures along the river, where she acquires a dog and lives off the land, bring to mind Huck Finn. Adaline draws on her wilderness skills and faces difficulties with growing self-confidence along the way to the satisfying conclusion to the story.

Peck, Richard. *A Long Way from Chicago: A Novel in Stories*. **1998. Hardcover: Dial. Paperback: Puffin. Ages 9–13.**

Although this book is narrated by a boy, Joey, the central character is his incomparable grandmother. Every summer from 1929 through 1935, Joey and his younger sister Mary Alice take the train from Chicago to a small Illinois town where they stay with Grandma Dowdel, a woman who is strong, determined, and supremely sure of herself. In a series of entertaining episodes, she takes matters into her own hands whenever it suits her, even if it means breaking the law. She often helps people who are down and out, which typically entails annoying arrogant town folk at the same time. She wields a shotgun and brews her own beer despite Prohibition. Although now and then her soft side shines through, most of the time Grandma Dowdel has a no-nonsense manner that her grandchildren learn to respect. Throughout the years, Joey and Mary Alice are friends and equals, and Mary Alice shows some signs of taking after Grandma. With characters the reader will grow to love, this Newbery Honor Book is a funny, warm, thoughtful novel. It's followed by the Newbery Medal winner *A Year Down Yonder*, which focuses on Mary Alice and Grandma Dowdel.

Robinet, Harriette Gillem. *Washington City is Burning*. **Illustrated by Gabriela Gonzalez Dellosso. 1996. Hardcover: Atheneum. Ages 9–13.**

Twelve-year-old Virginia, who has been a slave at James Madison's Virginia plantation, moves to Washington to work in the White House. Virginia soon realizes that the old slave

Tobias has arranged for her to be in D.C. Because Virginia recently risked searing physical pain to save her fellow slaves from harm, Tobias wants her to help with efforts to free slaves in the capital city. Authentic details of the beauty and luxury of life in the White House contrast with nearby slave markets. Virginia quickly gets involved in helping Tobias, and although she makes a mistake in judgment, she plays a key role in several escapes. Meanwhile, the War of 1812 is bringing British soldiers closer to the city, until the White House itself is endangered. This fast-paced novel offers a thought-provoking view of James and Dolley Madison, through the eyes of a young slave who longs for freedom and sees the flaws in a president who condones slavery.

Ryan, Pam Muñoz. *Esperanza Rising*. 2000. Hardcover: Scholastic. Ages 10–13.

Esperanza, whose name means "hope" in Spanish, starts life as the daughter of a wealthy farmer in Mexico. But in 1930 when she is fourteen, her father is killed, and she and her mother are forced off the farm. In a role reversal, they now depend on a family that had worked as their servants, including sixteen-year-old Miguel. Miguel and Esperanza had been friends all through childhood until recently, when Esperanza pointed out their class difference. Esperanza, her mother, and Miguel's family leave Mexico and travel to the United States where Miguel's relatives are migrant workers. Esperanza's once elegant mother starts to work in the fields until she becomes too ill to continue. Meanwhile Esperanza tries to help out by taking on simple chores that prove a challenge. Her new experiences make Esperanza grow up fast, as she deals with poverty, injustices, prejudice against Mexicans, hard physical work, and her mother's grave illness. A coming-of-age story replete with history and hope.

Ryan, Pam Muñoz. *Riding Freedom.* **Illustrated by Brian Selznick. 1998. Hardcover: Scholastic. Paperback: Scholastic. Ages 8–11.**

This short novel draws from the life of Charlotte Darkey Parkhurst, perhaps the first woman to vote in the United States, long before women were legally allowed to vote. Parkhurst spent her adolescence and adult life disguised as a male, and voted under the name she used as a man, "Charles Parkhurst." As the novel relates, her childhood was spent in an orphanage, where she grew to love horses. She made her mark as a highly skilled stagecoach driver, first in New England and then in California. In this readable fictionalized account, Charley flees the exploitative orphanage dressed as a boy, and works for a kind-hearted stable owner. She seeks her fortune driving stagecoaches in California during the gold rush, and fulfills her hopes of owning land and her own home. The afterword reveals liberties the author took with a few facts and gives more information about this fascinating rebel.

Smucker, Barbara. *Runaway to Freedom: A Story of the Underground Railroad.* **Illustrated by Charles Lilly. 1977. Paperback: Trophy. Ages 10–12.**

Before Julilly is sold away from the only home she's ever had, her mother tells her about following the North Star to Canada. On her new, much harsher plantation, the twelve-year-old befriends a girl named Liza and they resolve to escape together. With help from two male slaves, an abolitionist, and the Underground Railroad, the girls disguise themselves as boys and head North. "You have foresight and great courage," the abolitionist tells them before they leave, and they prove their courage again and again. Separated from the men, the girls battle pain, fatigue, and fear as they make their way toward Canada. Suspense builds as they elude the men and hounds following them from the plantation. Can Liza survive the ordeal despite her ill health? Can they really trust the members of the Underground Railroad? Even if they make it to Canada, will Julilly ever see her mother again? An exciting but sad story that will grip the reader from start to finish.

Sterman, Betsy. *Saratoga Secret*. 1998. Hardcover: Dial. Ages 10–13.

The farm families who live near Saratoga, New York, feel isolated and safe from the battles of the Revolutionary War. When news comes that the British are bringing an army down through the Hudson Valley, Amity Spencer's family is shocked. Her father joins the Revolutionary forces and Amity and her mother take care of the farm and protect Amity's baby brother. Conditions worsen as neighbors leave and one of Amity's friends reportedly dies in battle. Through an unexpected turn of events, Amity and her mother receive a secret British letter about a planned attack. Amity must make her way to the Revolutionary army to give them the letter. Although slow at first, the book's pace picks up when she leaves the farm and faces a series of dangers. Adventure, romance, and history combine to create a fine novel about a strong girl.

Streatfeild, Noel. *Ballet Shoes*. 1937. Paperback: Random House. Ages 9–12.

This wonderful, timeless story follows the fortunes of three adopted sisters—Pauline, Petrova, and Posy Fossil. A fossil hunter they call Great-Uncle Matthew, or GUM, has adopted them, then left the three with his niece Sylvia and her old Nanny. When GUM doesn't return after five years abroad, money starts to run out in their large London house. So Sylvia takes in boarders, including a dance teacher who encourages the girls to attend a special dance and acting school. There

Pauline shows great acting talent and Posy an equally great dancing ability. Petrova, in contrast, spends her spare time learning about cars, reading airplane magazines, and mending things. All three, especially Pauline, concern themselves with family finances and take their own interests very seriously. The girls are resolute and talented, but they suffer the everyday problems of all children. For more than fifty years, readers have shared the worries and dreams of these three sympathetic characters who have never lost their charm. Related books include *Theater Shoes*, *Dancing Shoes*, and more.

Sturtevant, Katherine. *At the Sign of the Star*. 2000. Hardcover: FSG. Ages 10–13.

Meg Moore, whose mother died when she was eight, is her father's only child and she expects to inherit his bookselling business in seventeenth-century London. She loves reading and witty conversation, and has never learned about the more traditional womanly arts of cooking and running a household. But her future is shattered when her father remarries. If his new young wife gives birth to a boy, Meg will lose her dreams. Consequently, first she tries unsuccessfully to prevent the marriage and then makes life miserable for her new mother. Meanwhile, she becomes intrigued with the work of Aphra Behn, a successful female playwright, who is based on a real person. Meg tries her hand at writing a play and realizes she has more avenues for a promising future than she had realized. Determined and intelligent, Meg grows in understanding throughout this short, lively novel.

Van Leeuwen, Jean. *Bound for Oregon*. Illustrated by James Watling. 1994. Paperback: Puffin. Ages 9–13.

Based on a true story, this memorable novel set in 1852 recounts the journey of nine-year-old Mary Ellen Todd and her family from their home in Arkansas to the rich farmland of Oregon. They must leave the girl's beloved grandmother behind, as well as the school Mary Ellen loves. The six-month-long trip in a covered wagon includes illness, an Indian attack, mountains, deserts, and much more. Vivid descriptions bring the trail to life and convey Mary Ellen's fear and excitement along the way, and show her growing in strength and courage. A moving story replete with historical detail.

Wells, Rosemary. *Mary on Horseback: Three Mountain Stories.* **Illustrated by Peter McCarty. 1998. Hardcover: Dial. Paperback: Puffin. Ages 8–12.**

Three moving stories tell about Mary Breckinridge, a remarkable woman who started the Frontier Nursing Service. In each fictionalized account of a true incident about a child, the reader can see the enormous need for health care among the mountain residents, and the courage and compassion of Breckinridge and her nurses. An afterword explains that Breckinridge came from a well-to-do family, but almost lost heart when her two children, and her first and second husbands all died before she reached thirty. She entered nursing school in 1907, nursed French children after World War I, and then turned her energy to Appalachia. There she started with three nurses in 1925 and in six years built a hospital and six clinics, saving countless lives. An inspiring and important piece of American history.

Whitmore, Arvella. *The Bread Winner.* **1990. Hardcover: Houghton. Ages 9–11.**

After moving from a farm to a shanty in town, sixth-grader Sarah Puckett realizes just how poor she and her parents are. It is the Depression, and a fourth of the men in the country are out of work. Her father tries desperately to find a job while her mother earns a pittance taking in laundry. After Sarah's father teaches her how to defend herself from neighborhood bullies, Sarah wins a few key fights and makes a good friend after one skirmish. She also uses her bread-baking skills—her bread was awarded a blue ribbon at the county fair—to earn a little money. She gets interested in how money works as she buys ingredients to make more bread and barters with the neighborhood grocer. Her skills at baking and business prove vital to her family as she truly becomes a "breadwinner." She learns to stand up for herself and try out her ideas, even if it means risking failure. A heartwarming story about an enterprising girl.

Fantasy and Science Fiction

Avi. *Poppy*. Illustrated by Brian Floca. 1995. Hardcover: Orchard. Paperback: Avon. Ages 9–12.

The striking dust jacket will draw readers into this fantasy in which a large family of mice live under the rule of Mr. Oxac, a most unpleasant owl. The clan's leader, Lungwort, believes that Mr. Oxac protects the mice despite the fact that the owl occasionally eats one of them. Lungwort's daughter Poppy begins to question her father's beliefs and defies Mr. Oxac by traveling to New House, a possible new home for the mice. One of the few female leads in an animal fantasy, Poppy gains in courage and resourcefulness as she pursues her goal and becomes a leader herself. Several of the engaging black-and-white illustrations show Poppy brandishing a porcupine quill as if it were a sword, a weapon that figures in the downfall of the owl. Ereth, a helpful porcupine, adds comic relief to this exciting tale of an increasingly bold female mouse. This outstanding animal fantasy is the first in a series.

Babbitt, Natalie. *Tuck Everlasting*. 1975. Hardcover: FSG. Paperback: FSG. Ages 9–12.

In this beautifully written novel, ten-year-old Winnie Foster starts her move toward independence, away from a loving but restrictive family. At first, she just ventures out of the yard and into the woods. But that step leads her into an unexpected adventure when she meets the Tucks, a family who will live forever after drinking from a nearby spring. Winnie grows to love the earthy, disheveled Tuck family. When Mae Tuck attacks a man to defend Winnie, Winnie does her best to help Mae, even though it means breaking the law and disappointing her proud family. This is a magical novel that draws the reader into the world of Winnie and the Tucks, and raises the perplexing question that Winnie will have to answer someday: Do you want to live forever? Don't miss this book.

Banks, Lynne Reid. *The Farthest-Away Mountain*. Illustrated by Dave Henderson. 1977. Hardcover: Doubleday. Paperback: Avon. Ages 9–11.

In this fairy-tale novel, fourteen-year-old Dakin refuses to get married and settle down, the usual fate in her village for a girl her age. Instead, she makes three resolutions: to visit the farthest-away mountain that she can see from her window, to meet a gargoyle, and to marry a prince. In her journey to the mountain she meets a troll and a talking frog, hides from a giant, and speaks to three lonely gargoyles. She is frightened several times but refuses to give up. She finally faces the evil spirit who rules the mountain, knowing that only one of them can survive the encounter. Every chapter holds a new danger for Dakin, which requires all her courage and ingenuity. A surprising twist near the end leads to a satisfying conclusion.

Coville, Bruce. *The Dragonslayers*. Illustrated by Katherine Coville. 1994. Hardcover: Pocket. Paperback: Minstrel. Ages 8–10.

Princess Wilhelmina, known as Willie, objects to her parents' plans to marry her off. She wants to be free to make her own choices and plan her own life. So when the king promises half his kingdom and Willie's hand in marriage to whoever can kill a troublesome dragon, she sees it as a way to win her own freedom. She disguises herself as a boy and uses her tracking skills to follow the official dragonslayers, an old squire named Elizar and a page named Brian, into the forest. Just in the nick of time, she swoops in on a vine to confront the dragon, which is about to devour young Brian. But will she be able to overcome the beast, by force or cunning? The final scene relies heavily on coincidence to tie the ends together, which is characteristic of Coville's pedestrian writing. Nevertheless, his fans will enjoy this story about a feisty princess and her exploits.

Curry, Jane Louise. *Moon Window*. 1996. Hardcover: McElderry. Ages 9–12.

JoEllen, who cannot believe her widowed mother is going to marry again, is behaving abominably to her future stepfather. When no relatives want to have her visit while her mother is on her honeymoon, JoEllen gets dropped off with Granty, an elderly cousin who lives in the old Winterbloom House. Planning to run away, one night JoEllen climbs out of a strange-shaped window in the attic and down a tree, but she realizes that the window is taking her into other times in the past. She meets earlier generations of females in her family and must ultimately match wits with Witch Ellen, a powerful woman from long ago who still haunts Winterbloom House. Headstrong and brave, JoEllen solves the mystery of the house and saves her cousin at the same time. An entertaining time-travel story.

Furlong, Monica. *Wise Child*. 1987. Paperback: Random House. Ages 11–14.

This fantasy's main character, nicknamed Wise Child, has no parents at home and lives with her aged grandmother. Her mother deserted her and her father is at sea. When the grandmother dies, only Juniper, a local woman said to practice magic, will take the girl. But to Wise Child's surprise, living with Juniper is a pleasure despite the hard work she must do. Juniper teaches her about herbs and their uses as well as how to keep house, milk a cow, and eventually practice magic. Despite her happy new home, Wise Child is tempted when her evil mother appears and promises her riches and a life of leisure. Wise Child grows in knowledge and courage, a courage that is put to a serious test. An entrancing fantasy about two memorable females. Fantasy fans will also want to read *Juniper*, which tells how Juniper gained her knowledge and magic.

Jacques, Brian. *Mariel of Redwall*. 1992. Hardcover: Philomel. Paperback: Avon. Ages 9–13.

Mariel is a warrior at heart. In this entry in the popular Redwall series, the young mousemaid seeks revenge on the cruel pirate Gabool the Wild. When the story opens, Mariel has lost her memory but retained her spirit. She fashions herself a weapon and makes her way to the Abbey Redwall, a delightful refuge of comfort, food, and kind souls. A piece of poetry sends her on her way again, this time with three animal companions. As she sets off, Mariel is "filled with a sense of freedom and adventure," for she is an adventurer at heart. She leads the group on their quest, which culminates in a large battle against Gabool. Although most of the characters are male, the hare Rosie shows unparalleled courage and the badger Mother Mellus takes up bow and arrows when necessary. Among the array of animals that makes up the friends and residents of Redwall, males and females respect each other and share authority far more than usual in fiction. For readers who enjoy long, exciting fantasies, this is highly recommended.

Kindl, Patrice. *Goose Chase*. 2001. Hardcover: Houghton. Ages 10–13.

The Goose Girl has lived a contented independent life thus far, tending her geese and living in a little hut. As the story opens, though, she is stuck in a tower until she chooses between a prince and a king who both want to marry her. Fairy-tale fans will recognize familiar themes as she explains how she ended up in captivity. With a sharp tongue and humorous asides, the Goose Girl tells her story and explains that she longs to return to independence. From the tower she embarks on a series of adventures that include ogresses, magical occurrences, romance, and her ornery geese. Her strong-minded nature sees her through dangers, but she also learns to appreciate occasional help and advice from others. The wonderfully wrought plot leads to an ending that ties up all the complications on a happy note.

Klause, Annette Curtis. *Alien Secrets*. 1993. Hardcover: Delacorte. Paperback: Dell. Ages 10-12.

Even before Puck boards the spaceship to journey to the planet Aurora, she witnesses what seems to be a murder. Early in the trip, which she is making because she was expelled from school, Puck befriends an alien nicknamed Hush who has enemies aboard the ship. But Puck and Hush cannot tell whom they can trust among the passengers and the crew; even the female captain of the ship may be in league with criminals. In one exciting scene, Puck risks her life climbing between the inner and outer hulls of the ship to recover a sacred treasure belonging to Hush. While gaining confidence as well as testing her courage, Puck learns to overcome her prejudices in dealing with aliens. In a final heartwarming scene all she has learned comes together to reward her in the best way possible. The gripping adventure also has touches of humor, such as the futuristic slang Puck uses. A quick-moving, highly enjoyable story.

L'Engle, Madeleine. *A Wrinkle in Time*. 1982. Hardcover: FSG. Paperback: Dell. Ages 10–13.

This modern classic describes the suspenseful quest of Meg Murry, her younger brother Charles Wallace, and their friend Calvin to rescue Meg's father from forces of evil. They travel to another planet through a "wrinkle in time" with the help of three wise and powerful women. Meg, a misfit at her high school, gains confidence and learns to rely on herself rather than on the males around her. The three wise women encourage her to draw on her "faults"—anger, impatience, and stubbornness. Though not usually encouraged in girls, these traits prove a source of strength for Meg who plays the central role in completing their mission. Meg is unusually good at math, better than Calvin, and her mother is a dedicated scientist who combines work and family. This exciting adventure, beautifully written, was well ahead of its time in its vision of the role females can play. Winner of the Newbery Medal, this is not to be missed.

Lindgren, Astrid. Translated by Florence Lamborn. *Pippi Longstocking*. Illustrated by Louis S. Glanzman. 1950. Hardcover: Viking. Paperback: Puffin. Ages 8–11.

Pippi Longstocking is unique. She lives with her horse and

her pet monkey, Mr. Nilsson, in an old house, supported by bags of gold from her missing seafaring father. To the astonishment of her sedate neighbors Tommy and Annika, Pippi does what she likes when she likes. She is so strong that she can lift two policemen and defeat the strong man at the circus. She can climb any tree, a skill she uses to rescue two children from the top of a burning building. After the rescue, the crowd watching gives her three cheers while Pippi characteristically gives herself four. Pippi gives school a try, in order to get vacations, but she finds it too confining. No adult intimidates her; she chastises the teacher for asking too many questions about arithmetic, calling her "my dear little woman." She is quite happy with herself and her life, and with living alone. It's too bad Annika tends to be easily scared, but Tommy is not much braver. They both overcome their prim upbringing to join Pippi in her adventures, as any child would want to. A most remarkable girl.

Lisle, Janet Taylor. *Forest*. 1993. Hardcover: Orchard. Paperback: Scholastic. Ages 9–12.

Angry at her father, twelve-year-old Amber has climbed a tree to spend the night. There she discovers mink-tailed squirrels living in the Upper Forest, who have a sophisticated civilization, complete with language and social structure. Most of the squirrels view her as an invader, certain to cause trouble. Only Woodbine, a young male squirrel, sees her differently. When her father comes to the Forest the next day to shoot squirrels, almost hitting Amber by mistake, war begins between the humans and the squirrels. Amber is determined to halt the war. Her brother Wendell believes she may succeed because she is, as he sees her, "a master of detail, a maestro of design, a thinker of dazzling cleverness." She and eight-year-old Wendell enlist the help of Professor Spark, a dynamic older woman who studies woodland animals and gives Amber a role model she desperately needs. On the squirrels' side, Woodbine, his sister, and her friend Laurel also take risks to avert the war. Packed with action and ideas, this is a unique novel about strong human—and squirrel—females.

Pierce, Tamora. *First Test*. 1999. Hardcover: Random House. Paperback: Random House. Ages 9–13.

Keladry knows that by law girls can study to be knights at the King of Tortall's court, but no girl has for years. When Kel applies, they put her on probation for a year just because she is female. One of the King's main knights, Lady Alanna, is female, but that doesn't seem to help. Plagued by bullies, Kel draws on her martial arts background to fight for fair treatment and to defend other students who are bullied. Eventually she makes close, loyal friends, and sometimes excels in warfare training, despite the hostility of the training master. Will they let her return for the second year? An engaging first book in the Protector of the Small series by a popular fantasy author.

Pierce, Tamora. *Sandry's Book*. 1997. Hardcover: Scholastic. Paperback: Point. Ages 9–13.

The first in the Circle of Magic quartet, this engaging novel introduces three girls and a boy who are misfits or outcasts. The four find a home in Winding Circle, a temple community, where the children begin to realize their magical talents. Sandry, an aristocrat whose family has died, works magic through weaving and thread. Daja, a seafarer cast out by her people, combines metalwork and magic. Tris can call down storms and change the weather, while the boy Briar is in touch with anything that grows. Although all prickly and independent, they start to rely on one another as they explore their remarkable talents. Meanwhile, a threat to the Winding

Temple arises—a threat that could destroy everything the four children have gained. This is one of several fantasy series from Pierce that gives courageous girls center stage.

Service, Pamela F. *Being of Two Minds*. 1991. Hardcover: Atheneum. Paperback: Juniper. Ages 10–12.

Ever since her birth, fourteen-year-old Connie has been having fainting spells. But what her parents and schoolmates don't know is that during her unconscious periods, she is in the mind of a boy born the same day. The boy Rudolph, prince of the small Central European kingdom Thulgaria, also experiences spells and enters her mind. They enjoy the exchanges, although regret having to worry their parents. Their unusual link becomes a matter of life or death when Rudolph is kidnapped and Connie has to convince skeptical adults to pay attention to her information about it. She flies to Thulgaria, where she finds her own life at risk as she tries to find the castle where Rudolph is being held. With the help of their psychic link, the two overpower a guard and escape—only to be captured again. Connie, whose parents have been overprotective because of her spells, has to face physical challenges, scrambling over rocks and down cliffs. She draws on all her powers of quick thinking and bravery in the final push to safety in this appealing story.

Springer, Nancy. *Rowan Hood: Outlaw Girl of Sherwood Forest*. Illustrated by Stephen Hickman. 2001. Hardcover: Philomel. Ages 9–12.

Rowan has always lived in the woods with her mother, Celandine, who is a healer. When Celandine is killed because she is believed to be a witch, Rowan's only living relative is her father, whom she has never met—Robin Hood, the famous outlaw. Since Sherwood Forest is some distance from her now-burned home, Rowan undertakes a difficult journey

to find him. On the way, she disguises herself as a boy and befriends a wolflike dog. She finds Robin Hood, but that doesn't
solve her problems. She rescues a fleeing princess and the two
of them join forces with a young minstrel to rescue Robin
Hood when the sheriff captures him. Plenty of action and adventure characterize this entertaining novel about a brave
young outlaw.

Sreenivasan, Jyotsna. *The Moon Over Crete.* **Illustrated
by Sim Gellman. 1994. Paperback: Holy Cow! Press.
Ages 9–11.**

This time-travel adventure, which was excerpted in *New
Moon* magazine, follows eleven-year-old Lily back in time to
the island of Crete. Lily has been harassed recently at school,
and she has noticed how obsessed with looks her best friend is
getting. She longs for a place where women are equal to men,
and she finds it in ancient Crete. This worthy theme dominates the book, which is stronger on message than plot. The
dramatic tension comes from Lily's desire to tell the queen of
Crete about a disaster that will overtake her people, which
Lily knows about from studying history. But her music teacher,
Mrs. Zinn, who has brought Lily to ancient times, forbids her
to alter history. Lily's struggle with her conscience and her observations about a more equal culture and its rituals comprise
most of the book. Noteworthy for its unusual setting.

White, E. B. *Charlotte's Web.* **Illustrated by Garth Williams. 1952. Hardcover: Harper. Paperback: Trophy.
Ages 7–11.**

When the pig Wilbur first meets the spider Charlotte A.
Cavatica, he likes her but finds her fierce and bloodthirsty.
Little does he know that she will do her best to save his
life. Charlotte is smart and articulate, a talented weaver like

her mother before her, and a loyal friend. Like the old female sheep in the barn where they live, Charlotte knows more than Wilbur does and gives him good advice. When Charlotte weaves the words "Some Pig" into her web, to make Wilbur more precious to his owners, the Zuckermans, Mrs. Zuckerman observes that it's the spider who's extraordinary, not the pig. Although Fern, the girl who raised Wilbur, grows more stereotypically girlish, and her mother and aunt are traditional farmer's wives, Charlotte and the other spiders she describes are strong females. Written in flawless prose and illustrated with memorable pictures, this modern classic is a joy to read aloud. A Newbery Honor Book.

Wrede, Patricia C. *Dealing with Dragons*. 1990. Hardcover: Harcourt. Paperback: Scholastic. Ages 10–13.

Cimorene finds being a princess boring. Every time she tries to study something interesting such as swordplay and politics, her father stops her. When her parents decide she must marry a dull prince, Cimorene runs away and lands a job as princess to a female dragon named Kazul. Although constantly having to discourage princes who try to rescue her, Cimorene is happy with her duties of cooking and putting the dragon's treasures and books in order. Her routine is interrupted when wizards try to poison Kazul, and Cimorene must lead a fight to outwit these enemies. Her allies are a businesslike witch named Morwen, a stone prince, and another dragon's princess. Cimorene is strong-willed, brave, and smart, as are Kazul and Morwen: definitely an unusual trio of females. Full of humor, this fantasy series has quickly become a popular one. The equally appealing sequels are *Searching for Dragons*, *Calling on Dragons*, and *Talking to Dragons*, although the final book focuses on a male relative of Cimorene.

Yep, Laurence. *Dragon of the Lost Sea*. 1982. Hardcover: Harper. Paperback: Trophy. Ages 10–13.

The young dragon princess Shimmer is determined to recover a magic pebble in order to restore the ocean—which has been magically removed by Civet, a powerful witch—to her people. In her pursuit of Civet, Shimmer befriends a human boy named Thorn. At first he seems like a burden but instead proves to be an unexpected help as well as a rare friend. They swoop through the sky on their journey, encountering various magical creatures and dangers that they can overcome only as a team. The dragon Shimmer is a strong and headstrong heroine, more interested in adventure than in caution. The sequels are *Dragon Steel*, *Dragon Cauldron*, and *Dragon War*.

Biography and Nonfiction

Leaders and Activists

Andronik, Catherine M. *Hatshepsut: His Majesty, Herself*. Illustrated by Joseph Daniel Fiedler. 2001. Hardcover: Atheneum. Ages 9–13.

A female pharaoh ruled ancient Egypt for more than twenty-one years, reigning over a peaceful, prosperous kingdom. The daughter of Tuthmosis II, Hatshepsut gained power when her male siblings died. At first she served as the regent for her young nephew, but slowly assumed power herself and was officially crowned as pharaoh. Full-page illustrations show the people, clothing, monuments and some customs of the time. The enjoyable text tells not only how she achieved and used her power, and something about her accomplishments, but also explains how archaeologists know so much about an unusual ruler from so long ago.

Bridges, Ruby. *Through My Eyes*. 1999. Hardcover: Scholastic. Ages 9–13.

In 1960, first grader Ruby Bridges integrated an all-white elementary school in New Orleans, walking through angry mobs each day to get there. When none of the white parents sent their children to join her, Ruby spent the days alone with her teacher. In this elegant book illustrated with glossy black-and-white photographs, the adult Ruby Bridges looks back at her feelings and understanding at the time of this important event. She describes how it affected her life, even though she didn't realize the implications for a long time, and describes her current activism to continue promoting justice and civil rights. A moving story of courage and faith in a beautifully designed book.

Colman, Penny. *Fannie Lou Hamer and the Fight for the Vote*. 1993. Hardcover: Millbrook. Paperback: Millbrook. Ages 8–10.

Fannie Lou Hamer was a true heroine. This attractive, brief biography opens with Hamer's experience at the 1964 Democratic Convention, where she and her fellow delegates were told to take a backseat to another, all-white delegation from Mississippi. Unwilling to accept a role as a token, Hamer protested publicly and then left. In 1968, she was seated at the Democratic Convention with a standing ovation. None of Hamer's political victories came easily. Determined to vote, she and her husband both lost their jobs and put their lives in danger. She was beaten cruelly by police, receiving injuries she never fully recovered from. She not only continued her quest, but she organized and inspired other blacks to join her. After the 1968 convention, she started the Freedom Farm Cooperative in Mississippi to form a community where poor people had work and housing.

Dash, Joan. *The World at Her Fingertips: The Story of Helen Keller*. 2001. Hardcover: Scholastic. Ages 9–14.

During her lifetime, Helen Keller fascinated people around the world who wanted to meet someone who had overcome such enormous difficulties. In spite of her blindness and deafness, Keller learned to read and write not just English, but also Latin, German, and French. Although most people now know the story of her younger years, her adult life is equally intriguing. She graduated from Radcliffe at age twenty-four, already a published writer, then gave lectures, performed in vaudeville, raised money for the blind, and traveled the world as an advocate for people with disabilities. Her Socialist beliefs drew criticism, but her popularity remained strong and she received the Presidential Medal of Freedom. This absorbing biography portrays Keller without idealizing her, but with well-deserved admiration. Inserts of black-and-white photographs enhance the text.

Hansen, Joyce. *Women of Hope: African Americans Who Made a Difference*. 1998. Hardcover: Scholastic. Ages 9–14.

The striking black-and-white photographs on every other page of this collective biography came from a series of posters created by Bread and Roses, a union-related activist group. Next to the photos, a page describes each woman and her impressive accomplishments. The book opens with Ida B. Wells-Barnett, a journalist who crusaded against lynching, and ends with Mae C. Jemison, the first black woman in space. In between are writers Maya Angelou, Toni Morrison, Alice Walker, and the Delaney sisters; leaders and activists Septima Poinsette Clark, Ella Josephine Baker, Fannie Lou Hamer, and Marian Wright Edelman; actress Ruby Dee; and neurosurgeon Alexa Canady. Beautifully designed and written, this is an extraordinary book likely to inspire all readers.

Karnes, Frances A., and Suzanne M. Bean. *Girls and Young Women Leading the Way: 20 True Stories about Leadership*. 1993. Paperback: Free Spirit Press. Ages 10–14.

These girls and young women have tapped their leadership abilities to make a difference in their communities and schools. Each describes her achievement and gives her views on how to lead. The first ten girls focused on needs in their

communities: hunger and homelessness, environmental problems, literacy, and more. Often they coordinated efforts with
other children, such as putting on a play to save an arts program. In school, several of the projects concerned recycling or
other ecological issues. One particularly impressive achievement was a booklet expressing the views and feelings of the
disabled children at the school to enlighten other students
and teachers. At the end of each essay is a short list of questions to prompt ideas in the reader, and the names of relevant
organizations. The final section of the book, a "Leadership
Handbook," gives suggestions, inspiration, and information
including a bibliography about women leaders. The messages,
that girls can be leaders and that a few people can make a big
difference, come across effectively through the many exciting
examples.

Krull, Kathleen. *Lives of Extraordinary Women: Rulers,
Rebels (and What the Neighbors Thought).* **Illustrated by
Kathryn Hewitt. 2000. Hardcover: Harcourt. Ages 9–14.**
 What a delightful way to learn about important women of
the past and present. "Well-behaved women rarely make history," a quotation from historian Laurel Thatcher Ulrich
opens this collective biography on just the right note for a
book that notes the accomplishments and eccentricities of
twenty influential leaders and activists. Each biographical
sketch of four to six pages starts with a full-page caricature
of the woman, surrounded by symbols of her life. Elizabeth I
of England, for example, holds a book and a musical instru-
ment, with a ship near her feet and courtiers bowing to her.
The text sums up key events and deeds, and adds quirky bits of
information, such as that Elizabeth wore white makeup she invented made of lead, egg whites, and poppy seeds. Cleopatra,

Catherine the Great, Indira Gandhi, and Wilma Mankiller are some of the powerful women who will captivate readers of this lively book.

Levin, Pamela. *Susan B. Anthony: Fighter for Women's Rights*. 1993. Hardcover: Chelsea House. Paperback: Chelsea House. Ages 9–12.

The name "Susan B. Anthony" is synonymous with the fight for women's right to vote. Raised in a liberal Quaker family, Anthony grew up with strong beliefs. Her first political cause was the temperance movement because she saw the harm done to families by alcohol, and she came to believe that women needed the vote to affect this and other issues. She was a powerful speaker and successful fund-raiser who made great strides in securing more rights for women. Although women didn't secure the vote until 1920, in 1906 at age eighty-six, Anthony characteristically told her fellow suffragists, "Failure is impossible!" This eighty-page biography succinctly sums up the career and accomplishments of this inspiring woman.

Professionals and Businesswomen

Brown, Drollene P. *Belva Lockwood Wins Her Case*. Illustrated by James Watling. 1987. Hardcover: Albert Whitman. Ages 8–11.

A remarkable nineteenth-century American, Belva Lockwood was the first woman admitted to practice law before the U.S. Supreme Court. Her life was a series of accomplishments. In the successful schools she started and ran, girls learned public speaking and practiced sports, both innovations. She put herself through college and law school despite opposition from within the schools, then ran a lucrative law office. Lockwood was the first woman to run for president; she won more than four thousand votes, all from men, although she lost the election. She was a noted and popular public lecturer and an active suffragist, working for the vote and fair laws for women. This interesting biography interlaces facts with catchy anecdotes, such as her habit of riding a three-wheel bicycle when it was not yet an accepted practice for women.

Ferris, Jeri. *Native American Doctor: The Story of Susan LaFlesche Picotte*. 1991. Hardcover: Carolrhoda. Paperback: Carolrhoda. Ages 9–11.

Any woman who wanted to become a doctor in 1886 faced many obstacles, but Susan LaFlesche had the additional challenge of being an American Indian (as she referred to herself) in a hostile world. After graduating from the Hampton Institute in Virginia, where she was inspired by the school's woman doctor, she moved to Philadelphia to attend the Women's Medical College. She and her classmates studied medical sciences (such as anatomy and histology), dissected human bodies, and watched operations, to the astonishment of those who believed women too delicate for such work. She returned to the reservation permanently after getting her M.D. and served as its doctor. Despite her ill health, she became an important advocate for her Omaha tribe, once traveling to Washington, D.C., to secure the tribe's control over their own finances, a striking accomplishment. This serviceable biography relates how Susan LaFlesche Picotte attained nearly impossible goals and went on to benefit her tribe for many years.

Fredeen, Charles. *Nellie Bly: Daredevil Reporter*. 2000. Hardcover: Lerner. Ages 10–13.

In her first big assignment for a New York newspaper in

1887, Nellie Bly had herself committed to an asylum for the mentally ill in order to give an insider's report on the asylum. She detailed the indignities and harsh living conditions in her reports, thus earning acclaim for herself and helping improve life for the mentally ill. Such "stunt" reporting was popular at the time, and Nellie Bly, whose real name was Elizabeth Cochran, excelled at it. She also took a personal interest in the people involved in the stories she wrote, such as visiting the homes of union workers during the famous Pullman strike to see how the company really treated them and adding their voices to her writing. In a time when newspapers usually confined female writers to reporting on fashion and the like, Bly worked hard to get more exciting assignments. Her most famous feat was traveling around the world in seventy-two days to beat the hero in Jules Verne's *Around the World in Eighty Days*. She suffered numerous setbacks and endured discouraging sexism but nevertheless made an impact on her time.

McLuskey, Krista. *Entrepreneurs*. 1999. Hardcover: Crabtree. Paperback: Crabtree. Ages 9–13.

This slim volume focuses on six women who have made their fortunes in business, with an appendix that briefly describes eleven other entrepreneurs. "Women entrepreneurs need even more courage and imagination than men because business traditionally has been considered a 'man's world,'" states the introduction. The women highlighted fill that description, starting with fashion designer Coco Chanel, who spent most of her teenage years in an orphanage, yet overcame her poverty by establishing a series of stores, fashion houses, and a perfume factory. Mary Pickford joined with four other actors to found United Artists; Anita Roddick made millions by establishing the Body Shop franchises. Oprah Winfrey and Martha Stewart are familiar figures, but readers probably don't know of Jannie Tay, an award-winning business owner who founded a chain of watch stores. Each profile gives personal background and a short version of the woman's success story, illustrated by color photographs.

McPherson, Stephanie Sammartino. *Peace and Bread: The Story of Jane Addams.* **1993. Hardcover: Carolrhoda. Ages 8–12.**

Jane Addams was the first American woman to win a Nobel Prize; she won the 1931 Nobel Peace Prize for her efforts to end war around the world. When she died four years later, thousands crammed the streets of Chicago to pay their respects. As a young woman, Jane Addams chose to share her prosperity and her life with people who had less money. She bought a large house, later called Hull House, in a poor section of Chicago and opened it up to her neighbors, providing child care, a range of classes including citizenship classes, housing for working women, a museum, a laboratory for studying science, and much, much more. She lobbied for better laws and conditions for the poor, worked for women's suffrage, and dedicated herself to trying to establish peace in the world. Her work at Hull House drew national admiration and served as a model for other settlement houses, as they were called. This straightforward biography, illustrated with photographs, effectively presents a woman whose fame should endure today.

Meltzer, Milton. *Mary McLeod Bethune: Voice of Black Hope.* **Illustrated by Stephen Marchesi. 1987. Paperback: Puffin. Ages 9–12.**

Mary McLeod Bethune, a educator of great note, was founder and president of the school that became Bethune-Cookman College in Florida. At a time when education for African-Americans was poorly funded and often unavailable,

Bethune dedicated herself to offering education at all levels to blacks. She also became an influential national leader and an advisor to President Franklin Delano Roosevelt. Bethune organized the Federal Council on Negro Affairs, a group of blacks in federal government, and created the National Council of Negro Women. This biography effectively conveys the spirit of this tireless, influential crusader, one of the most important women of this century.

Peck, Ira. *Elizabeth Blackwell: The First Woman Doctor*. 2000. Hardcover: Millbrook. Ages 8–12.

Twenty-nine medical schools turned down Elizabeth Blackwell before the Geneva Medical College reluctantly accepted her application in 1847. When she graduated two years later, she was first in a class of 130, the rest of whom were men. Although she felt she was treated well at school and excelled there, she could find no hospital in the United States that would give her practical experience. Instead she was forced to travel to France, where a hospital for women finally agreed to allow her to work, followed by a British hospital. When she returned to New York, she met more resistance and eventually opened her own clinic to treat the poor. She later started a medical college for women in New York and the first one in England, too. This short biography focuses on her pioneering career with enough personal information to set her work in the context of her life.

Wadsworth, Ginger. *Julia Morgan: Architect of Dreams*. 1990. Hardcover: Lerner. Ages 10–13.

At a time when few women were architects, Julia Morgan ran her own architectural office in San Francisco and designed more than seven hundred buildings. She graduated from the University of California in engineering in 1894 and proceeded to Paris, where she was the first woman to receive a certificate from the Ecole des Beaux-Arts, an eminent architectural school. Morgan was also the first woman to be licensed as an architect in California. Her largest project was at the Hearst estate in San Simeon, where she designed and supervised the construction of several large, ornate buildings, including the well-known "Hearst Castle." Wadsworth's fluent text, amply illustrated with photographs and sketches, focuses on Morgan's work, the all-consuming center of her life. Her success was partly thanks to the patronage of women, including the millionaire Phoebe Hearst who gave her many commissions. A pioneer in a man's world, Morgan offers inspiration to future architects and engineers. An appendix lists a large selection of buildings with their addresses.

Scientists and Inventors

Dewey, Jennifer Owings. *Bedbugs in Our House: True Tales of Insect, Bug, and Spider Discovery.* 1997. Hardcover: Marshall Cavendish. Ages 9–13.

In this entertaining memoir about her childhood in New Mexico, Owings describes adventures involving insects and spiders, at school and with her friends, including one about a black widow bite. She liked to take stink bugs for walks with kite string around their middles, and she filled her room with jars of insects and spiders. Factual sections at the end of each chapter, combined with the beautifully rendered drawings, provide a lot of information about insects in a readable manner. Owings's childhood contradicts stereotypes that suggest girls have long been afraid of bugs. On the contrary, she loved them as a child and still does.

Dudzinski, Kathleen. *Meeting Dolphins: My Adventures in the Sea*. 2000. Hardcover: National Geographic. Ages 8–12.
   This striking photo-essay provides a lot of information about dolphins while also tracing the career path of the author, a marine biologist. Dudzinski explains that her love of animals and the sea started in her childhood, and was solidified by an internship during college at a research center, where she collected data about dolphins and whales. She went on to earn a Ph.D. in Wildlife and Fisheries Science, with a specialty in dolphin communication in the wild. Spectacular photographs show many dolphins, as well as Dudzinski working and participating in the filming of the IMAX film *Dolphins*. Dudzinski describes her equipment for recording dolphin communication and, in general terms, how she processes the data using computers. The final pages list organizations and other resources for future dolphin researchers.

Gallardo, Evelyn. *Among the Orangutans: The Biruté Galdikas Story*. 1993. Paperback: Chronicle. Ages 8–11.
   Biruté Galdikas has been studying orangutans in Borneo since 1971. A pioneer in her field, Galdikas set up camp in an unpopulated area of Borneo, where she tracked orangutans, learned to identify individuals, and rescued orphaned young to be raised at the camp. The text describes the problems her work has presented in Galdikas's personal life, but it focuses on her impressive strides in the study of orangutans. Galdikas has also concentrated on helping orangutans survive despite the threats of poachers and declining rain forests. Color photographs on every page, many of orangutans, add interest to this short biography of a dedicated scientist.

Goodall, Jane. *My Life with Chimpanzees.* **1996 revised edition. Paperback: Pocket. Ages 9–11.**

Using a conversational style, prominent ethologist Jane Goodall tells her own story from childhood through her twenty-five years of studying chimpanzees. Her groundbreaking work in the study of animal behavior stems from her strong interest in animals as a child. She credits a supportive family as well as her own initiative and good luck for her start in the field. She and her mother are so close that Goodall invited her mother to live with her for several months at her first research site in the Gombe Stream Game Reserve in what is now Tanzania; her mother started a medical clinic while Goodall observed chimps. Despite encounters with dangerous buffalo and leopards, and the knowledge that scorpions and poisonous centipedes infested the camp in damp weather, nothing stopped her from her work. Goodall gives fascinating details about the chimps she watched and learned to love, and about life in the wilderness. The small black-and-white photographs have the feel of a family album, which suits the autobiography's informal tone.

Johnson, Rebecca L. *Braving the Frozen Frontier: Women Working in Antarctica.* **1997. Hardcover: Lerner. Ages 9–13.**

Until the 1960s, women were not welcome to work in Antarctica, the huge cold continent around the South Pole. That has changed over the last four decades, and now women have an array of jobs, many in scientific research, and others in the support services that keep the scientists functioning. The first woman introduced is a helicopter pilot who transports people and supplies, often facing bad flying conditions and the challenges of landing on ice. Bulldozer operator and carpenter are two of the other jobs held by women who are included in the book. Most of the women featured are scientists from different fields and different universities. They study volcanoes, glaciers, penguins, seals, soil ecology, and more. Due to conditions, many of them need wilderness survival skills, sleeping in tents and navigating snowmobiles through wind and snow. The range of jobs and the unusual setting, shown in well-chosen photographs, make this a wonderful read for future scientists or anyone who enjoys vicarious adventures.

Karnes, Frances A., and Suzanne M. Bean. *Girls & Young Women Inventing: Twenty True Stories about Inventors plus How You Can Be One Yourself.* **1995. Paperback: Free Spirit. Ages 9–14.**

The impressive stories about girl inventors in the first part of this book make inventing look like fun. The second section gives practical advice on how to set about it. Essays by each of the twenty inventors, who range in age from elementary school to college, describe the process of thinking up an invention and making it. They make inventing seem not just possible but enjoyable and satisfying. In many cases, the girls improved on something they used themselves for chores, like a mop, or for entertainment, like a board game for girls. Some of the young inventors have applied for patents and explored ways to sell their products. All of them agree that the challenge and rewards of inventing are an end in themselves. The directions on how to set about inventing reduce an intimidating concept to manageable steps. Information at the back includes useful addresses, a list of books about inventors, and inspiring quotations. Read this valuable book and you will look at inventing in a new way.

Lasky, Kathryn. *The Most Beautiful Roof in the World: Exploring the Rainforest Canopy*. Photographs by Christopher G. Knight. 1997. Hardcover: Harcourt. Paperback: Gulliver. Ages 9–12.

Meg Lowman, a scientist who specializes in the relationships between plants and insects in the rain forest treetops, often climbs one hundred feet to do her work. This exciting photo-essay shows her climbing, then walking along skywalks and platforms in the treetops of a Central American rain forest. Through clear, colorful photographs, the reader sees the animals and plants Lowman sees, and learns about her experiments and measurements. Her two sons, who appear to be of grade school age, accompany her up the trees in the afternoon, then take a walk with her at night, both expeditions full of interesting sights. The essay integrates information about the rain forest and its importance with fascinating details about Lowman's studies in this excellent portrait of a woman scientist at work.

McPherson, Stephanie Sammartino. *Rooftop Astronomer: A Story about Maria Mitchell*. Illustrated by Hetty Mitchell. 1990. Hardcover: Carolrhoda. Ages 8–11.

Maria Mitchell deserves to be far better known than she is. A Nantucket native, she was the first woman to discover a comet. As a result of her discovery, Mitchell was voted the first female member of the American Academy of Arts and Sciences and of the Association for the Advancement of Science. Trained in math and science mainly by her father, she had no college education. In 1865, Vassar, one of the first women's colleges, hired her to teach, a job into which she poured her energy. Despite her accomplishments, Vassar paid her less than male professors received, and her formal protest resulted only in a small raise. Increasingly involved in the movement for women's rights, Mitchell served as president of the American Association for the Advancement of Women. The first woman astronomer in the United States, Mitchell will be an inspiration to anyone who reads about her.

Parker, Steve. *Marie Curie and Radium.* **1995. Hardcover: Chelsea House. Ages 9–12.**

Marie Curie won two Nobel Prizes for her pioneering scientific work: one in physics, which she shared with two male scientists, and one alone in chemistry. This attractive short biography, abundantly illustrated with photographs and other pictures, discusses her life and work. Polish by birth, she attended the Sorbonne, then continued to live in Paris with her husband and fellow scientist Pierre Curie. Except for time spent bicycling and with their two children, the Curies devoted themselves to their research. Marie Curie spent years purifying radium, helped by male assistants, and working on other research with male peers. Her husband's father moved in with the family to care for their two children. After her husband's early death, Curie became the first female professor at the Sorbonne. This inviting biography provides a useful page of information on atoms and radioactivity, and sidebars on well-chosen topics such as Curie's daughter's work as a scientist.

Ross, Michael Elsohn. *Fish Watching with Eugenie Clark.* **Illustrated by Wendy Smith. 2000. Hardcover: Carolrhoda. Ages 8–11.**

"I plan to keep diving and researching and conserving until I'm ninety years old," Eugenie Clark once declared. Now nearly eighty, the well-known shark expert still conducts research in her field, which includes trips to the Red Sea, Papua New Guinea, and the Solomon Islands. This attractive book will introduce readers to this remarkable woman, while also giving them basic information about fish. It begins by showing how Clark's interest started as a child and continued through her schooling, in a time when women who wanted to be scientists faced serious barriers because of bias against women. She persisted and made the most of her opportunities, learning to dive before scuba gear was even available. Clark directed a shark research lab in Florida and became a college professor. Her writing influenced the public's perception of whales and increased concern about the environment. While touching briefly on her personal life, this biography primarily covers Clark's work and success.

Scott, Elaine. *Adventure in Space: The Flight to Fix the Hubble*. Photographs by Margaret Miller. 1995. Paperback: Hyperion. Ages 8–11.

After the $1.6 billion Hubble space telescope was launched in 1990, scientists realized it didn't work properly. A group of seven astronauts traveled 4.4 million miles and eleven days to fix it in space. This photo-essay describes that mission, with a slight emphasis on the role of Kathy Thornton, the most experienced woman astronaut in the world. Physicist Thornton was one of the four astronauts who donned space suits and went outside to fix the telescope. The mother of three daughters, Thornton advises girls to study the hard sciences, and to take calculated risks, just as she risks the dangers of space flight to gain the benefits of being an astronaut. Photographs show Thornton and the other astronauts planning, practicing, and accomplishing their goal in space. An attractive book about an important space mission.

Thimmesh, Catherine. *Girls Think of Everything: Stories of Ingenious Inventions by Women.* **2000. Hardcover: Houghton. Ages 9–13.**

This attractive collective biography introduces women and girls responsible for useful, creative inventions. After a short overview that points out the bias many women faced in trying to receive credit for their work, the book devotes two to three pages to each inventor, beginning with the woman who created the chocolate chip cookie. Some of the inventions took place at work, like those of chemists Stephanie Kwolek, who invented the remarkably strong fiber Kevlar® while working for Du Pont and Patsy O. Sherman, who came up with Scotchgard™ for 3M. Others started their own businesses, like the woman who created the Snuggli® for carrying babies and a girl who devised a way to write in the dark by placing paper on top of a glowing sheet. The well-chosen profiles describe the process of inventing and the aftermath in a readable manner, illustrated with jazzy collages. A final few pages give advice for the reader on becoming an inventor.

Women in the Arts

Allman, Barbara. *Her Piano Sang: A Story about Clara Schumann.* **Illustrated by Shelly O. Haas. 1997. Hardcover: Carolrhoda. Ages 8–11.**

This short biography opens in 1828 on the day of Clara Schumann's first performance as a professional pianist, when she was nine. Choosing apt anecdotes, the author describes the pianist's childhood and family problems, her marriage to composer Robert Schumann, and her extraordinary, long career as a pianist. Clara trained under her demanding father and was successful starting with her first concert. She and Robert Schumann had many children, but unfortunately he suffered from mental illness. Clara supported him and the children, traveling extensively to perform throughout Europe. Readers get a sense of the enormous demands of her life but also the joy she experienced thanks to music, family, and friends. Black-and-white full-page watercolors add atmosphere more than information to this attractive introduction to a fine musician.

Lyons, Mary E. *Stitching Stars: The Story Quilts of Harriet Powers.* 1993. Paperback: Aladdin. Ages 8–11.

This beautifully designed book explores two story quilts sewn by Harriet Powers, an African-American born into slavery and freed by the Civil War. Although little is known about her early life, the book discusses typical conditions of the times and region where she lived, including the importance of quilting bees. Despite poverty and a hard life, Powers created two remarkable story quilts. The first, based on biblical stories, she made for herself but had to sell during hard times. When that quilt went on display at an exposition, a second quilt was commissioned. This one incorporated religious stories and historic natural events such as an enormous meteorite shower. The text and captions explain and analyze many of the individual quilt panels, in which graceful textile figures tell stories and express religious feelings. With no art training, Powers took everyday materials and an everyday craft and turned them into enduring art.

Lyons, Mary E., editor. *Talking with Tebé: Clementine Hunter, Memory Artist.* 1998. Hardcover: Houghton. Ages 9–12.

This intriguing biography portrays the life of folk artist Clementine Hunter, known as Tebé, a black woman in Louisiana who was born in 1886 and died in 1988. She spent most of her adult life on a plantation, where she worked in the fields, cooked, raised a family, and taught herself to paint. She painted the world around her: baptisms, weddings, wakes, farming, laundry, cooking, and even "Saturday Night at the HonkyTonk." She also painted religious scenes with flying angels and floral pictures. Reproductions of her colorful folk art convey a sense of time, place, and spirit, amply matched by her own words as edited from tapes and written quotations. Her voice resonates with wisdom and humor, recalling memories of hard times and good times. The combination of her lively words and equally vibrant paintings is entrancing.

Martinez, Elizabeth Coonrod. *Sor Juana: A Trailblazing Thinker*. 1994. Hardcover: Millbrook. Ages 8–11.

Juana Ines de Asbaje y Ramirez, who lived in Mexico in the 1600s, was determined to become educated even though higher education was reserved for males. She was exceedingly intelligent, learned to read at age three, and mastered Latin and other ancient languages as a teenager. She so impressed the royal court that the officials decided to have her tested by experts when she was fifteen; she answered all their questions perfectly. Because nuns were the only women who could pursue studies, Juana joined a convent and became Sor Juana. She wrote plays and poetry, studied sciences, and played music. Only when the church officials forbade her to continue writing because she was female was this brilliant woman silenced, four years before her death at age forty-seven. Her writings expressed her belief that women should be allowed to think and study, goals she herself attained despite the odds.

Pettit, Jayne. *Maya Angelou: Journey of the Heart*. 1996. Paperback: Puffin. Ages 9–11.

This seventy-page biography describes both the difficulties

and the notable accomplishments in the life of writer Maya Angelou. In her childhood she was often separated from her parents, living with her grandmother in Arkansas and later her grandmother in St. Louis. The book briefly discusses that she was raped at age eight by a friend of her mother's, who was murdered before he could be imprisoned. Although she has also encountered many troubles as an adult, Angelou has succeeded as an actress, an activist, and a writer of striking prose and poetry. She has been honored in several fields, nominated for an Emmy for her acting role in the television series *Roots* and nominated for a Pulitzer Prize for poetry. Her inaugural poem for President Clinton moved listeners throughout the country. The rich life of this distinguished woman reads like a dramatic novel.

Ringgold, Faith, Linda Freeman, and Nancy Roucher. *Talking to Faith Ringgold*. 1996. Hardcover: Crown. Paperback: Crown. Ages 9–13.

Innovative artist Faith Ringgold, who combines fabric and painting in her art, is perhaps best known for her extraordinary story quilts. She has also written and illustrated award-winning children's books. In all her ventures she draws on her African-American heritage to create striking artwork. In this unusual book, she speaks directly to readers about her background and artwork, and asks questions in sidebars to help readers explore their own creativity. Photographs of her artwork appear on most pages, interspersed with photos of the artist and her family taken over her lifetime. She combines stories about growing up in Harlem, thoughts about art, information about other artists, reflections on important black leaders, and more, in a fresh approach that draws readers in. A highly enjoyable introduction to an artist.

Sills, Leslie. *In Real Life: Six Women Photographers.* **2000. Hardcover: Holiday. Ages 9–14.**

Moving from the beginning of the twentieth century to the end, this excellent overview of women photographers features beautifully reproduced examples of each person's work. It starts with Imogene Cunningham, whose exquisite black-and-white images reflect trends in photography and her own original approach. Cunningham's near contemporary, Dorothea Lange, is best known for her photographs during the Depression. The other artists, each discussed in about ten pages, are Mexican photographer Lola Alvarez Bravo; Carrie Mae Weems, who reveals aspects of African-American life with her camera; Elsa Dorfman, known for her large portraits; and the innovative Cindy Sherman. A beautifully designed book with thoughtful, informative text and well-chosen photographs.

Sports Biographies and Nonfiction

Anderson, Joan. *Rookie: Tamika Whitmore's First Year in the WNBA.* **Illustrated by Photographs by Michelle V. Agins. 2000. Hardcover: Dutton. Paperback: Puffin. Ages 9–14.**

Not long ago, no one would open a book about a professional basketball rookie expecting to read about a woman, but times have changed for the better. This essay illustrated by large color photographs looks behind the scenes at Tamika Whitmore's first year playing for the WNBA's New York Liberty. Several pages and photographs convey her childhood in Mississippi, growing up in a house without electricity but with a strong, supportive mother. The book then discusses her remarkable high school and college basketball careers. Most of the book focuses on her routine during her first professional basketball season, with lots of quotations from Whitmore herself. Photographs show her in action on the court as well as relaxing with her teammates off-court. The final segment covers the day of a key game against the Washington Mystics, from morning through Whitmore's excellent performance that night. An inspiring treat for basketball fans about a hardworking talented young athlete.

Breitenbucher, Cathy. *Bonnie Blair: Golden Streak.* **1994. Paperback: Lerner. Ages 9–12.**

As of the 1994 Winter Olympics, speed skater Bonnie Blair had won more medals—five gold and one bronze—than any other U.S. athlete in the Winter Olympics. She has participated in four Olympic games and numerous other speedskating events. Only great athletic ability combined with intense dedication could produce such a record, and Bonnie Blair has both. This upbeat biography with its admiring tone focuses mainly on her career with details of her race history and her many successes.

Christopher, Matt. *On the Court with Lisa Leslie.* **1998. Paperback: Little, Brown. Ages 8–13.**

In this biography about the career of basketball great Lisa Leslie, popular sports fiction writer Matt Christopher gives facts about her upbringing and schooling, but writes most enthusiastically about her basketball games. Important, close games get special attention, from her high school championships to her NCAA games. The victory of the U.S. team at the 1996 Olympics, on which Leslie was a key player, comes across as truly exciting. The athlete's hard work and dedication to her sport and to providing a role model are unmistakable. Although it touches on her personal life, the book's focus is squarely on basketball and will satisfy sports fans. An inset of mediocre black-and-white photographs mostly shows Leslie in her role as a member of the WNBA's L.A. Sparks.

Macy, Sue, and Jane Gottesman, editors. *Play Like a Girl: A Celebration of Women in Sports.* **1999. Hardcover: Henry Holt. Ages 8–12.**

This short, inspiring book brings together powerful photographs and moving words about a wide variety of women's sports. Each double-page spread has crisp color photos of athletes participating in tennis, skiing, swimming, track, soccer, skateboarding, rowing, and more. The women grimace, sweat, lunge, yell, and strain their muscles as they pursue excellence. Readers may recognize such well-known athletes as Venus Lacey, Martina Navratilova, Shannon MacMillan, Kristine Lilly, and others, while other photographs show unknown female athletes giving it their all. The quotations from athletes and writers that accompany the photographs express the excitement and emotion of competing. The images of strong women provide a welcome contrast to the many media images of women chosen for their conventional looks.

Olney, Ross R. *Lyn St. James: Driven to Be First.* **1997. Paperback: Lerner. Ages 8–12.**

If Lyn St. James had an ambition as a child, it was to be a pianist, not a major race car driver. She enjoyed cars as a teenager and sometimes raced boys she knew, but her first long-term exposure to racing was through her first husband, who was a racer. She helped his crews but wanted to get into the action herself, so she attended school for racing and got her competition license in the mid-1970s. When her marriage ended, St. James opened and managed an auto parts store, and continued racing. The third woman to participate in the Indy 500, she placed eleventh in 1992 and was named Rookie of the Year. She has raced in the Indy in other years and in many other races, despite the difficulty as a woman of getting sponsors. This brief biography, illustrated with color photographs, gives examples of the bias St. James has faced as a female racer but also conveys her intense love of the exciting sport.

Savage, Jeff. *Julie Foudy: Soccer Superstar.* **1999. Hardcover: Lerner. Paperback: Lerner. Ages 8–12.**

Julie Foudy well deserves the enthusiastic following she has among soccer fans. Not only has she excelled on the field, she has encouraged her teams with her spirit and leadership, while also dedicating herself to studying hard in school. Readers will enjoy the color photographs of Foudy throughout her career, starting when she was seven. The shots from her college and national team games show her throwing herself completely into the game, heading balls, jumping, running, and dribbling, all with intensity. Her competitive spirit comes across in the text, which balances a moderate amount of information about her personal life with much more about her soccer career, including some descriptions of tense moments in specific games. Off the field, Foudy has been accepted by Stanford Medical School, an impressive academic feat, and has become an advocate for better labor conditions in sports companies. With a glossary for those not familiar with soccer, this is a solid introduction to one of the soccer greats.

Steiner, Andy. *Girl Power on the Playing Field: A Book about Girls, Their Goals, and Their Struggles.* **2000. Hardcover: Lerner. Ages 10–14.**

This unusual nonfiction book looks at how girls approach

sports, the benefits of being athletic, and the obstacles girls still face on the playing field. The author quotes from girls she has interviewed, as well as adults concerned about girls and sports. She notes a shift as girls reach adolescence and may feel less comfortable defining themselves as athletic. The chapters outline specific obstacles and offer some steps to take to overcome them. For example, girls who have been shut out from certain sports like ice hockey have countered by organizing leagues themselves. Packing a lot into ninety-six pages, the book gives practical advice about getting into sports, describes famous and less famous female athletes to emulate, and provides a host of resources such as organizations, Web sites, books, and more.

Stewart, Barbara. *She Shoots . . . She Scores! A Complete Guide to Girls' and Women's Hockey.* **1998. Paperback: Firefly. Ages 9–14.**

A lot of information fills the two hundred pages of this nicely designed guide to ice hockey. It covers the history of the sport, famous female players, with an emphasis on Canadians, and the basics of how to play. Chapters cover skating, stickhandling, passing, shooting, and goaltending, with diagrams, illustrations, step-by-step directions, checklists of equipment, and more. In addition, a whole chapter discusses equipment, with more checklists, tips, and sample prices. Yet other chapters advise coaches and officials, and describe how to start a league. Short descriptions highlight various hockey teams around the world, followed by paragraphs about each member of Team Canada and Team USA. Finally, a resource section lists addresses of organizations and college programs. Every serious ice hockey player will want to read this thorough book, and fans will enjoy it as well.

More Dynamic Girls and Women

Cummins, Julie. *Tomboy of the Air: Daredevil Pilot Blanche Stuart Scott.* **2001. Hardcover: Harper. Ages 8–12.**

Daredevil Blanche Stuart Scott was the first American woman to fly. This enjoyable biography starts with Scott's trip as the second woman to drive cross-country, a trip that reinforced her love for adventure and fame. Soon she took up flying and had her first solo flight the same year. Enamored by the dangerous thrill of flying, she became the first woman test pilot and then the first woman stunt pilot. She also starred in a silent movie as a pilot. The well-written text describes her feats and her personality, amply illustrated with black-and-white photographs and other visual material. Scott's accomplishments as a pioneer in aviation richly deserve the attention they receive in this excellent biography.

Fleming, Candace. *Women of the Lights.* **1996. Hardcover: Albert Whitman. Ages 9–12.**

From 1768 until 1947, two hundred and fifty women staffed lighthouses in the United States, a dangerous job that took physical strength, mental toughness, and an expert knowledge of weather. This fascinating book describes five such lighthouse keepers, with a final chapter about the exploits of several other women. Ida Lewis, a lighthouse keeper in Newport, Rhode Island, rescued many people from boating accidents and became a national celebrity. Kate Walker of New York, who succeeded her husband as a lighthouse keeper, saved more than fifty people—and one little dog—in her time. Most surprising is Emily Fish, who turned her Monterey peninsula lighthouse into a gracious social center, complete with pedigreed poodles. Her daughter emulated her mother by becoming a lighthouse keeper on an island in San Francisco Bay. All the women described broke traditions and proved the ability of women to equal men at this difficult job.

Fritz, Jean. *The Double Life of Pocahontas.* **Illustrated by Ed Young. 1983. Hardcover: Putnam. Paperback: Puffin. Ages 9–12.**

This biography with its soft, evocative illustrations provides an antidote to the Disney version of Pocahontas. The verified facts about her life are combined with speculation to give the sense of her as a real person. The "double life" of the title refers to her roles in the world of her tribe and in that of the English settlers and later in England. As the daughter of a chief, Pocahontas knew the privileges and responsibilities of a powerful family. When she was sent to negotiate with the settlers for captured Indians, her father admonished her not to beg, but to leave that to her companions. Later, when the English kidnapped her and her father refused to pay the ransom, Pocahontas turned her intelligence and energies to learning English ways. She married Englishman John Rolfe and bore a son, but died on a trip to England in 1617 at the age of twenty-one. Although best known for her friendship to John Smith, whose life she saved, her life was a more complex and poignant one than many realize.

Fritz, Jean. *You Want Women to Vote, Lizzie Stanton?* **Illustrated by DyAnne DiSalvo-Ryan. 1995. Hardcover: Putnam. Paperback: Paper Star. Ages 9–12.**

Skillful biographer Fritz turns her hand to a key figure in the women's suffrage movement: Elizabeth Cady Stanton. Using apt anecdotes and fascinating details, this short biography explores the factors that turned Stanton into a writer and orator for the cause. Struggling to raise seven children with little help from her husband, she participated when she could in the movement that eventually won women the vote. She was outspoken and unafraid of the negative reactions to her views. The book highlights the harsh conditions that affected women at the time: No married woman could own property; men could legally beat their wives; only men had the power to obtain a divorce; and more. The highly readable and entertaining text will open the eyes of readers unfamiliar with the history of women in this country. Occasional black-and-white illustrations add humor and interest. An excellent introduction to a remarkable woman and a vital cause.

Hart, Philip S. *Up in the Air: The Story of Bessie Coleman*. 1996. Paperback: Carolrhoda. Ages 9–12.
The courage and determination of African-American aviator Bessie Coleman was truly extraordinary. She became the first black woman to earn a pilot's license at a time when flying was dangerous, and flying the kinds of planes she could afford was often fatal. Coleman grew up poor in Texas, but her intelligence and ambition eventually took her to Chicago where she began to pursue her dream of flying, saving money and learning French so she could train in France. Encouraged by a newspaper owner, Bessie accomplished her goal of earning a pilot's license in France and came back to a storm of publicity. She hoped to make it easier for others to learn to fly by opening her own flying school, but in 1926—five years after she became a pilot—she died as a passenger in a plane crash. This balanced, accessible biography, with its black-and-white photographs and enticing dust jacket, sets Coleman's accomplishments in a historical framework that emphasizes the significance of what she did.

Johnston, Johanna. *They Led the Way: Fourteen American Women.* **Illustrated by Deanne Hollinger. 1973. Paperback: Scholastic. Ages 9–11.**

This simple introduction to fourteen important women extends from colonial times until women won the vote in 1920. Five to ten pages, with occasional black-and-white illustrations, tell the women's stories, using some fictionalized dialogue. First comes Anne Hutchinson, who argued that women could receive signs from God and had the right to speak out on their religion; she was banished from the Massachusetts Bay Colony for her boldness. Anne Bradstreet was the first American poet published in England, and Phillis Wheatley the first black poet published in the colonies. Lady Deborah Moody, a wealthy widow, started the town of Gravesend, now in Brooklyn, for which she wrote the laws and planned the design. Ernestine Rose, a Polish Jew, defied convention by speaking out publicly against injustice in Europe and the United States in the nineteenth century. Other better known women discussed are Abigail Adams, Elizabeth Blackwell, Clara Barton, and Harriet Beecher Stowe. Victoria Woodhull, one of the first women brokers and a presidential candidate before women could even vote, is described briefly, as is journalist and adventurer Nellie Bly. A good way to spark an interest that may lead to longer biographies.

Katz, William Loren. *Black Women of the Old West.* **1995. Hardcover: Atheneum. Ages 10–14.**

This attractive volume, illustrated with black-and-white photographs and prints, fills a gap in most history books: the role of black women in settling the American West. Full of anecdotes and examples, it describes African-American women suing for their rights and working to form successful communities. It emphasizes the importance of blacks in helping others escape from slavery, in providing homes for the underground railroad, and more. The emphasis women put on their children's and their own education comes through again and again. They organized to fight segregated schools in the West, and achieved higher literacy rates than white women on the frontier. To avoid isolation in sparsely populated areas, black women banded together in cultural societies and charitable organizations. Black women owned real estate, ran businesses, worked a wide range of jobs, and sometimes made a lot of money. Profiles of individuals tell their stories, and captions under the numerous photographs add more information. Although some of the photographs are damaged or hazy, there is something powerful and haunting about these faces looking out from the past. An outstanding photo-essay.

Landau, Elaine. *Heroine of the Titanic: The Real Unsinkable Molly Brown.* 2001. Hardcover: Clarion. Ages 10–13.

A musical and movie have given the wrong impression about the so-called Unsinkable Molly Brown, a heroine of the *Titanic* sinking. Margaret Brown, not known as Molly in her lifetime, had many more aspects to her life than that one episode. Raised in Missouri, she moved to Leadville, Colorado, as a teenager and married a hardworking mining engineer, J. J. Brown, who soon struck it rich in a gold mine. Enormously wealthy, they moved to Denver, where Margaret immersed herself in charitable and civic causes, while also leading an active social life. She absorbed culture with great energy and loved to travel. She worked for women's suffrage and supported unions, among other causes. This enjoyable biography, amply illustrated with photographs, paints a picture of an influential woman who also had the courage to help her fellow travelers when the *Titanic* went down.

Macy, Sue. *Bull's-Eye: A Photobiography of Annie Oakley.* **2001. Hardcover: National Geographic. Ages 9–13.**

Starting with a photograph of Annie Oakley looking thoughtful and composed on the cover, this fine biography replaces legends about the famous sharpshooter with a more accurate story. It describes Oakley's difficult Ohio childhood, during which she learned to hunt but also faced tragedies and pain. The graceful text goes on to describe her stellar career with Wild West shows and her steady marriage to fellow shooter Frank Butler. The book quotes from Annie Oakley and her relatives as it separates fact from fiction. It also emphasizes little-known qualities such as Oakley's dedication to teaching women to shoot and her support of charities. The elegant design incorporates many black-and-white photographs as well as other visual materials like posters and postcards, adding to the pleasure of reading about a woman who broke barriers and fascinated people around the world.

Roessel, Monty. *Kinaaldá: A Navajo Girl Grows Up.* **1993. Hardcover: Lerner. Paperback: First Avenue. Ages 9–12.**

Thirteen-year-old Celinda McKelvey lives near the Navajo Reservation in New Mexico, where she celebrates her coming of age with a two-day event called Kinaaldá. The ceremony, which welcomes a girl into her role as a Navajo woman, includes singing, running, sitting up all night, and cooking a large corn cake. The tasks challenge Celinda's endurance while teaching her about her future. Family and friends gather during the days to share in prayers and help with the ceremony. The photo-essay reveals contemporary aspects of Celinda's life and explains Navajo traditions without romanticizing the past.

Stanley, Diane. *Joan of Arc.* **1998. Hardcover: Morrow. Ages 9–14.**

Sumptuous acrylic paintings dominate this picture-book biography of the French saint. To set the scene, the book opens with two pages about the Hundred Years' War, followed by a pronunciation guide and a map of France. The story itself begins with Joan of Arc's childhood, family, and village life, and moves quickly into her first vision. Although Stanley describes the young saint's many visions, she also reminds readers about medieval beliefs that made the visions plausible then. The ample text continues with Joan's mission to reach the French dauphin and help him get crowned as king. Her leadership and later betrayal are conveyed with apt details in the words and paintings. A final note looks at the reversal of heresy charges after her death, and her subsequent canonization, with thoughtful comments from the author about how she researched the life of this brave, beloved young woman.

Szabo, Corinne. *Sky Pioneer.* **1997. Hardcover: National Geographic Society. Ages 9–13.**

Black-and-white photographs on nearly every page are the strength of this biography of the famous aviator who was the first woman to fly solo across the Atlantic. Earhart bought her first plane in 1922 when she was twenty-five and earned her pilot's license the next year. In an era of record setting, she was the first woman to make a solo round-trip flight across the United States, and in 1930 she set three women's world speed records. Ignoring the widespread belief that flying was too dangerous for women, Earhart repeatedly challenged herself, and died—like many early aviators—during such a challenge, trying to fly the longest route ever taken around the world. This eye-catching biography emphasizes Earhart's feats as a flier and her spirit of adventure.

Warren, Andrea. *Pioneer Girl: Growing up on the Prairie.* **1998. Hardcover: Morrow. Paperback: Harper. Ages 9–13.**

History comes alive in this account of one girl's life on the frontier. As a young child, Grace McCance Snyder moved to Nebraska where she lived in a sod house, herded cattle, harvested, and reveled in her outdoor life. "I couldn't have asked for a more wonderful life," she said, despite the many hardships and disasters over the years. Based on interviews and Grace's memoir, the book brims with lively incidents and absorbing details about life on the prairie during the late 1800s and early 1900s. Black-and-white photographs, including one of ninety-year-old Grace on horseback, add information and atmosphere. Readers will be sorry to reach the end of this wonderful journey to the past.

5

Books for Older Readers

Many fine writers focus on writing for adolescents, so the selection that follows is a rich one. The best of these books are more sophisticated in plot and vocabulary than most books in the previous chapter. Some challenge readers with more complex characters, more layers of meaning, and more ambiguous endings. At their finest they enable readers to stretch their imaginations as they enter the lives of the characters. The annotations and age ranges will indicate which books are appropriate for advanced younger readers and which are best for readers with more emotional maturity. Although the age ranges only go up to fourteen, older teenagers may also enjoy some of these books.

At this age, approximately twelve to fourteen, many readers start reading books written for adults, a few of which are listed here. Fantasy and mystery fans are particularly likely to supplement their reading with adult fiction. But all adolescents should be encouraged to read the "young adult" literature written for them, which speaks directly to their concerns and interests.

This chapter, as in chapter 4, is divided into two large sections: Fiction, and Biographies and Nonfiction. Within Fiction are adventure and survival stories; contemporary life; sports stories; mysteries and ghost stories; historical fiction; and fantasy and science fiction. Biographies and Nonfiction is divided into leaders and activists; professionals and businesswomen; scientists and inventors; women in the arts; sports biographies and nonfiction; and more dynamic girls and women, a catch-all area of interesting titles including books on the women's suffrage movement.

Be sure to check for more suggestions in chapter 4 and in the collections of folklore in chapter 2. And keep in mind that the picture-story books associated with younger children can offer teenagers excellent examples of writing and art, and a kind of comfort to readers on the verge of growing up.

Fiction

Adventure and Survival Stories

Alexander, Lloyd. *The Illyrian Adventure*. **1986. Paperback: Dell. Ages 10–14.**

Sixteen-year-old Vesper Holly is a unique heroine, a female Indiana Jones living in the 1870s. She "has the mind of a chess master," knows six languages, and can swear in all of them. She can use a slide rule but would rather do calculations in her head. Curious about the country Illyria, which her now-dead father had visited, Vesper organizes an expedition to go there with the help of Professor Brinton Garrett, her guardian and the narrator of the story. They find themselves caught up in a rebellion and at odds with an evil power. Vesper, whose life is in danger more than once, plays a key role in the future of the small country, thanks to her intelligence and courage. A lark to read. Others in the series are *The El Dorado Adventure*, *The Drackenberg Adventure*, and more.

Avi. *The True Confessions of Charlotte Doyle*. **1990. Hardcover: Orchard. Paperback: Avon. Ages 10–14.**

"Not every thirteen-year-old girl is accused of murder, brought to trial, and found guilty," is the opening line of this thrilling tale. When ladylike Charlotte Doyle boards the *Seahawk* in 1832 to sail from England to Rhode Island, she expects to be chaperoned by two families. Instead, she finds herself the only female aboard a ship on which a mutiny is planned. At first disdainful of the scruffy crew, Charlotte comes to realize that they hate the cruel captain for good reason. She herself joins the crew and, though she has never done any manual labor, learns to climb the riggings and shoulder her share of the work. As her spirit and strength flourish, the hatred the captain feels for her grows until it culminates in trying her for a murder she didn't commit. The book's ending is enough to make readers cheer for this heroine who has too much courage and spirit for the conventional life she has left behind. A Newbery Honor Book.

Dickinson, Peter. *A Bone from a Dry Sea*. 1993. Hardcover: Delacorte. Paperback: Dell. Ages 11–14.

Alternating chapters tell the stories of two girls, one in the present who is visiting a paleontological dig in Africa; the other, Li, a hominid living four million years earlier in the same area. Vinny, whose father works on the dig, discusses evolution and geology with him, and advocates a theory she has read about how humans may have evolved from hominids who lived partly in water. She holds her own, even when he scoffs at her, and she later defies the leader of the dig when he tries to intimidate her into becoming part of the dig's publicity campaign. Wrangling among the males on the dig is paralleled in Li's time by males vying for dominance, one of the many intriguing parallels between the two times. Li is a genius in the context of her primitive life. She devises innovations to help her tribe, fashioning a net to catch shrimp and swimming with dolphins who drive fish toward shore for Li. Both girls are emotionally strong as well as intelligent. In the satisfying conclusion, they are linked across time by a shark bone, which Li has bored with a primitive awl and which Vinny recognizes as important. A thought-provoking, beautifully written book.

George, Jean Craighead. *Julie of the Wolves.* **Illustrated by John Schoenherr. 1972. Hardcover: Harper. Paperback: Trophy. Ages 11–14.**

Miyax is an Eskimo girl on a journey across the tundra, running away from a bad situation, who finds herself lost and without food. Remembering her father's teachings, she befriends a small pack of wolves and with their aid tries to survive the light months until the North Star appears again. The details of her survival and how she carefully learns the ways of the wolf pack make fascinating reading. She works diligently to make a place in the wilderness, but then must face the question of whether to leave. An extraordinary but convincing adventure of a remarkable girl. Winner of the Newbery Medal. The sequels are *Julie* and *Julie's Wolf Pack.*

Marsden, John. *Tomorrow, When the War Began.* **1993. Hardcover: Houghton. Paperback: Laureleaf. Ages 13–14.**

Teenager Ellie and six of her friends decide to go wilderness camping in a hard-to-reach valley not far from their homes in a country that resembles Australia. When they return home they discover that their country has been invaded. At the sheep farms where Ellie and several others live, they find dead animals and empty houses. Once they realize that their families and other citizens are confined to a large fairground by the invaders, they retreat back to the wilderness. Eventually they choose to fight back, executing dangerous sabotage operations. Narrator Ellie, who is strong and extremely competent, turns out to have leadership skills and daring she didn't know she had. The three boys and four girls share the risks and planning, and some romance, in this utterly gripping page-turner that is the first in a series. Highly recommended.

Mikaelsen, Ben. *Stranded*. 1995. Hardcover: Hyperion. Paperback: Hyperion. Ages 10–13.

Koby lives on one of the Florida Keys in a boat named the *Dream Chaser*. She spends her happiest time out in her dinghy, where it doesn't matter that half of one of her legs is missing, lost in an accident. On her way home from fishing one evening, she spies a pilot whale in trouble, caught in a net. Koby bravely cuts the net, knowing the whale could hurt her, then rescues the whale's newborn calf. Not too many days later, she finds the whales stranded on the shore and stays with them through the night to keep them wet. A rescue squad, including a female marine veterinarian named Dr. Michaels, takes charge of the whales and tries to rehabilitate them. Koby volunteers to help and, as the only person the whales respond to, ensures their survival. Although she has trouble dealing with her parents' troubled marriage, Koby faces most of her challenges with courage and determination, forging ahead even when she is afraid. An appealing adventure especially for animal lovers.

Nelson, O. T. *The Girl Who Owned a City*. 1995. Hardcover: Runestone. Paperback: Dell. Ages 11–14.

This survival story set in the near future takes as its starting point the unlikely premise that everyone over twelve has died from a virus. Left in a world of children and dwindling supplies, ten-year-old Lisa discovers her extraordinary talent for leadership. She organizes the children on her suburban block, carefully strategizing to convince them to follow her. She fearlessly confronts Tom Logan, leader of a marauding gang. Eventually she moves her followers into a well-fortified high school, ending up with hundreds of children under her guidance, but their problems continue. The author's philosophy about self-reliance figures blatantly in the writing, but even more disturbing for some readers is the emphasis on fighting and violence. Great enthusiasm goes into forming a militia and fortifying the school. While the focus on violence may be realistic and doesn't come near what appears nightly on television, it is unusual in children's books. However, Lisa shows strong leadership abilities rarely attributed to girls. A gripping, disturbing novel.

O'Brien, Robert C. *Z for Zachariah*. 1975. Hardcover: Atheneum. Paperback: Aladdin. Ages 11–14.

This futuristic thriller hums with suspense. Fifteen-year-old Ann Burden thinks she may be the last person alive, having survived a nuclear holocaust thanks to the microclimate of the valley she lives in. Although she is coping well alone on her family's farm, she gets excited when a man appears dressed in a radiation-resistant suit. But the man, John Loomis, becomes increasingly dangerous to her, intent on taking control of the farm and of her life, until one night she barely escapes when he comes into her bed. A stalwart heroine, Ann is adept at farming, driving a tractor, doing mechanical tasks, and shooting. But little in her protected childhood has prepared her to face the increasingly disturbed man. Finally she takes the offensive. The book is genuinely hard to put down as the reader waits for the next fateful move in this gripping game of survival.

Thesman, Jean. *Rachel Chance*. 1990. Paperback: Avon. Ages 11–14.

"Nothing ever happens that we don't make happen," declares fifteen-year-old Rachel Chance to her wise neighbor Druid Annie. After Rachel's two-year-old brother Rider is stolen by a traveling revival show, Rachel's already troubled family can barely cope. So Rachel decides to get Rider back. She, her irascible grandfather, Druid Annie, and Hank, the boy who helps at their farm, set forth in an unreliable old truck to a meeting of the revival. They experience so many setbacks that finally Rachel goes off on her own. Although suffering from self-doubt, Rachel does what she has to. Love motivates her, but strength and intelligence keep her going. A subplot about Hank's aunt, an abused wife who shoots her husband, raises questions for Rachel about how women are treated and how they should be. A fine novel of adventure, romance, and courage.

Voigt, Cynthia. *Jackaroo*. **1985. Paperback: Fawcett. Ages 12–14.**

In this adventure set in an imaginary kingdom in the past, Gwyn, an innkeeper's daughter, feels constrained by being lower class and female in a strictly traditional society. She learns to read, even though it is forbidden to her class, and develops her strengths in unconventional ways. Her goal is to help the poor and hungry, who are preyed upon by thieves and thieving soldiers. Yet what can a sixteen-year-old girl do, even if she is strong and smart? When she discovers the clothing of Jackaroo, a legendary hero from the past, she secretly dons the costume, enjoying the freedom of men's clothing, and sets off on horseback to bring help to those who need it. With the help of a man who cherishes her forceful nature, Gwyn ultimately makes a path in life that suits her, boding well for her future. A long but very satisfying adventure.

Contemporary Life

Bauer, Joan. *Rules of the Road*. **1998. Hardcover: Putnam. Paperback: Puffin. Ages 10–14.**

Sixteen-year-old narrator Jenna Boller is as smart and

strong as she is funny, but it takes a strange road trip for her to realize it. She spends her summer driving an elderly businesswoman named Mrs. Gladstone from Chicago to Texas, stopping along the way to inspect shoe stores in the large Gladstone chain. As they go along, Jenna not only learns about business, she learns some of her strengths as well. Their journey reaches a climax at a stockholder's meeting where issues of quality and greed clash, and Jenna surprises herself with her courage. Despite a serious subplot about Jenna's alcoholic father, the tone is upbeat and often downright funny. Savvy working women of three generations make this an unusual, welcome novel that offers tips on selling along with rules about life's hard roads.

Bauer, Joan. *Squashed.* **1992. Paperback: Laurel Leaf. Ages 9–14.**

Sixteen-year-old Ellie devotes herself to raising a huge pumpkin to win the Rock River Pumpkin Weigh-In. But she faces hazards like pumpkin thieves, bad weather, and a father who thinks she should study more and garden less. Her father, a motivational speaker, tries to use his talents to get Ellie to change her goals. Ellie adopts some of her father's techniques to motivate her pumpkin to grow, making this a very funny book. A new boy in town, who grows champion corn, catches Ellie's eye and they start to get to know each other. While pumpkin growing may seem like a strange topic, Ellie's hilarious voice and the eccentric citizens of Rock River make this a pleasure to read. Like most of Bauer's fine, funny books, this one introduces a girl pursuing a strong interest. Highly recommended.

Bloor, Edward. *Crusader.* **1999. Hardcover: Harcourt. Paperback: Scholastic. Ages 13–14.**

Although smart and strong-minded, Roberta Ritter doesn't

get much encouragement in her life. At fifteen, with her mother murdered years before, Roberta spends her time outside of school working in the unsuccessful video arcade owned by her father and uncle. The arcade is in a Florida shopping mall that has seen better days, now in competition with a fancy new mall down the road. Roberta's father pays little attention to Roberta. The concerned adults in her life are her two journalism teachers, who recognize her talent, and Mrs. Weiss, a kind widow who owns a card shop in the mall. Roberta puts her energy into learning to be a reporter and when it looks like the mall will be closed, she turns her new skills to saving it. At the same time, she starts researching news archives about her mother's murder and discovers a painful truth about the past. Bloor creates a remarkably real cast of characters in an unmistakably modern American setting, with a heroine well worth knowing. An outstanding novel that provides a long, satisfying read.

Garden, Nancy. *The Year They Burned the Books*. 1999. Hardcover: FSG. Ages 13–14.

Senior Jamie Crawford faces an unexpectedly dramatic year as editor in chief of her high school newspaper. Her editorial endorsing the school's plan to distribute condoms draws fire when she can't get anyone to write a piece with another viewpoint. Conservative forces on the school committee object to the editorial, the new school policy, and the health curriculum that covers homosexuality. The small Maine town is deeply divided, and ugly homophobic incidents occur, directed against Jamie and her best friend Terry who are struggling with their sexual identities. Terry falls in love with another boy but fear limits their relationship, while Jamie is attracted to a new student, Tessa. No easy solutions emerge in this realistic, sometimes inspiring, novel about freedom of the press and the issues confronting gay high school students, which ends on a hopeful but ambiguous note.

Johnson, Angela. *Toning the Sweep*. 1993. Hardcover: Orchard. Paperback: Scholastic. Ages 11–14.

Wonderful older women inhabit the desert community where fourteen-year-old Emily's grandmother Ola lives. Ola, who has cancer, is packing up her house and saying goodbye to her close friends, with the help of Emily and her mother. Emily makes a videotape for Ola as a memento, learning a lot about her mother and grandmother in the process. As she tapes Ola's friends, Emily sees the strength and love of a community of confident, sometimes boisterous, women. Emily gains an appreciation, rarely seen in children's books, of the support women give each other. Enriched by this community, the intrepid Ola, a fast driver and world traveler, has lived happily by herself for many years, and now must face moving in with Emily's family. The relationship between Emily, a young woman who is growing stronger, and Ola, a wise woman who is facing change and death, is fully realized. A brilliant, beautifully written novel about an African-American family.

Moore, Yvette. *Freedom Songs*. 1991. Paperback: Puffin. Ages 12–14.

Fourteen-year-old Sheryl, who aspires to be pretty and popular, changes her values after a visit to the South in 1963. In North Carolina she encounters blatant prejudice and understands why her college-age uncle Pete has joined the nonviolent protesters known as Freedom Riders. Knowing he is risking his life for the cause, Sheryl returns to Brooklyn wanting to help. She and her friends band together to raise money for the Freedom Riders by giving a concert. In the process,

Sheryl starts to take her artistic talent seriously and struggles with being a leader. Strong female relatives abound in Sheryl's family, such as her aunt whose carpentry business is at risk because of her belief in equality. The family needs all its strength when tragedy strikes close to home. A moving story about the evil of racial prejudice, and the courage of those who fought for freedom in the sixties.

Naidoo, Beverley. *Chain of Fire*. Illustrated by Eric Velasquez. 1990. Paperback: Trophy. Ages 12–14.

Set in South Africa in the 1980s, this intense novel follows the fate of fifteen-year-old Naledi, her family, and her friends when the government announces plans to move them to a bleak "homeland." Devastated, Naledi and the others slowly start to fight back. She earns the respect of her peers by defying their unfair school principal, and the others elect her as one of their leaders. They organize a peaceful march made violent by the police. The resistance brings painful retaliation, but Naledi also feels a growing sense of solidarity. Her own voice gets stronger as she speaks out against the inhumane acts of the government. Courageous older women provide leadership and inspire Naledi to keep strong. No unrealistic happy ending mars the story's dignity. Instead the sense of hope for Naledi and the others comes from their bond as they continue the struggle for what is right. Full of tragedy and injustice, this novel will grip the reader from beginning to end. An earlier book about Naledi is *Journey to Jo'burg*.

Singer, Marilyn, compiler and editor. *Stay True: Short Stories for Strong Girls*. 1998. Paperback: Scholastic. Ages 11–14.

These eleven stories by well-known children's writers all center on a girl, usually a girl with a mind of her own. Several of the main characters are trying to preserve their dreams in the face of opposition. A smart Hispanic girl longs to go on an astronomy field trip to further her dream of becoming an astronomer, but her family believes she should stick to traditional female roles. In another case, an African-American girl insists on taking a summer job working on the Brooklyn Bridge despite her grandmother's hope that she will work in the local hair salon. Still another girl, who struggles with being large and liking activities such as fishing, experiences a moment of hope when she glimpses a world where she might fit in. Although a few of the stories seem out of place, most of them will give encouragement to adolescents who want to march to their own drummers.

Staples, Suzanne Fisher. *Shabanu: Daughter of the Wind.* 1989. Hardcover: Knopf. Paperback: Random House. Ages 12–14.

Growing up in contemporary Pakistan, Shabanu has little in common with American adolescents. She and her family are nomads in the Cholistan desert who rely on camels for their livelihood. Shabanu's thirteen-year-old sister Phulan will be married soon to a man her parents have chosen, and Shabanu knows her turn will be next. Since she has no brothers, she has had more freedom than most girls while helping her father with the camels. But there is no escaping her fate in such a patriarchal society, and Shabanu knows that soon she will have to leave her beloved freedom in the desert. Her aunt Sharma, who built up her own herd and then left her abusive husband, gives Shabanu a sense of hope when the future looks most bleak. The realistic ending suggests that Shabanu's strength of character will see her through future struggles. A beautifully wrought portrait of another culture and a sympathetic young woman. A Newbery Honor Book. The sequel *Haveli* is about Shabanu's daughter.

Temple, Frances. *Tonight, by Sea.* **1995. Hardcover: Orchard. Paperback: Trophy. Ages 13–14.**

This painful novel takes place in Haiti in 1993, when brutal soldiers and other terrorists are making life unbearable for ordinary people. Paulie lives with her uncle and grandmother, barely getting enough to eat. During an American journalist's visit, Paulie's neighbor Jean-Desir speaks out against the government. When the soldiers retaliate, Paulie courageously makes her way to the city to find the journalist again, risking her life. She puts her safety in jeopardy more than once for the cause of freedom and the love of her country. She also risks her life to try to save a neighbor. She keeps on trying, as she has learned from her uncle and grandmother, even after tragic events surround her. An afterword gives more details about the modern history of Haiti.

Voigt, Cynthia. *Bad Girls.* **1996. Hardcover: Scholastic. Paperback: Scholastic. Ages 11–13.**

Margalo and Mikey, new girls in the fifth-grade class, sit next to each other and quickly become friends. Margalo could be friends with more sedate girls, but she is drawn to Mikey, who is never boring. Mikey, who has no interest in being nice like other girls, objects loudly to boys dominating the soccer field. A talented, aggressive player, she and a few other girls insist on joining the recess games, then join the school's all-boy team. Mikey's main rival and enemy is Louis, but she also offends a self-satisfied girl named Rhonda, who lashes back publicly. When Margalo decides to defend her friend, she pulls some outrageous tricks on Rhonda. Their escapades liven up an already rambunctious class and keep the stern teacher hopping. Both strong personalities, the two girls clash as they work out their friendship in a realistic way. This unconventional, refreshing novel is the first in a series.

Voigt, Cynthia. *Homecoming*. 1981. Hardcover: Atheneum. Paperback: Fawcett. Ages 11–14.

Dicey Tillerman is a stubborn, resourceful thirteen-year-old, "a fighter," as she calls herself. When their mentally ill mother deserts Dicey and her three siblings, Dicey struggles valiantly to keep the family together, leading them on an arduous journey to find an unknown aunt. Along the way, Dicey invents solutions to every problem that arises, including their desperate need for money; her ideas don't always work, but she never gives up. Her relationship with her two younger brothers and younger sister is loving but tough. After many hard miles, they find a possible home, but it will take all Dicey's ingenuity and more hard work to keep them there. Dicey is a sympathetic modern heroine who is making her way through a difficult world. The excellent sequels include the Newbery Medal winner *Dicey's Song* and *Seventeen Against the Dealer*.

Wolff, Virginia Euwer. *The Mozart Season*. 1991. Paperback: Scholastic. Ages 11–14.

In this well-paced novel, twelve-year-old Allegra spends a watershed summer practicing for a violin competition and growing up. She learns about tenacity, defined by her violin teacher as "holding on when it would be more comfortable to let go," and confronts her fears of performing. Like training for serious softball, which Allegra did in the spring, practicing violin requires discipline but also the ability to relax. Tension builds as the competition comes closer and Allegra tries to make the Mozart concerto her own. Allegra has an unusually cherished existence, surrounded by supportive friends and family, and a rich relationship with her mother, a professional violinist who loves and admires her daughter. Evocative, almost magical, writing about music makes this an exceptionally beautiful novel.

Young, Karen Romano. *The Beetle and Me: A Love Story.* **1999. Hardcover: Greenwillow. Paperback: Avon. Ages 11–14.**

Fifteen-year-old Daisy wants to repair and eventually drive her family's old, broken-down 1957 Volkswagen Beetle, which her parents drove when Daisy was younger. Her Porsche-loving father, her aunt who's an automobile mechanic, and her race-car driving uncle discourage her from the difficult task. Ignoring their advice, Daisy talks her way into the auto mechanics class at her high school, where she starts to learn what she needs to know. Her project is full of setbacks and only her determination keeps her going. Cars are such a big part of her life that even her brushes with romance revolve around them. A refreshingly original novel about a girl whose pursuits shatter stereotypes.

Sports Stories

Cebulash, Mel. *Ruth Marini of the Dodgers.* **1983. Hardcover: Lerner. Ages 10–14.**

When this sports novel opens, senior Ruth Marini has pitched better than any player in New Jersey high school baseball in years. Still, she doesn't expect the Los Angeles Dodgers' owner to contact her after graduation, much less to sign her to a contract. Eighteen-year-old Ruth leaves the modest apartment in Union City where she lives with her mother, who works in a dress shop, to work on her pitching with a coach in South Carolina. He is tough but fair, and his wife welcomes Ruth into their home. Next it's off to spring training in Florida, where not all the guys are friendly but most improve when they see Ruth's pitching. Tense but determined, she holds her own and earns a place on a minor league team. Meanwhile, Ruth has to work out a relationship with her best friend, now turned boyfriend, who vacillates between being supportive and jealous. Plenty of baseball action characterizes this optimistic but not impossible scenario about what it might be like for a woman in men's professional ball.

Levine, Anna. *Running on Eggs*. **1999. Hardcover: Front Street/Cricket Books. Ages 11–14.**

Karen, who lives in a kibbutz in Israel with her mother and brother, misses her father, who was killed as a soldier. She is determined to do well in track partly because he was a runner, but the long-standing conflict between Arabs and Jews even affects school sports. When Karen and an Arab girl named Yasmine start a tentative friendship, Karen's friends and Yasmine's brother chide them. Then Yasmine's father insists she run in a skirt, which causes the track coach, who is neither Jewish nor Arab, to take her off the team. Karen and Yasmine secretly start training together, cementing their friendship but putting them in a precarious situation. While the story's message of reaching out dominates, running is an important element in the story and the girls' relationship.

Levy, Marilyn. *Run for Your Life*. **1996. Hardcover: Houghton. Paperback: Paper Star. Ages 13–14.**

Based on a true story, this compelling novel follows the fate of a girls' track team at a community center in Oakland, California. Most of the girls on the team, including the narrator Kisha, live in a housing project. Most have serious difficulties in their lives, such as poverty, sexual abuse, and troubled parents, but the team gives them a source of security. Darren, the center's director, understands their situations but requires hard work and good grades. Several of the girls including Kisha come close to quitting as they struggle with their personal lives. Dramatic tension builds as the team prepares for a national track meet. A powerful, hopeful novel that shows how important sports can be to young women.

Macy, Sue, editor. *Girls Got Game: Sports Stories and Poems*. 2001. Hardcover: Holt. Ages 11–14.

This fine anthology of original stories and poems explores a wide range of emotions and experiences of athletic girls, giving voice to fresh material and viewpoints. What is it like for a girl to clash with a female coach? What happens when a girl loves football and has the physical build to play it? Can a romantic friendship between a girl and boy survive when the girl beats the boy at a sport? The short stories and poems hinge on these and similar issues that girls deal with in the world of sports, covering swimming, stickball, soccer, horseback riding, tennis, track, baseball, and more. A gift to girls who love sports and reading.

Spinelli, Jerry. *There's a Girl in My Hammerlock*. 1991. Paperback: Aladdin. Ages 10–13.

Although Maisie tries out for the wrestling team because she has a crush on one of the members, she finds she loves wrestling. She takes grief from the coach, players, and her friends, but sticks with her resolve and makes the team. Maisie is a terrific athlete, but it takes a special show of physical courage before her teammates will accept her. Even then, boys on opposing teams default rather than wrestle a girl. Students and town members vent their hostility at wrestling matches and in the town newspaper. But Maisie persists through it all, and in the end she triumphs in an unpredictable way. A warm, amusing story with a realistic picture of how unwelcome a girl can be in a boy's sport.

Voigt, Cynthia. *Tell Me If the Lovers Are Losers.* **1982. Hardcover: Atheneum. Paperback: Fawcett. Ages 12–14.**

Set at a New England women's college in 1961, this is the story of Ann Gardner, her two freshman roommates, and their volleyball team. One roommate, Niki, is an intensely competitive athlete with a sharp tongue and no patience for lesser players. The other roommate, Hildy, a North Dakotan farm girl with an unshakable moral code, brings out the best in her fellow volleyball players. The team gets increasingly serious about defeating the other freshmen teams and challenging the sophomores. Ann, who is not athletic, grows in strength and sureness on the volleyball court; the team becomes her main social circle. The sports interest ultimately takes second place in the plot to friendship issues and a final tragedy. This thought-provoking novel does a fine job of capturing the intensity of female athletes and their bonding through sports.

Wolff, Virginia Euwer. *Bat 6.* **1998. Hardcover: Scholastic. Paperback: Scholastic. Ages 10–14.**

In this powerful novel set in 1949, girls' baseball teams from Bear Creek Ridge and Barlow Schools in Oregon gear up for the fiftieth anniversary game between the two towns and two schools. All their lives, most of the girls have attended the game and looked forward to their chance to play. But World War II has left some scars on the towns and the girls, and the painful memories interfere with the upcoming game. Told in the voices of the players, switching frequently, the text builds up tension between a newcomer whose father was killed at

Pearl Harbor and a girl of Japanese descent whose family was banished to a camp during the war. As the girls watch the problem grow, the question is, will anyone address the issues or will they continue the silence and animosity of many of the adults around them? A challenging and original book that combines girls' voices, baseball, and important social issues.

Mysteries and Ghost Stories

Cross, Gillian. *Tightrope*. 1999. Hardcover: Holiday House. Paperback: Harper. Ages 12–14.

Ashley, who has more responsibility than most fourteen-year-olds, rebels by spray-painting graffiti. When her chronically ill mother falls asleep at night, Ashley sneaks out and uses skills gained in gymnastics to climb buildings and write her graffiti tag, "Cindy." Her exploits bring her to the attention of Eddie Beale, a powerful young man in her working-class neighborhood. At the same time, Ashley receives anonymous letters and other signs that she is being stalked by someone who knows she is Cindy. Ashley turns to Eddie for help—only to land in worse trouble until she takes matters into her own hands. Ashley breaks stereotypes with her nightly graffiti, her fearless climbing, and her willingness to fight the forces of evil. A compelling British thriller.

DeFelice, Cynthia. *The Ghost of Fossil Glen*. 1998. Hardcover: FSG. Paperback: Camelot. Ages 9–13.

This supernatural thriller opens with sixth-grader Allie clinging to a cliff face, where she has been looking for fossils and climbed too high. A calm voice encourages her to save herself, but when she does she discovers that there's no one around. Could it have been the voice of a sixth-grade girl who died before Allie moved to town? Was she murdered? Allie endangers her own life as she tries to find out the truth and bring the murderer to justice. A fast-paced combination of murder mystery and ghost story about two gutsy girls.

Haddix, Margaret Peterson. *Running Out of Time*. 1995. Hardcover: Simon & Schuster. Paperback: Aladdin. Ages 11–13.

In this intriguing thriller, Jessie believes that she lives in 1840 in an Indiana village where her friends and family are dying from diphtheria. Recognizing Jessie's courage, her mother tells the thirteen-year-old the truth: it is really 1996, and they live in a reconstructed village that tourists view through hidden cameras. The forces that run the village have quit giving medicine or letting people leave. Jessie must escape from the village into the modern world and quietly get help. She gathers her strength and copes with the strange new world, but just as it seems all is well, she realizes that she is about to be killed. She needs to save her own life and figure out a way to save those dying in the village, a seemingly impossible task for someone who has never used a telephone, seen a car, or watched television. How can she come up with a scheme that will work in the dangerous modern world? A well-crafted page-turner about a resourceful girl.

Nixon, Joan Lowery. *The Name of the Game Was Murder*. 1993. Paperback: Dell. Ages 11–14.

Impetuous fifteen-year-old Samantha invites herself to spend two weeks with her great-aunt and her aunt's husband, the famous writer Augustus Trevor. Little does she know she will be trapped on an inaccessible part of an island off the coast of California with a murderer. Trevor has invited five famous guests for the weekend and threatened to reveal a dark secret about each of them in his forthcoming book. Their only chance to avoid the public humiliation is to solve a mystery Trevor has devised. But before the game can continue, the writer is found murdered. The guests are desperate to find Trevor's manuscript and destroy it, while Samantha is determined to find out who the killer is. Unusually good at breaking codes, she pieces together clues to solve the crime, but then must decide what to do with the answer. Initially underconfident and impetuous, Samantha thrives on her ability to outwit the adults around her. A fast-paced mystery with an Agatha Christie–like setting and a group of glamorous characters.

Pullman, Philip. *The Ruby in the Smoke*. 1987. Paperback: Knopf. Ages 12–14.

An incomparable stolen ruby, a dangerous secret society, mysterious sailors and evil landladies all come together in this gripping melodramatic story. Living in London in 1872, sixteen-year-old orphaned Sally Lockhart makes a first-class heroine. She always carries a gun and is an excellent shot. Her father has schooled her in bookkeeping and in the stock market, and skipped the traditional female lessons. "Problems," he taught her, "were things you faced, not things you ran away from." Her cool head comes in handy as she becomes embroiled in the intrigue surrounding the lost ruby of Agrapur. She makes friends, including an attractive young male photographer who treats her as an equal, and soon all of their lives are in danger. Nonstop action keeps the reader breathless until the very end, when the mysteries of Sally's life are unraveled. A plausible, strong and smart heroine in an exciting historical thriller. The sequels are *The Tiger in the Well*, *Shadow in the North*, and the related book *The Tin Princess*.

Springer, Nancy. *Looking for Jamie Bridger*. **1995. Hardcover: Dial. Ages 11–14.**

Who are Jamie Bridger's parents? The fourteen-year-old has been raised by her meek grandmother and domineering grandfather. Neither will tell her anything about her parents, although she knows she's not adopted. When her grandfather dies suddenly and her mentally ill grandmother becomes dependent on her, Jamie resolves to seek her answers soon. She gathers information, taking several trips on her own including a dangerous one to New York City. Her loyal friend Kate, a woman lawyer, and an eccentric turtle-loving old woman help her out along the way until at last Jamie learns the strange secret about her life.

Tate, Eleanor E. *The Secret of Gumbo Grove*. **1987. Paperback: Bantam. Ages 10–13.**

Living in modern South Carolina, narrator Raisin Stackhouse has a strong interest in history. When a neighbor, Miss Effie, needs help cleaning up an old cemetery, Raisin helps out and becomes fascinated by the history of the local African-American community. But when she starts to pass on the stories that Miss Effie tells her about black ancestors, the adults around Raisin get nervous. They don't want anyone digging up the past, even if it reveals how important African-Americans were in the town's early history. But once Raisin gets involved in something, she doesn't give up. She slowly unravels a mystery from the past. Raisin is an appealing combination of smart, persistent, impulsive, and a bit rebellious. She is surrounded by strong women and girls who have strong opinions and speak their minds.

Tolan, Stephanie S. *Who's There?* **1994. Hardcover: Morrow. Paperback: Beech Tree. Ages 10–13.**

Drew and her younger brother Evan have lost their parents

in an explosion. After staying with friends, they move to another town to stay with an aunt and grandfather they've never met or even heard about. Aunt Jocelyn and their chronically sick grandfather live in a huge house called Rose Hill, a house that Drew comes to believe is haunted. She teams up with Will, a boy who does gardening on the estate, and they research the house's history. They learn about the deaths of Jocelyn's little brother, also named Evan, and his mother Amalie, who was Jocelyn's beautiful and well-loved stepmother. When Drew and Will suspect Amalie wasn't the saint she seemed, Jocelyn reacts with fury, and Drew puts her new security in jeopardy. Meanwhile, Evan, who hasn't spoken since his parents died, gets drawn into the mystery and danger of Drew's investigation. This exciting combination of murder mystery and ghost story is a real page-turner.

Historical Fiction

Armstrong, Jennifer. *Steal Away*. 1992. Paperback: Scholastic. Ages 11–14.

What would it be like for two lonely girls, one a white orphan, the other a black slave, to escape to the North together in 1855? Living in the South, Susannah longs to return to her home in Vermont after the death of her parents, while Bethlehem has no hope for happiness as a slave and fears the intentions of her young master. They set off disguised as boys, scarcely knowing each other or the danger they are getting into. Each girl tells the story from her perspective as they slowly make their way North. Shy Susannah blossoms under the freedom of being disguised as a boy, free from worry about her behavior or threats from men. Bethlehem struggles with her desire to learn to read, knowing it is illegal for a slave, and with the burdens freedom brings. Underlying themes about the powerlessness of girls and blacks give deeper meaning to this exciting adventure. In the book's layered structure, Susannah and Bethlehem are telling their story forty years later to two thirteen-year-old girls, whose reactions add another dimension. A sophisticated novel about freedom, females, and our country's troubled history. Highly recommended.

Barrett, Tracy. *Anna of Byzantium*. 1999. Hardcover: Delacorte. Paperback: Laurel Leaf. Ages 11–14.

Anna of Comnena, the daughter of a Byzantium emperor, lived from 1083 to 1153. After her father's death, the well-educated Anna wrote an eleven-book epic about his feats as a warrior and ruler, in which she also describes her own life and family. She is known to have plotted unsuccessfully with her mother to assassinate her brother John, who became emperor and exiled Anna to a convent. In this fictionalized version of her life, Anna expects to inherit her father's throne. She studies history and learns how to rule from her nefarious grandmother. But when she clashes with her grandmother, the powerful woman switches alliances to John. Unusual in its focus on the political intrigue among three women—Anna, her mother, and her grandmother—this novel paints a detailed picture of palace life one thousand years ago.

Bruchac, Joseph. *Sacajawea: The Story of Bird Woman and the Lewis and Clark Expedition*. 2000. Hardcover: Harcourt. Ages 10–14.

This fine historical novel alternates between the voices of Sacajawea, the teenage Shoshone woman who helped guide the Lewis and Clark Expedition, and William Clark, an expedition leader. The journey from North Dakota to the Pacific Ocean and back, full of hardships and danger, keeps the plot moving quickly. Sacajawea's intelligence and strength, which are set in historical context, are indispensable for the group's survival. Folktales and excerpts from the expedition journals open each chapter, and quotations are amply used to bring the journey to life. A map shows the route, and an author's note separates fact from fiction. This historical novel will grab reader's interest in the perilous trip and the important role Sacajawea played.

Carter, Dorothy Sharp. *His Majesty, Queen Hatshepsut*. Illustrated by Michele Chessare. 1987. Hardcover: Lippincott. Ages 10–14.

Hatshepsut ruled for more than twenty years as the king of Upper and Lower Egypt. The daughter of Thutmose I and wife of Thutmose II, she defied her husband's dying wish that his young son become ruler and declared herself Pharaoh. This fictionalized account of her life from age thirteen until her death portrays Hatshepsut as a shrewd and accomplished ruler who strengthened her country internally. Hatshepsut narrates her own story, describing the constant resistance she felt from the powerful priesthood and other men, and the network of spies she created to learn of plots against her. Although she is painfully besotted with one of her advisors, she also believes herself superior to him and everyone else. The few black-and-white illustrations show Hatshepsut, known to her subjects as "His Majesty," dressed both as a man and as a woman. A study in power and intrigue in the ancient world, with a woman at its center, this novel is one of a kind.

Collier, James Lincoln, and Christopher Collier. *War Comes to Willy Freeman*. 1983. Paperback: Dell. Ages 10–13.

A free black girl living through the Revolutionary War,

Willy Freeman sees the war and the colonies through an unusual perspective. After her father dies fighting for the colonies and the British take her mother, she questions what good either side will do for her people. Willy uses her sailing skills to flee from Connecticut by boat to New York City, where, disguised as a boy, she finds work at a tavern. The freedom the disguise gives her leads Willy to reflect on women's lack of freedom: "When I came to think about it, when you was a woman you was half a slave, anyway." Willy has her eyes wide open as she looks at the world around her, and it is all she can do, some days, to suppress her anger. Losing her temper gets her involved in an important legal case for blacks, with surprising results. The bittersweet ending promises no easy life to Willy, but her courage and intelligence give the reader hope for her future.

Cushman, Karen. *Catherine, Called Birdy.* 1994. Hardcover: Clarion. Paperback: Trophy. Ages 12–14.

Catherine, daughter of a small-time nobleman in medieval England, is hilarious. In a diary format she records her daily life, the outrages she suffers as a girl, and her often humorous assessment of things. She longs to be outside frolicking instead of inside sewing, and she chafes at her lessons in ladylike behavior. Birdy is the sort of girl who organizes a spitting contest and starts a mud fight. She makes a list of all the things girls cannot do, such as go on a crusade, be a horse trainer, laugh out loud, and "marry whom they will." She battles with her father who wants to marry her off to the highest bidder, no matter how repulsive. Many of her best sarcastic remarks are reserved for him, and she irritates him whenever possible. She has a bawdy sense of humor and a palpable love of life. Few fictional characters are so vivid and funny—do not miss this one. A Newbery Honor Book.

Cushman, Karen. *The Midwife's Apprentice.* **1995. Hardcover: Clarion. Ages 11–14.**

The heroine of this book starts so low in life she doesn't even have a proper name, but is known as Brat and then Beetle. Taken in by a cranky midwife, Beetle very slowly gains some sense of self and confidence, eventually renaming herself Alyce. By secretly watching the midwife at births, Alyce learns something about delivering babies. On her way to becoming a midwife, Alyce learns that risking and failing is unavoidable, but that giving up is the worst thing she can do. This classic lesson that boys are taught far more often than girls makes this book valuable. Alyce makes herself keep trying in the face of discouragement, a real act of courage. A Newbery Medal winner.

Donaldson, Joan. *A Pebble and a Pen.* **2000. Hardcover: Holiday. Ages 10–13.**

Before typewriters and computers existed, some men and fewer women made their living through their penmanship. In this charming novel, Matty, a fourteen-year-old farm girl who has excelled in school, resolves to master penmanship and earn her living. She runs away to the Ohio school of master penman Platt Rogers Spencer, a real person whose Spencerian Script became America's most widely taught system of handwriting. Despite the hostility and teasing of her male classmates, Matty perseveres and makes progress. She exchanges housework for tuition and starts to see her dreams coming true, when a setback occurs that could prevent her future as a "penman." The story ends realistically, with uncertainty tempered by hope and a hint of romance. An appealing combination of fact and fiction, with elegant handwriting samples throughout.

Duffy, James. *Radical Red.* **1993. Hardcover: Atheneum. Ages 11–14.**

It is 1894 and Susan B. Anthony is in Albany, New York, to tell the legislature why women have a right to vote. Twelve-year-old Connor O'Shea, who has a boy's name because her father wanted a son, knows nothing about women's rights. But she does see her alcoholic father beat her mother, and she sees how hard her mother works as a laundress only to have her father take the money. She also knows she does better in school than many boys who will eventually have the vote when she won't. Connor and her friend Doreen volunteer to help the suffragists, then so does Connor's mother. When her father finds out, he gets more violent than ever and the mother and daughter have to make a choice about their future. This engrossing novel, in which Susan B. Anthony appears as a character, brings an era and a movement to life in a way that readers can understand. The legislators' argument that women's delicate natures will be harmed by the vote looks ludicrous in view of the kind of life Connor's mother has. Sympathetic characters combine with important history to make this a book well worth reading.

Garden, Nancy. *Dove and Sword: A Novel of Joan of Arc.* **1995. Paperback: Scholastic. Ages 12–14.**

In this fictionalized account about Joan of Arc (in French, Jeannette d'Arc), the main character is Gabrielle, another peasant girl from Jeannette's village. Gabrielle, a friend of Jeannette's brother, follows Jeannette on her quest. Disguised as a boy, Gabrielle expands her talents as a healer to help care for those wounded in battle. An observant girl who chafes at the roles assigned to women, Gabrielle aspires to be a great doctor and makes the most of her chance to study with

Christine de Pisan, a famous writer of the time and a great proponent of women. Gabrielle serves as an excellent narrator of Jeannette d'Arc's quest to see the true French king crowned. Both these young women from a small village are strong and brave. Gabrielle is the dove who heals instead of fights, and Jeannette, the bearer of the sword. Theirs is an exciting tale, full of danger and love.

Gregory, Kristiana. *Earthquake at Dawn.* 1992. Paperback: Harcourt. Ages 11–14.

This historical novel dexterously blends fact and fiction in its story about the 1906 San Francisco earthquake. Told by a fictional character named Daisy Valentine, a fifteen-year-old servant who grew up in mining country, it follows the adventures of Daisy and her employer, Edith Irvine. Edith, a real person, was a twenty-two-year-old photographer, daughter of a wealthy mine owner. She plans to take Daisy with her on a world tour, but when they reach San Francisco, the earthquake hits. They take refuge with friendly strangers with whom they flee to Golden Gate Park. There they camp out with thousands of others experiencing the aftershocks and waiting for fires to abate. Defying the mayor's orders against photography, Edith records the pain and ruin around them in photographs only made public eighty years later. Daisy surprises herself with her own bravery, defending Edith against the attack of a soldier and fighting off rats in the park. An exciting survival story laced with intriguing details about a true historical event.

Hendry, Frances Mary. *Quest for a Maid.* 1988. Hardcover: FSG, o.p. Paperback: FSG. Ages 10–14.

"When I was nine years old, I hid under a table and heard my sister kill a king." This tantalizing first sentence sets the tone for this exciting adventure novel about a hardy Scottish girl named Meg. The youngest daughter of a shipbuilder, Meg is outspoken and brave. After she rescues a young lad named Davie from danger, and another named Peem from a cruel master, the three of them swim and sail together, often breaking rules and taking the punishment. When Meg goes with a delegation to fetch the young Norwegian princess for her wedding to an English prince, a storm wrecks their ship on the way back. Once again, Meg's unflagging courage comes into play as she and her friends fight to keep the princess safe. The suspense and excitement rarely slow down in this gripping novel that blends history and magic. All the children have strengths, but Meg is the center of the group, a heroine not to be missed.

Houston, Gloria. *Mountain Valor*. 1994. Paperback: Paper Star. Ages 11–14.

Valor longs to live up to her name and the medal of valor her father gave her when he left to fight for the Confederacy. In her mountain life, she finds several women to emulate, including an herb gatherer who rides her horse astride in men's clothes, rather than sidesaddle. This old woman introduces Valor to the phrase "sister of the wind," meaning a woman who goes her own way with freedom and courage. Furious at Yankees who have devastated her family, Valor disguises herself as a boy and follows them to retrieve stolen livestock. She faces a series of dangers on the way and gets some unexpected help. Based on a true story, this is an exciting adventure about a girl who grows up to become a "sister of the wind."

Ingold, Jeanette. *Pictures, 1918*. 1998. Hardcover: Harcourt. Paperback: Puffin. Ages 11–14.

In this engaging novel, high school junior Asia falls in

love with the camera in a store window in her small Texas town. Determined to have it and to capture the images that haunt her, she saves her money and borrows some from her strong but fading grandmother. Asia also persuades the owner of the local photography studio to take her on as an apprentice. Her hard work and dedication convince him to teach her how to develop pictures as well as how to compose them. Her parents doubt the suitability of her pursuit, but with her grandmother's support, Asia changes her family's belief in what a girl can do. Meanwhile, she falls in love with her good friend Nick and deals with romantic complications. The book's conclusion, which coincides with the end of World War I, leaves Asia on the brink of following her dreams into a hopeful future.

Kline, Lisa Williams. *Eleanor Hill.* **1999. Hardcover: Front Street/Cricket Books. Ages 10–14.**

Twelve-year-old Eleanor Hill wants more from life than to stay in the North Carolina fishing village where she grew up. She looks for inspiration in her older brother, Frank, who has left home to travel, and her new school teacher, Miss Rosalie, who believes that women should have the right to vote. But it's 1912, and Miss Rosalie's views prompt the village parents to dismiss her. She continues to influence Eleanor through her letters when she moves West. When Frank comes to visit, he brings his Model-T and teaches Eleanor to drive, but he leaves after quarreling with their conservative father. More determined than ever, Eleanor soon leaves home herself to further her education and gets a job involving cars. She learns, travels, and forms her own ideas, breaking tradition when it seems best and embracing it at other times. Over five years, Eleanor grows in strength and courage, and creates the life she wants in this engaging novel.

Konigsburg, E. L. *A Proud Taste for Scarlet and Miniver*. 1975. Hardcover: Atheneum. Paperback: Dell. Ages 11–14.

This novel explores the life of Eleanor of Aquitaine, the most powerful woman in the twelfth century. It opens with four people—an abbot, a knight, Eleanor, and her mother-in-law—sitting around heaven, reminiscing. Each narrates a part of Eleanor's life, with Eleanor herself describing her final years. Although fictionalized, the story is faithful to the facts of her life and times. She was a queen who steeped herself in luxury, music, and art. She loved to travel and even went on one of the Crusades. A political force in her own right, Eleanor became the queen of France through her first marriage and the queen of England through her second. At times she had the authority to collect taxes, administer lands and castles, and sit in judgment in the courts, but more often her power was indirect, through her husbands and sons. In either case, she was a shrewd politician who reveled in power. This sophisticated novel, punctuated with humorous observations, brings a fascinating woman to life.

LaFaye, A. *Edith Shay*. 1998. Hardcover: Viking. Paperback: Aladdin. Ages 10–13.

Although Katherine Lunden's family has lived in the Wisconsin woods for generations, she longs to see the world. In 1869, at the age of sixteen, she seizes her chance and takes the train to Chicago. With hard work and courage, she works several jobs and gains skills as a seamstress. She finds friendship in Chicago but still wants to see more. Having found an abandoned suitcase labeled "Edith Shay" at the train station, Katherine adopts the name and then tries to find her way in war-torn Richmond, Virginia. She works as a printer's apprentice and a cook as she gains independence. An engaging character, Katherine struggles with homesickness and with expectations for young women of her time.

Namioka, Lensey. *Ties That Bind, Ties That Break*. 1999. Hardcover: Delacorte. Paperback: Laurel Leaf. Ages 11–14.
Ailun is growing up in a changing China at the beginning of the twentieth century. Although her grandmother, mother, and older sisters have bound feet that make them hobble when they walk, Ailun's thoughtful father sides with her request to keep her feet unbound. He also sends her to a public school where she masters English and especially loves learning about the rest of the world. When her father dies, though, Ailun is left without allies. She must quit school and feels lucky to get a governess job with an American family. Their return to the United States offers her an opportunity to begin an entirely new life. Told in the first person, this short novel incorporates information about Chinese history into a fast-moving story about a girl who bravely breaks with tradition and forges her own life.

O'Dell, Scott. *Carlota*. 1989. Paperback: Dell. Ages 11–14.
Because her brother died as a baby, Carlota has been raised as a boy. Her father has taught her to ride, to wield a lance and a lasso, and to help run their large ranch in Spanish California in the mid-1800s. At sixteen, Carlota dresses in leather pants and jacket, and rides astride instead of sidesaddle, to her grandmother's disgust. The dictatorial old woman rolls and smokes her own cigarillos, and argues constantly with her son and granddaughter. Carlota's love of horses makes it easier to follow her father's unconventional wishes, but as she gets older, she doesn't always agree with him. When she goes off with him to fight the American army, Carlota starts to follow her own conscience and to speak her mind. Combining physi-

cal courage and strength, kindness and honesty, Carlota is an original heroine in a captivating setting.

O'Dell, Scott. *Sarah Bishop*. 1980. Hardcover: Houghton. Paperback: Scholastic. Ages 12–14.

After Sarah Bishop's home and family are destroyed at the beginning of the Revolutionary War, a British officer unfairly accuses her of setting a fire. Lonely and scared, Sarah escapes and flees westward, buying a musket on the way and selling her hair to buy supplies. Her musket saves her from an unwanted approach by a man she meets on the road, but the encounter convinces her to get away from people. Within walking distance of a village, she finds a cave and sets about preparing to stay there for the winter. She grows more confident when she finds she can survive on her own, and she learns to love her solitude. Although the ending hints that she may seek the company of others soon, her time apart has made her independent and strong. An outstanding survival story.

Paterson, Katherine. *Lyddie*. 1991. Hardcover: Dutton. Paperback: Puffin. Ages 11–14.

Lyddie Worthen faces her hard life in the 1840s with unflagging determination, hard work, and unexpected help from other women. Forced to leave the family's farm, she makes her way to Lowell, Massachusetts, to work in the textile mills, one of the few places females could get a relatively well-paying job. The work is dangerous and difficult, but Lyddie masters it while also learning to read well. As the hours and work increase and Lyddie has to ward off the overseer's unwanted advances, she has to decide whether to join other workers in protesting poor work conditions. A friendship with a new worker leads Lyddie to a painful choice between keeping her integrity or her job, but she emerges from the struggle stronger in spirit, with clear goals for the future. Skillfully crafted by a talented writer, this story portrays a fiercely independent young woman who battles for a place in a harsh world. Highly recommended.

Pfitsch, Patricia Curtis. *The Deeper Song.* **1998. Hardcover: Simon & Schuster. Ages 12–14.**

In this novel that imagines a woman might have written part of the Old Testament, the main character Judith lives in Jerusalem in the time of King Solomon. She is a teenage girl whose father, one of Solomon's priests, has begrudgingly given in to his wife's request to educate Judith, who has become a skilled storyteller. The strong-minded girl has begun to worship secretly at the Temple of the Goddess, a traditional religion that is at odds with her family's Jewish faith. Increasing tensions in the city lead to violence against the Goddess worshipers but also inspire Judith to write down the stories in the first five books of the Old Testament. Danger and intrigue characterize her struggles, which also lead her to romance and an uncertain future. A short, well-written novel with an interesting premise.

Rinaldi, Ann. *Girl in Blue.* **2001. Hardcover: Scholastic. Ages 10–14.**

Based on true stories about women who disguised themselves as soldiers and served during the Civil War, this historical novel invents Sarah Wheelock, a Michigan farm girl who enlists in the Union Army. Miserable at home, where her father beats her and plans to marry her off to a brutal neighbor, fifteen-year-old Sarah enlists dressed as a boy and goes as part of the Second Michigan Infantry to fight in the Battle of Bull Run. An excellent shot, Sarah has never killed anyone before the battle, which is bloody and confused. She spends time working in an army hospital where, after completing an errand across enemy lines one night, she is revealed as a woman. Having proved herself resourceful and brave, Sarah does dangerous work for Allan Pinkerton, a detective who coordinates spying for the Union. An engaging story full of action and intrigue.

Roberts, Willo Davis. *Jo and the Bandit.* **1992. Hardcover: Atheneum. Ages 11–13.**

In this action-packed Western adventure, twelve-year-old Josephine Whitman, known as Jo, and her younger brother Andrew go to live with their uncle, a judge in Texas, surviving a stagecoach robbery on the way out. When Jo and Andrew arrive in Muddy Wells, they find that Judge Macklin doesn't much like children, especially girls. He does start to appreciate Jo when he realizes she can help do the accounts and staff the counter at the general store he owns. Jo learned her assertiveness from her grandmother, the Judge's mother, who taught her to "learn to like to work, because you're going to have to earn a living." She also told Jo that "a smart woman could outwit a man anytime if she set her mind to it." Adventures abound when the bandits from the stagecoach robbery show up in town. A little romance, a lot of action, and a feisty heroine make this great fun to read.

Sappéy, Maureen Stack. *Letters from Vinnie.* **1999. Hardcover: Front Street. Ages 11–14.**

In the years after the Civil War, a sculptor named Vinnie Ream created a life-size statue of Abraham Lincoln that stands in the U.S. Capitol building rotunda. A teenager when she began the sculpture, Ream had already completed a bust of

Lincoln sculpted from life. This intriguing novel tells about her experiences through letters to a fictional friend. It details her job as a clerk at the post office and her lessons from a famous sculptor, who was impressed by her talent. She was devoted to Lincoln and to the Union, though both her brother and her suitor fought for the South. Ream even played a role in preventing President Johnson, Lincoln's successor, from losing his office. The letters are deliberately formal and sometimes flowery, echoing the style of the time, but the fictionalized life of this talented, courageous artist will nevertheless grip readers.

Speare, Elizabeth George. *The Witch of Blackbird Pond*. 1958. Hardcover: Houghton. Paperback: Dell. Ages 10–14.

Kit has been raised to think for herself and to enjoy life. When her grandfather dies and she must leave Barbados for colonial Connecticut, her headstrong impulses and love of life lead her into friendship and trouble. She chafes under the grim Puritan authority of her uncle but doesn't let him break her spirit. When Kit befriends a neglected little girl and an old Quaker woman who is branded a witch, she risks being accused of witchcraft herself. Despite the patriarchal nature of their lives, the women Kit encounters manage to develop strength and wisdom of their own, although men have more freedom and opportunities. This engaging modern classic received the Newbery Medal.

Taylor, Mildred D. *Roll of Thunder, Hear My Cry*. 1976. Hardcover: Dial. Paperback: Puffin. Ages 10–14.

Cassie Logan has a strong, proud family who struggle against virulent racial prejudice in their rural area in the South. They farm their own land, but are in constant danger of losing it during the Depression. Nine-year-old Cassie, who narrates the dramatic events in their lives, has a fierce temper and a habit of speaking her mind that can be dangerous in her world. Cassie's valiant mother, who risks her teaching job by teaching black history, and her grandmother Big Ma, who still works the fields, try to prepare Cassie and her brothers for an unjust world without stifling their spirits. Readers will be moved to anger and tears by the evils of racial prejudice that endanger the Logan family. A powerful novel, beautifully written. Winner of the Newbery Medal. Other books about the Logan family include *The Land*, *Let the Circle Be Unbroken*, and others.

Tomlinson, Theresa. *The Forestwife*. 1995. Hardcover: Orchard. Ages 11–14.

In this wonderful reworking of the Robin Hood legend, Maid Marian precedes Robin into Sherwood Forest. She is fleeing from an arranged marriage with the help of her old nurse Agnes. Wise Agnes leads them to the Forestwife, a woman who lives in the forest and helps all who ask. There Marian learns about herbs and healing and how to survive in the forest. Poor folk, broken by the greedy lords, come seeking cures, food, shelter, and understanding. Marian grows more indignant as she sees the results of injustice. She and her friends attract a group of strong women and a few men, including Agnes's son Robert, who joins in the useful work when he isn't off fighting. Although he and Marian find romance together, Marian's first loyalty is to her work and those who need her help. In this superb reworking of an old legend, independent women take fate into their own hands and change it. Highly recommended. Followed by *Child of the May*.

Watkins, Yoko Kawashima. *So Far from the Bamboo Grove*. 1986. Hardcover: Lothrop. Paperback: Beech Tree. Ages 11–14.

In 1945, eleven-year-old Yoko Kawashima, her sixteen-year-old sister Ko, and their mother made an arduous journey from northern Korea to their homeland of Japan. They tramped through harsh countryside, disguised themselves as Korean soldiers, and finally arrived by boat in Japan, only to find their relatives had died in the war. They lived for months on end in train stations and warehouses, scavenging for food in garbage cans. Ko kept up her disguise as a male to protect herself, and their mother relied on a small concealed sword. At first the bewildered Yoko complains about their hardships, but she gains courage and endurance as their trials continue. This fictionalized version of a real-life story about two strong girls is hard to put down.

Fantasy and Science Fiction

Alexander, Lloyd. *The Arkadians*. 1995. Hardcover: Dutton. Paperback: Puffin. Ages 11–14.

This frolic through Arkadia, a country much like mythological Greece, follows the fortunes of Lucian, a palace bean counter. After he discovers embezzlement by powerful officials, Lucian has to flee the palace of the fierce King Bromios with the help of the poet Fronto, who has been changed into a donkey. The two meet up with Joy-in-the-Dance, a young woman who leads and protects them as they travel to the land of the Lady of Wild Things to cure Fronto. Although Lucian is the central character, Joy-in-the-Dance is a close second, and is clearly the wiser and stronger of the two. On their way they meet different peoples and hear wondrous tales, including versions of Greek myths in which women look wise and men look foolish. Women once ruled in Arkadia and still hold important powers. The inevitable happy ending points to a future in which women will regain their power. This charming adventure combines storytelling and fights, calamities and romance, with a large dose of humor and an unusual tribute to women.

Dickinson, Peter. *Eva*. 1989. Paperback: Dell. Ages 12–14.

When Eva wakes in a hospital bed after a car accident, she is in for a shock that few human beings could face: Her brain has been transplanted to the body of a chimp. Only a masterful writer like Dickinson could handle such a strange plot, but he makes it believable and fascinating. Because she was raised interacting with chimpanzees, as part of her father's work, she survives the blow. As Eva adjusts to her new life, she finds her loyalty divided between humans and chimps, and begins to question how humans treat chimpanzees. Eva grows into a thoughtful, powerful leader who must make difficult choices. Set years in the future, the story raises issues about the environment and the nature of progress, but the issues never get in the way of the gripping story. An utterly original, thought-provoking novel.

Dickinson, Peter. *The Ropemaker*. 2001. Hardcover: Delacorte. Ages 11–14.

For twenty generations, the Valley where Tilja lives has been protected from outsiders. But now the magic that keeps out enemies is breaking down. When Tilja and her grandmother attend a gathering about the changes, only the old man Alnor and his grandson Tahl agree that something must be done. The four of them travel to find a magician in the far-off city of Talagh, encountering many dangers. Tilja discovers her unexpected power to ward off magic, without which their mission would be lost. But even with her growing ability to defeat evil sorcery, their world's safety hangs in the balance until the very end. This long, entrancing fantasy creates a strong heroine, a cast of compelling characters, and a new world imagined in full detail. Highly recommended.

Engdahl, Sylvia Louise. *Enchantress from the Stars.* **1970. Hardcover: Walker. Ages 12–14.**

Elana, a member of an advanced civilization, appears to be an enchantress to Georyn, who is a native of the planet Andrecia. Elana, her father, and the man Elana plans to marry are trying to save the planet from colonization by the Imperials, people from a civilization less sophisticated than Elana's but more advanced than Georyn's. The interaction among these three groups raises intriguing questions about what it means to "help" another group of people, and when such help may actually harm them. Elana ponders these questions as, despite her inexperience, she takes on a central role in their mission. She learns rapidly because she takes risks, even when it means disobeying her father's orders. Thrusting herself into dangerous situations, she must rely on her wits to get out. In the end, success is mixed with pain in this suspenseful adventure that is also a moving love story. A challenging book in which excitement, ideas, and romance will keep the reader captivated. A Newbery Honor Book.

Fletcher, Susan. *Dragon's Milk.* **1989. Paperback: Aladdin. Ages 12–14.**

Kaeldra knows she is different from the people of Elythia, where she lives with her foster family, but she doesn't realize that she is a dragon-sayer, one of those who can speak with dragons. While trying to save her younger sister from death, Kaeldra becomes attached to three young dragons and finds herself responsible for them. The four set off on a perilous journey, pursued by men intent on killing the dragons. Only through Kaeldra's courage and ingenuity do they reach their final destination. Kaeldra has undertaken her mission at great danger to herself and in the process learned to cherish her unique strengths. This fast-moving fantasy adventure is the first in The Dragon Chronicles series.

Griffin, Peni R. *Switching Well.* **1993. Hardcover: Mc-Elderry. Paperback: Puffin. Ages 11–14.**

In this outstanding time-travel book set in San Antonio, two girls switch places in time a hundred years apart. Amber is tired of urban life in 1991 and longs for a simpler, cleaner age. Ada finds the role of females in 1891 too constricting and wishes she were living in the future. Each gets her wish but finds the other time to be less wonderful than expected. Amber finds poverty and more restrictions than she's used to. Her forthright ways cause her to clash with the adults she meets, and she feels frustrated at every turn. Ada gets by only with the help of Violet, a strong and generous girl at Ada's 1991 foster home. Ada and especially Amber draw on reserves of courage and resourcefulness they didn't know they had, which lead to a heartwarming conclusion. Bound to make the reader contrast past and present roles of women and African-Americans, this is an unusually thoughtful and enjoyable story.

Jones, Diana Wynne. *Year of the Griffin.* **2000. Hardcover: Greenwillow. Paperback: Greenwillow. Ages 11–14.**

Elda, the griffin offspring of human parents who are both wizards, is thrilled to be attending the only wizard school in Derkholm. She immediately becomes part of a circle of students that includes a dwarf, a poverty-stricken prince, a pirate's daughter, an emperor's sister, and the brother of an emir.

Most of her friends have come to the school secretly to develop their magical powers. But when the inept faculty sends out fund-raising letters to the students' relatives, their secrets are revealed and havoc ensues. The six friends must use their newly learned magic to ward off the assassins, armies, and furious dwarves. Filled with action and magic, and peopled with a host of magical creatures and teenage human wizards, this fantasy is another page-turner from one of the best fantasy writers for young people. It is the sequel to *The Dark Lord of Derkholm* but can be enjoyed perfectly well on its own.

Mahy, Margaret. *The Changeover: A Supernatural Romance*. 1984. Paperback: Puffin. Ages 13–14.

Fourteen-year-old Laura Chant has known for some time that she has extrasensory powers, and she gets warnings about the future. When her three-year-old brother is imperiled by an evil male witch, she explores her powers in order to save him. With the help of three witches—an older boy named Sorenson, his mother, and his grandmother—Laura goes through a perilous rite of passage in hopes of becoming a witch herself. An engaging supernatural story in which a girl mines her inner strength to overcome evil.

McKinley, Robin. *Beauty: A Retelling of the Story of Beauty and the Beast*. 1978. Hardcover: Harper. Paperback: Trophy. Ages 11–14.

Beauty, whose real name is Honour, is an intelligent, courageous teenager in this retelling of the familiar fairy tale. While her family is rich, she studies intensely in hopes of attending the university, a rare dream for a woman. She enjoys translating Sophocles, but also loves horses. When the family falls on hard times, Beauty takes on tasks a boy would ordinarily do—chopping wood, gardening, and helping her brother-in-law, a blacksmith—and learns to fish and snare small animals. Known for her temper and stubborn will, she can't be talked out of her choice to go to the Beast in her father's place. At the Beast's magical castle, Beauty deals with her loneliness by horseback riding every day. Her relationship with the Beast develops through their love of literature and proceeds in an understated manner. Unlike the envious fairy-tale sisters, Beauty's are loving and respectful. The happy ending results less from magic than from Beauty's integrity and strong sense of self. A masterful retelling about an unconventional girl coming of age.

McKinley, Robin. *The Blue Sword*. 1982. Hardcover: Greenwillow. Paperback: Ace. Ages 10–14.

In this outstanding fantasy, Harry, a girl restless with her life in what seems to be a British colony, is kidnapped by the desert king Corlath. She discovers that she has magical powers when she trains with one of Corlath's soldiers and becomes an extraordinary swordswoman and rider. Corlath, who senses Harry will play a key role for his kingdom, gives her the blue sword of Aerin, a sword that only a woman can bear. Visions of Aerin, the female dragon-killer who is the main character in *The Hero and the Crown* (see following entry), appear to Harry and bolster her spirit. In a culture where women had once been warriors, Harry is welcomed as the damalur-sol, a lady hero. She plays a major role in a battle against a formidable enemy, leading an extraordinary group of women and men, including some experienced soldiers who willingly follow a woman into battle, a rare scenario in fiction or reality. One of the best books with strong heroines, this is definitely not to be missed. A Newbery Honor Book.

McKinley, Robin. *The Hero and the Crown*. 1984. Hardcover: Greenwillow. Paperback: Ace. Ages 10–14.

In this prequel to *The Blue Sword*, another extraordinary heroine makes a place for herself in an unfriendly world through her courage and strength. Aerin is the daughter of the king of Damar, but the Damarians fear her because they believed her mother was a witch. Her only real friend is her cousin Tor, heir to the throne, who teaches her the skills of hunting, fishing, riding, and swordplay. After Aerin rehabilitates her father's injured war horse Talat and learns to ride him without stirrups and reins, Talat and Aerin start to fight small dragons that plague the kingdom. But when they meet a fearsomely large dragon, Aerin the Dragon-Killer barely survives. Her hero's welcome back to the city honors her as no woman in recent history had been honored. In her next challenge, which looks even more hopeless, she faces an evil sorcerer with the help of the Blue Sword, a weapon of great magic. A magnificent story, this Newbery Medal winner well deserves its many fans.

Nix, Garth. *Sabriel*. 1996. Hardcover: Harper. Paperback: Harper. Ages 12–14.

In this complex fantasy, a teenage girl named Sabriel inherits a powerful magic position from her father, Abhorsen. Although born in the magic Old Kingdom, Sabriel has lived at a girls' boarding school in a nearby more modern country where magic is weak. Sabriel's own magic and that of Abhorsen is necromancy, the ability to go into the kingdom of the dead. Sabriel is determined to rescue her father from the dead, but journeying into the Old Kingdom, she realizes that her quest is a larger one. A powerful force from the Dead is destroying the Old Kingdom, and Sabriel joins forces with a mysterious man from the past and a magical cat to try to defeat it. Although difficult to follow at times, the fantasy pulls the reader in and builds to a gripping climax. Followed by *Lirael*.

Pattou, Edith. *Fire Arrow: The Second Song of Eirren*. 1998. Hardcover: Harcourt. Paperback: Voyager. Ages 12–14.

In this long fantasy, the main character, Brie, travels to a new country where she defeats a fearful enemy. She starts her journey planning to avenge her father, who was slain in her presence when she was a child. Her close friend Collun believes that seeking revenge will harm her, but she ignores his advice. First, a message redirects her path to her uncle's home, where Brie finds a magic arrow that will guide her destiny. On her extended journey, she meets friendly fairies, powerful sorcerers, cruel goat-men, a stalwart female storyteller, and finally, her unknown enemy from long ago. She leads an army to battle and discovers the true power of her fire arrow. Although this is the second book in a trilogy that began with *Hero's Song*, in which Collun is the main character, readers will find it a satisfying story without having read the first book.

Peck, Richard. *Ghosts I Have Been*. 1977. Paperback: Dell. Ages 11–13.

Nothing fazes Blossom Culp, as she'll tell you herself. She is used to making her own way in the world and doesn't let living on the wrong side of the tracks stop her. It's 1914, so folks place a big premium on gentility, but Blossom can't afford it: "To turn me ladylike might have rendered me useless and possibly ornamental. Then I would not be able to fend for myself." Blossom thrives on excitement and creates it herself when necessary, such as the time she dresses as a ghost and scares a gang of boys. Ghosts play a bigger role when she discovers that she has inherited her mother's gift of Second Sight and finds herself in a trance aboard the *Titanic*—while it is sinking. Blossom, who tells the story in her wonderfully original voice, is wry and shrewd. She gets the most out of life and sometimes gets the good fortune she deserves.

Blossom first appears in *The Ghost Belonged to Me*, which focuses on another character. She continues her adventures in *The Dreadful Future of Blossom Culp* and *Blossom Culp and the Sleep of Death*.

Pierce, Tamora. *Alanna: The First Adventure*. 1983. Hardcover: Atheneum. Paperback: Random House. Ages 11–13.

Eleven-year-old Alanna follows the time-honored tradition of disguising herself as a boy to seek adventure. She goes to the king's castle to train as a knight, a task made harder because she is smaller than the boys she learns with. As her first challenge she fights a bully who has chosen her as his favorite target; to prepare she practices fighting techniques for hours on end. The bout is a nasty one, described in detail, but Alanna triumphs and goes on to her next challenge, drawing on her inner strength and her magical powers of healing to try to save a dying friend. Her final test of strength comes in a sword fight with an evil magical opponent. No fictional boy has ever been more determined than Alanna to master the fighting arts and become an outstanding knight. The other three books in the Song of the Lioness series about this heroic fighter are *In the Hand of the Goddess*, *The Woman Who Rides Like a Man*, and *The Lioness Rampant*.

Pierce, Tamora. *Wild Magic*. 1992. Hardcover: Atheneum. Paperback: Random House. Ages 11–14.

Few novels offer such strong roles to females as this fantasy series does. Daine, the main character, is an unsurpassed archer and outdoorswoman who can communicate with animals through magic. She works for a woman who is in charge of horses for a group of male and female champions led by the country's queen. Alanna, a female knight from Pierce's Song of the Lioness series, also figures in the story. Encouraged by these strong women and a male mage, Daine expands her magical powers and learns to believe in herself. After playing a key role against an invasion of evil creatures, Daine finds a place where she belongs among people who believe in her and in the equality of men and women. Original and exciting. Daine tests her increasingly strong magical abilities in *Wolf-Speaker*, *The Emperor Mage*, and *The Realms of the Gods*.

Pullman, Philip. *The Golden Compass*. 1996. Hardcover: Knopf. Ages 11–14.

This complex four-hundred-page fantasy follows the quest of Lyra Belacqua and her daemon Pantalaimon, the animal companion who is as close to her as her own soul. Lyra has grown up in a college in Oxford, in a world only partly similar to ours. She has run wild under the lenient care of the professors, playing with servants' children, wandering the streets of Oxford, and climbing around the college roofs. Her bold-spirited escapades have prepared her for the adventure she undertakes to free her imprisoned father and find her friend, who has been kidnapped along with many other children. From the very start, Lyra enjoys taking risks and mastering her fears. She uses her keen intelligence to plan strategies against the many enemies she meets and finds help on the way from Gypsies, witches, other children, and a fierce armored bear. Her quest takes her to the brutally cold North and a surprising, inconclusive climax. Lyra is a daring heroine on a journey more important than even she understands. Lyra plays a less important role in the sequel *The Subtle Knife* and then returns to center stage in *The Amber Spyglass*.

Thompson, Kate. *Switchers*. 1998. Hardcover: Hyperion. Paperback: Hyperion. Ages 11–14.

In this creative fantasy, thirteen-year-old Tess enjoys the fact that she can switch to be any animal when she wants, but is lonely being the only Switcher she knows. When she firsts meets Kevin, another Switcher, he seems obnoxious and skittish. Even once she likes him, she doesn't want to get involved in his mission, which is unclear even to him. It is related, though, to the incredibly cold weather in Ireland—their home—and elsewhere around the globe. Reluctantly Tess agrees to go with Kevin to see if they can fight against the cause of the cold. The two head north as birds, dolphins, whales, and polar bears to combat huge monsters recently awakened, who are causing the cold. Both teenagers prove brave and tenacious, and share in the brainstorming that leads to several unexpected, wonderful twists in the plot. Highly original and suspenseful, this is the first of a trilogy of well-written page-turners about Tess.

Biography and Nonfiction

Leaders and Activists

Beals, Melba Pattillo. *Warriors Don't Cry*. 1995 abridged edition. Paperback: Pocket. Ages 13–14.

This painful autobiography tells about a girl and her family who rank among the bravest of all Americans. In 1957, fifteen-year-old Melba Pattillo was one of the nine African-American students to integrate Central High School in Little Rock, Arkansas. In a voice remarkably lacking in self-pity, Beals tells of the horrors that awaited the nine inside and outside the doors of Central High: viciously screaming adults, endless physical and verbal attacks by other students, cruel telephone calls and threats. Beals relied on her mother and grandmother for the emotional and spiritual support they provided even as they themselves suffered. Worried about threats, Beals's grandmother, an expert shot, sat up nights with a rifle across her lap. She convinced her granddaughter to view herself as a warrior: "You're a warrior on the battlefield for your Lord. . . . The women of this family don't break down in the face of trouble." Beals's mother, one of the first blacks to integrate the University of Alabama, almost lost her teaching job in another district because the school board was against integration. Truly a modern hero, Melba Beals faced a battlefield that called for more courage than any teenager should have to summon. She tells her story without bitterness, in well-crafted prose. The book will hook readers with its suspense, stir their anger and shame, and probably make them cry. Don't miss it.

Bober, Natalie S. *Abigail Adams: Witness to a Revolution.* 1995. Hardcover: Atheneum. Paperback: Aladdin. Ages 11–14.

Abigail Adams's wit and intelligence come through clearly in this biography, thanks to extensive use of her letters. Quotations from her correspondence are woven into the text almost as if they are dialogue. As the wife of John Adams, who was often gone for months and sometimes years, Abigail Adams used her managerial skills to run their farm and a large household. She made financial decisions, including stock investments she kept secret from her husband that were crucial for their retirement. She believed in the intelligence of women and the need to educate them; she was outspoken and politically shrewd. She urged her husband to institute legal rights for women, to no avail. Although this lively biography glosses over her faults, it skillfully conveys an exciting historical time and the spirit of an important American woman.

Brooks, Polly Schoyer. *Beyond the Myth: The Story of Joan of Arc.* 1990. Paperback: Houghton. Ages 11–14.

Joan of Arc lived from 1412 to 1431, and in that short time helped the king of France get rightfully crowned. Raised in a small village, Joan could neither read nor write, yet this biography shows her to be articulate and intelligent beyond her years. She said that, starting at age thirteen, she heard voices of saints who directed her to help King Charles. She persisted despite enormous resistance, led men to battle, suffered wounds, and paved the way for the king's coronation. Captured by the enemy, she endured prison and a mockery of a trial, and was burned to death. Her independent spirit infuriated the men in power, who objected among other things to her wearing men's clothes and armor. But the people of France ultimately cleared her name of heresy and she was declared a saint. An excellent biography of a young woman who changed history.

Fireside, Bryna J. *Is There a Woman in the House . . . or Senate?* **1994. Hardcover: Albert Whitman. Ages 11–14.**

This is a valuable book that brings to life a neglected area of American history: women who are or have been in the U.S. Congress. First of these remarkable women is Jeannette Rankin, the first woman elected to Congress in 1917, before women could even vote in some states. Six Democrats and four Republicans are discussed with details about their childhood and their political careers, illustrated with black-and-white photographs. All have made an impact and served as advocates for women, while dealing with obstacles men in office do not face. The inspiring stories demonstrate that a woman can succeed in politics. As Barbara Mikulski said when elected as a Senator from Maryland, she had proved it was possible for "someone who is not male, wealthy, or possessed of good looks, who is fiercely outspoken, to take a place among the wealthy white males who traditionally dominate the Senate." That sums up the spirit of this fascinating volume.

Fradin, Dennis Brindell, and Judith Bloom Fradin. *Ida B. Wells: Mother of the Civil Rights Movement.* **2000. Hardcover: Clarion. Ages 12–14.**

This biography of the courageous Ida B. Wells describes in detail her crusade against lynching in the late 1800s and early 1900s, with painful stories of innocent people killed and explicit photographs of lynchings. Born a slave, Wells became a newspaper writer and public speaker, using both roles to promote civil rights and end lynching. Throughout her life, she fought injustice. As a young woman, she sued the Chesapeake and Ohio Railroad for forcing her out of the Ladies' Coach and putting her in the "Colored" car. She initially won the suit in 1884 but lost on appeal. As the years went on, she also became a strong advocate for women's right to vote. Quotations from her writings, and photographs and other visual materials from the time, give the biography a sense of immediacy. Ida B. Wells's willingness to speak her mind and bear witness to the truth regardless of dangerous consequences makes hers an inspiring life story.

Freedman, Russell. *Eleanor Roosevelt: A Life of Discovery*. 1993. Hardcover: Clarion. Paperback: Houghton. Ages 11–14.

This compelling biography covers Eleanor Roosevelt's life from childhood through old age. Written in an inviting manner and beautifully illustrated with photographs, it emphasizes her many accomplishments, including her advocacy for women's rights. Roosevelt made her mark as an outstanding woman in many ways: her writing and speaking, her influence on the nation through her husband, her service to the United Nations, and her abiding concern for social justice and world peace. As the biography shows, she came into her own in middle age, blossoming from a shy woman into a self-confident one. "You must do the thing you think you cannot do," she once said, and she lived her life according to those words. In 1943 she traveled twenty-three thousand miles in cramped military vehicles to visit American servicemen in the Pacific. Later in life she traveled around the world many times in her quest to learn more and advance world peace. Eleanor Roosevelt ranks among the great women of all time, and this exemplary biography makes it a pleasure to read about her. The photographs that illustrate the text are supplemented by an additional fifteen pages of photos at the end of the book, followed by information on visiting sites related to her life; a bibliographic essay; and an extensive index. Highly recommended. A Newbery Honor Book.

Fritz, Jean. *Harriet Beecher Stowe and the Beecher Preachers*. 1994. Hardcover: Putnam. Paperback: Paper Star. Ages 12–14.

Harriet Beecher Stowe's novel *Uncle Tom's Cabin* electrified the United States and helped bring about the Civil War. This excellent biography, illustrated with black-and-white photographs, puts Stowe in the context of her family, a group of powerful New England preachers. Her father, a famous minister, raised his sons to follow in his footsteps and cultivated the same spirit in his daughters, even though he believed women belonged in the home. Harriet Beecher Stowe raised six children, writing most of those years and providing much of the family income. Thanks to her influential novels, she met with Abraham Lincoln and was friends with important abolitionists. Hers is the story of an intelligent, hardworking woman who used two of the few paths open to women, writing and public speaking, to make a vital difference in her country.

McKissack, Patricia C., and Fredrick McKissack. *Sojourner Truth: Ain't I a Woman?* 1992. Hardcover: Scholastic. Paperback: Scholastic. Ages 10–13.

This well-written biography draws on Sojourner Truth's writings and speeches, combining them with facts about her life and apt illustrations. She was an extraordinary woman who was determined to get her rights and to help others obtain theirs. She was one of the first black women in the country to win a court case, suing when her son was sold illegally out of state. The authors acknowledge her mistakes, such as trusting some fraudulent religious schemers, but dwell on her strengths. Sojourner Truth was best known as a superlative speaker who advocated abolition and women's rights. Famous in her lifetime, she addressed senators and met with presidents. The story of how she rose out of slavery to become an influential activist is fascinating and inspiring.

Meltzer, Milton. *Ten Queens: Portraits of Women of Power.* **Illustrated by Bethanne Andersen. 1998. Hardcover: Dutton. Ages 10–14.**

This large, elegant book introduces ten important rulers in history from the biblical Esther to Catherine the Great, illustrated with full-page portraits and many smaller paintings. Each essay describes what is known of the monarch's childhood and rise to power, with her exploits and governing experiences set in historical context. The author does not shy away from the negative deeds, such as Queen Isabel's role in persecuting Jews during the Inquisition. Each chapter includes a map that defines the area the woman ruled, and a bibliography of sources. Lesser-known women such as Boudicca and Zenobia take their places next to famous leaders such as Eleanor of Aquitaine, Isabel of Spain, and Elizabeth I of England.

Parks, Rosa, with Jim Haskins. *Rosa Parks: My Story.* **1992. Hardcover: Dial. Paperback: Puffin. Ages 11–14.**

Rosa Parks sets the record straight in her own account of her role in the Montgomery Bus Boycott, an event distorted by history. Legend has it that she was an old woman who was simply too tired to give up her seat near the front of the bus. In fact, she was forty-two, sitting in the black section, and she wasn't especially tired: "No, the only tired I was, was tired of giving in." She was already active in the civil rights movement, secretary of the local NAACP, and well-informed about the legal implications of her actions. Rosa Parks's own words show her to be an intelligent, thoughtful, calm, private woman with a subtle sense of humor. She describes her childhood in segregated Alabama, her education and jobs, and her role in the civil rights movement. It is a pleasure to read her clear, straightforward account of what she has done and seen, and what she thinks about it. A graceful autobiography.

Soto, Gary. *Jessie De La Cruz: A Profile of a United Farm Worker*. 2000. Hardcover: Persea. Ages 13–14.

Jessie De La Cruz was the first woman to work as an organizer for the United Farm Workers of America, the union of migrant workers started by Cesar Chavez. In this short biography, readers learn about De La Cruz's work for the movement, *la causa*, but also about her life as a migrant worker since childhood. Soto, a well-known writer for young people, paints vivid pictures of the poverty and back-breaking work De La Cruz and her family did on California farms for appallingly low wages. As Jessie De La Cruz and her husband raised their children, they also dedicated themselves to making conditions better for their fellow workers. This commitment proved dangerous especially during strikes because of angry growers, who were sometimes violent, and the law enforcement officials who sided with the growers. Jessie De La Cruz comes across as a persuasive, hard-working advocate for justice who persisted in the face of discouraging setbacks.

Thomas, Jane Resh. *Behind the Mask: The Life of Queen Elizabeth I*. 1998. Hardcover: Clarion. Ages 13–14.

Queen Elizabeth I ruled longer than any other British monarch before her, man or woman. This lucid biography presents the intricate facts of her life and her political career in a smooth, readable style. It gives the reader enough historical background to make sense of her life, with special attention to the queen's powerful father, King Henry VIII. Details of everyday life are woven into the text, building a picture of her households, clothing, food, entertainment, and religious practices. Occasional prints and a series of reproductions of her portraits add to the picture. The biography focuses on her extraordinary powers as a ruler and diplomat, and how she dealt with the dangers and intrigues that surrounded her. Her faults are clearly presented, but they pale beside her enormous intelligence and skills. An accessible portrait of one of the most powerful women of all time.

Professionals and Businesswomen

Bayer, Linda. *Ruth Bader Ginsburg*. 2000. Hardcover: Chelsea House. Paperback: Chelsea House. Ages 12–14.

Ruth Bader Ginsburg made history as the second woman appointed to the U.S. Supreme Court. Her road to that high office was that of a pioneer, breaking new ground as a woman in the field of law and working toward equal rights for all women. When she entered Harvard Law School in 1956, she was one of nine women in a class of five hundred. Her impressive intelligence and hard work earned her a place on the prestigious law review, but when she graduated, after transferring to Columbia Law School and tying for first in her class, no law firm would hire her, an experience shared by fellow justice on the Supreme Court, Sandra Day O'Connor. Ginsburg's perseverance led to a career teaching law school and trying cases that affected women's rights for the ACLU. Her dedication to justice comes across in this readable, well-written biography of one of the great women of our time.

Briggs, Carole S. *Women in Space*. 1999 revised edition. Hardcover: Lerner. Ages 9–14.

Women have made enormous strides over the last few decades in securing their place in space exploration. Eleven women are highlighted in this useful volume, which also gives basic history about NASA and, to a lesser extent, space programs in other countries. After an overview, the book looks first at three female pioneers: Valentina Tereshkova, a Soviet who became the first woman in space in 1963; Sally Ride, the first American woman in space, in 1983; and Svetlana Savitskaya, also from the Soviet Union, the first woman to walk in space. With the advent of the space shuttle and space stations, astronauts gained a wider range of duties, as shown in profiles of four women, including Mae Jemison, the first black woman in space. Another chapter discusses pilots such as Eileen Collins, the first woman to pilot a space shuttle. The profiles give brief details about their personal lives but focus mainly on these women's important roles in space exploration.

Bundles, A'Lelia Perry. *Madam C. J. Walker*. 1991. Hardcover: Chelsea House. Paperback: Chelsea House. Ages 12–14.

This attractive biography, illustrated with many photographs, tells the memorable story of Madam C. J. Walker, America's first black female millionaire. Born Sarah Breedlove, the daughter of former slaves, she was a self-made businesswoman who invented and sold her own hair products door-to-door and through mail order. She excelled at marketing her products, shrewdly analyzing what customers wanted and training her workers to provide it. Known for her popular speeches urging black women to get into business for themselves, Madam C. J. Walker, as she came to be called, successfully extended her business around the country, ignoring the doubts of her husband and male advisors. Written by her great-great-granddaughter, this biography paints a glowing picture of Walker's impressive rags-to-riches story.

Gorrell, Gena K. *Heart and Soul: The Story of Florence Nightingale.* **2000. Hardcover: Tundra. Ages 11–14.**

Known as "The Lady with the Lamp," Florence Nightingale was not the gentle soul that many people picture when they hear her name. As this solid biography reveals, Nightingale was enormously intelligent, hard-working, and persistent, once she found her calling. A young woman from a wealthy family, she spent her early years frustrated at the limitations placed on women in nineteenth-century England, even those as educated as she was. But eventually she wore down her proper family and started to train as a nurse. Nursing had a reputation in England as a job of alcoholics and women of low character, a reputation transformed by Nightingale in her lifetime. She gained a place in the heart of the British public by her unrelenting service to soldiers in Crimea, then used her popularity and many contacts to establish nursing schools, reform medicine in the military, and improve life in British colonies such as India. Her leadership abilities were phenomenal, she wrote voluminously, and she changed the world for the better. This balanced biography, which acknowledges her more difficult side, is enjoyable to read as well as highly informative.

Karnes, Frances A., and Suzanne M. Bean. *Girls & Young Women Entrepreneurs: True Stories about Starting and Running a Business.* **1997. Paperback: Free Spirit. Ages 9–14.**

One in a fine series of three books about successful girls and young women, this unusual volume describes successful businesses and nonprofits, most of which were started by teenage girls. Each sketch opens with a general description of the girl and a black-and-white photograph, followed by an essay in the girl's voice about her enterprise. One girl, who opened a small store to sell goods for people with disabilities, describes her planning and success, based in part on her listening to her customers. Two sisters have turned their hobby of learning magic tricks into a small business entertaining at parties and elsewhere. A Girl Scout troop that needed to raise money for a trip began making and selling crafts. In each essay, the entrepreneurs discuss strategies, setbacks, and successes, and give practical advice. An appendix expands on the advice on how to start a business and includes directions for a business plan. A must-read for future businesswomen.

Pasachoff, Naomi. *Frances Perkins: Champion of the New Deal.* **1999. Hardcover: Oxford. Ages 12–14.**

"Every man and woman who works at a living wage, under safe conditions, for reasonable hours, or who is protected by unemployment insurance or Social Security, is her debtor," said a cabinet member about Frances Perkins. One of the great social reformers of the twentieth century, Perkins was the first woman to be a member of the president's cabinet, serving as Secretary of Labor from 1933 to 1945. This cogent biography focuses on her professional accomplishments, which were many, with only a passing glimpse into her personal life, which she kept very private. She began her work in New York where she advocated safer factories and better working conditions. Her purpose—to make life better and safer for the workers of America—never wavered. She was vital to instituting enduring measures during Roosevelt's New Deal that changed the workplace and our society.

Rosen, Dorothy Schack. *A Fire in Her Bones: The Story of Mary Lyon.* **1995. Hardcover: Carolrhoda. Ages 11–14.**

Mary Lyon, who founded Mount Holyoke Seminary for women in 1837, was a brilliant student and an educational pioneer. She made education her highest priority, leaving home as a child to attend school. Enrolled at Sanderson Academy at eighteen, Lyon stunned her teacher and fellow students by memorizing an entire Latin grammar over one weekend. She resolved to establish an affordable school for training female teachers, although many criticized her goal as inappropriate for women. She didn't live to see her goal of making Mount Holyoke a college, but her work has lived on after her. This chronological retelling of her life incorporates information about historical conditions for women and the history of education. Another strong woman whose story deserves to be heard.

Rubin, Susan Goldman. *Margaret Bourke-White: Her Pictures Were Her Life.* **Photographs by Margaret Bourke-White. 1999. Hardcover: Abrams. Ages 11–14.**

Margaret Bourke-White, who forged new paths in her field, led a remarkably exciting life as a photographer. She pioneered industrial photography, taking stunning black-and-white pictures of bridges, factories, steel mills, and building sites. She endured any discomfort, and she risked her life many times to get important photographs, such as when she went on bombing missions during World War II and refused to take shelter in Moscow as the Germans bombed it. As a result of her courage and her ability to persuade famous people to be photographed, she took some of the most dramatic and influential photographs of her time. This excellent biography incorporates a well-chosen array of her photographs to tell the story of her life, concentrating on her achievements as a photographer rather than her personal life. Highly recommended.

Wheaton, Elizabeth. *Myra Bradwell: First Woman Lawyer*. 1997. Hardcover: Morgan Reynolds. Ages 10–14.

Although Myra Bradwell gained official recognition as a lawyer only shortly before she died, she made an enormous impact on the legal world years earlier. With her attorney husband, she started a legal press that printed law books and a newspaper that greatly influenced the profession. The newspaper gave Bradwell a widely read outlet for her opinions, including her support of women's suffrage and other liberal causes. Born to an abolitionist family in 1831, she spent most of her adult life in Chicago and took an active role in civic affairs, acting as one of the organizers of the 1893 World's Columbian Exposition. Her leadership skills and her energy level were extraordinary. She fought and lobbied, often successfully, to change laws to improve life for women and other groups that lacked power. This straightforward biography tells her life story and accomplishments chronologically, ending with her long-hoped-for official recognition as a lawyer; since it was made retroactive to the time she applied, it made her the first woman lawyer in the country.

Whitelaw, Nancy. *Clara Barton: Civil War Nurse*. 1997. Hardcover: Enslow. Ages 10–14.

Clara Barton pioneered the role of nurses in this country and founded the American Red Cross. Although she spent years as a teacher, it didn't fulfill her ambitions. When the Civil War started, she was working in Washington, D.C., and got involved in volunteer efforts to help the soldiers. She traveled to battlefields in a time when many thought it a scandalous act for a single woman. She brought supplies, nursed the sick, and comforted the dying, earning the title Angel of the Battlefield. She came close to dying more than once as she rescued soldiers in the midst of battle. After the war Barton provided a much-needed service by locating prisoners of war, identifying the dead, and notifying their families. On a trip to Europe, she saw the work of the Red Cross there and determined to start a similar organization in the United States. She succeeded, expanded its role, and spearheaded the organization for many years. A woman of impressive organizational skills and leadership, Clara Barton overcame biases against women to accomplish her enduring goals.

Scientists and Inventors

Baker, Beth. *Sylvia Earle: Guardian of the Sea.* 2001. Hardcover: Lerner. Ages 10–14.

Marine biologist Sylvia Earle has made a strong impact on her field through her work and the attention it has drawn. She has spent more than six thousand hours underwater, including two weeks as the head of an underwater expedition of female scientists. She has pioneered many of the technologies for spending time underwater, most of them new since she entered the field. She has even been part owner of a company to develop such technologies. This readable biography, illustrated by many photographs of Earle at work, describes the childhood influences that led to her interest in the ocean and tracks her impressive career and travels. It concludes by highlighting Earle's work to preserve the environment and listing useful resources on that topic.

Barron, Rachel Stiffler. *Lise Meitner: Discoverer of Nuclear Fission.* 2000. Hardcover: Morgan Reynolds. Ages 13–14.

"I love physics with all my heart. I can hardly imagine it not being part of my life," wrote Lise Meitner to a friend around 1905, when she was in her late twenties. Meitner had no way of knowing then how close Hitler would come to depriving her of her work. Born and raised in Austria, Meitner moved to Germany to pursue her career as a physicist, an unusual role for a woman then. She became the first female professor in Germany, and worked primarily with a chemist named Otto Hahn. Together they isolated a new radioactive element, the ninety-first element in the periodic table. In 1938, when Nazi Germany became too dangerous for Meitner, who was Jewish, she fled to Sweden. She and Hahn had been in the midst of experiments that led to the discovery of nuclear fission. Despite her major contribution to the discovery, Hahn claimed it as his own and so received the Nobel Prize in chemistry. Despite this betrayal, Meitner won many other awards and widespread recognition among her colleagues. This short biography tells the dramatic story well, introducing a major scientist of the twentieth century.

Fine, Edith Hope. *Barbara McClintock: Nobel Prize Geneticist.* 1998. Hardcover: Enslow. Ages 12–14.

American geneticist Barbara McClintock was the third woman to win an unshared Nobel Prize in science, and the first to do so in physiology or medicine. She had devoted her professional life to studying genetics, following the genetic patterns of maize year after year, and won her Nobel Prize when she was eighty-one. Her early research made a big impact on her field, an unusual success for a woman in genetics, but for many years some in her field doubted or minimized her findings. Unable to secure a research professorship because she was female, McClintock nevertheless found a way to pursue her work at a research institution. This biography conveys her intense enjoyment of her work through many quotes from McClintock and her friends. In reflecting on her decades of scientific research, McClintock made a statement that should inspire future scientists: "I've had such a great time. I can't imagine having a better life."

Mark, Joan. *Margaret Mead: Coming of Age in America*. 1999. Hardcover: Oxford University Press. Ages 13–14.

At age seventy-four, Margaret Mead, who helped pioneer the field of anthropology, served as president of the American Association for the Advancement of Science, an important force in the science world, and was elected to the National Academy of Science, a great honor. After she died in 1978, she was given the Presidential Medal of Freedom, the highest civilian honor. When she was twenty-four, Mead did field work in the South Pacific, then wrote the immensely popular book *Coming of Age in Samoa*, mainly about adolescent girls in that country. It was the first of the many books that, in conjunction with her frequent public speaking, made her famous. This enjoyable biography combines Mead's personal life, complicated by several marriages, and her professional accomplishments. It treats her work even-handedly, mentioning criticisms, mostly late in Mead's career, about her research and conclusions. Mead's powerful personality and her deep commitment to her field are palpable and inspiring.

Stille, Darlene R. *Extraordinary Women Scientists*. 1995. Paperback: Children's Press. Ages 11–14.

This is an inspiring array of fifty women scientists from the nineteenth and twentieth centuries. Arranged alphabetically, the biographical sketches describe a wide range of work from anthropology to astronomy to medicine. The women are from all parts of the world, with a majority from Europe and the United States. The sketches, which are two to six pages, speak briefly of their childhoods and personal lives, and include at least one black-and-white photograph. Strikingly, many of them were helped by, or themselves helped, other women in their fields; many were products of women's colleges. During their extraordinary careers, many won Nobel Prizes and other major honors, overcoming strong biases against women. Well written, with an attractive design, this is an exemplary introduction to fifty eminent scientists. A companion volume is *Extraordinary Women of Medicine*.

Vare, Ethlie Ann, and Greg Ptacek. *Women Inventors and Their Discoveries*. 1993. Hardcover: Oliver Press. Ages 11–14.

Ten American women inventors are profiled in this readable volume, arranged chronologically. It opens with Elizabeth Lucas Pinckney, an eighteenth-century Southerner who developed the commercial crop of indigo that sustained the South Carolina economy for thirty years. The final entry is Stephanie Kwolek, a Du Pont chemist who patented Kevlar, a synthetic fiber five times stronger than steel. Other women described invented signal flares for military use, the first modern-day cookbook, Liquid Paper, and more. The women were scientists, a public health doctor, a secretary, and a naval officer. One inventor, Ruth Handler, was responsible both for the Barbie doll and a well-designed artificial breast called Nearly Me. All faced obstacles, often sexism, but they persisted, put in long hours, and reaped the rewards of their efforts.

Wadsworth, Ginger. *Rachel Carson: Voice for the Earth.* **1992. Hardcover: Lerner. Ages 11–14.**

This well-written biography traces the origins of Rachel Carson's ability to write in a powerful, beautiful way about nature. Her books helped prompt the government's role in preserving the environment, specifically through the Environmental Protection Agency. She studied biology in college and had a successful career with the U.S. Bureau of Fisheries. When she wasn't at work, she wrote bestselling books about the ocean, which garnered her many honors, some never previously given to women. Her most influential book, *Silent Spring*, published in 1962, took unusual courage to write because the subject of dangerous pesticides drew hostile reactions from large corporations. A quiet, modest woman who loved nature and her extended family, Carson combined talent, hard work, and integrity to make a lasting difference.

Yount, Lisa. *Contemporary Women Scientists.* **1994. Hardcover: Facts on File. Ages 12–14.**

This collective biography discusses ten twentieth-century scientists, seven of whom are still living and working. A biographical sketch describes each woman's work and career, with some words about how her professional life affected her personal life. A chronology and list of further reading follows each sketch, while photographs and diagrams in the text add more information. The women's fields vary from medicine to physics to astronomy; their successes include more than one Nobel Prize and a host of other prestigious awards. Readers may recognize some of them, such as shark expert Eugenie Clark and Navy Rear Admiral Grace Murray Hopper, but the majority are not well know. Regardless of their fields or fame, they all convey the message that, in one woman's words, science is "incredibly great fun."

Women in the Arts

Drucker, Malka. *Frida Kahlo.* **1991. Paperback: University of New Mexico Press. Ages 13–14.**

Frida Kahlo, perhaps Mexico's most renowned painter, led a life full of tragedy and excitement. This lively biography describes her life and her artwork, interweaving personal details, descriptions of paintings, and other information about her life as an artist. Born in 1907, Kahlo grew up outside of Mexico City and went to school in the city when she was fourteen. When she was eighteen, Kahlo was in a terrible accident. She recovered but experienced pain for the rest of her life. During her recovery she began to paint. Several years later she married Diego Rivera, the famous muralist; their marriage was a tumultuous one. They traveled often to the United States, and Kahlo was increasingly recognized as an outstanding painter. Readers may want to read this with a volume of Kahlo's paintings on hand, since this has only a handful of color reproductions. But Kahlo's story is a fascinating one, even without more examples of her work, and well worth reading.

Freedman, Russell. *Martha Graham: A Dancer's Life.* **1998. Hardcover: Clarion. Ages 11–14.**

Elegant black-and-white photographs add an extraordinary dimension to this biography of one of the great modern dancers. After a short first chapter that extols Graham's accomplishment and spirit, the text turns to her childhood and quickly to her interest in dance that began in 1911 when she was sixteen. She attended a dance performance by Ruth St. Denis, who danced barefoot in exotic costumes, and, Graham said, "From that moment on, my fate was sealed." She studied with St. Denis and her husband Ted Shawn, and danced in their troupe. After moving to New York City, Graham formed her own troupe, began to choreograph, and evolved her own personal style of dance. This well-written biography discusses her career in detail, set in the context of dance history, with many photographs of her in dance costumes and poses. It also offers information about her personal life, noting both her strengths and weaknesses. Even readers without a strong interest in dance may be entranced by the power of Graham's personality and dreams.

Lazo, Caroline. *Alice Walker: Freedom Writer*. 2000. Hardcover: Lerner. Ages 10–13.

Alice Walker's own words appear often in this solid biography, giving it an immediacy that will draw in readers. The book documents Walker's early life and the importance of her mother's strength and support. It also emphasizes Walker's involvement in the civil rights movement and its effect on her writing and world view. From as early as her college days, Walker's writing impressed those in the literary world. Muriel Rukeyser, a professor and poet, helped her find a publisher for her first poetry collection, and renowned poet Langston Hughes included her first short story in an anthology. Walker's third novel, *The Color Purple*, won the Pulitzer Prize—the first awarded to a black woman—the American Book Award, and was made into an award-winning movie. The biography discusses Walker's political activism and her personal life, but focuses mainly on her outstanding contributions as a writer.

Lyons, Mary E. *Sorrow's Kitchen: The Life and Folklore of Zora Neale Hurston*. 1990. Paperback: Aladdin. Ages 12–14.

The author combines a lively, biographical narrative with

Hurston's own writings to portray this trailblazing black woman. Hurston wrote seven books as well as short stories, plays, and essays. She was the first black Southerner to collect folklore from her own subculture, providing an invaluable resource for the future. Samples are given from the folktales she collected and from the voodoo traditions she studied. Hurston's life was both exciting and fraught with problems. She struggled with poverty as a child and again as an adult; she died poor and was buried in an unmarked grave. In 1989, writer Alice Walker erected a stone marker at Hurston's grave in Florida, with the epitaph "A Genius of the South." In recent years, Hurston's works have been reprinted and gained recognition. Hers was a truly original life, well worth reading about.

Meyer, Susan E. *Mary Cassatt*. 1990. Hardcover: Abrams. Ages 11–14.

This lovely biography uses many full-page color reproductions to illustrate Mary Cassatt's work. The conversational text combines information about her life with commentary on her artwork, setting her accomplishments in the context of the late nineteenth and early twentieth century when few women earned their living as artists. Cassatt had conventional manners but also unconventional artistic ambition. One of her greatest contributions to the future was persuading wealthy friends and relatives to invest in paintings, many from the Impressionists, that are now a part of important museum collections. A beautifully designed book that pays tribute to an incomparable artist.

Orgill, Roxane. *Shout, Sister, Shout! Ten Girl Singers Who Shaped a Century*. 2001. Hardcover: McElderry. Ages 13–14.

Music critic Orgill has chosen ten singers who each

capture the spirit of music during a decade of the twentieth century. Each chapter describes one of the women, her background, how she pursued her singing career, and the impact that she made. The chapters, less successfully, also try to sum up each decade's current events and technological advances in music. Starting with Sophie Tucker and ending with Lucinda Williams, the collective biography also covers Ma Rainey, Bessie Smith, Ethel Merman, Judy Garland, Anita O'Day, Joan Baez, Bette Midler, and Madonna. While their personal lives were often tragic, all the women worked strenuously at their careers and attained impressive financial as well as professional success.

Partridge, Elizabeth. *Restless Spirit: The Life and Work of Dorothea Lange*. 1998. Hardcover: Viking. Paperback: Puffin. Ages 12–14.

Beautifully reproduced black-and-white photographs, most of them by Lange, combine with strong writing and thorough research to create an outstanding biography about a photographer dedicated to her work. The many large photographs are well-integrated into the text, which encompasses Lange's personal life as well as her professional accomplishments. The writing draws from oral histories of Lange and her second husband, Paul Taylor; her letters and journals; interviews; books and magazine articles; and the author's personal memories. It also integrates social history as reflected by Lange's work. Partridge's willingness to examine not just Lange's successes, but also her problems, including those of balancing family and career, makes this an unusually vivid biography. Highly recommended.

Reich, Susanna. *Clara Schumann: Piano Virtuoso*. 1999. Hardcover: Clarion. Ages 11–14.

Concert pianist Clara Schumann, who started performing

at age nine, had a career that lasted longer than that of almost any other musician of the nineteenth century. Concert programs exist for more than 1,299 performances in her lifetime. Married to composer Robert Schumann, she gave birth to eight children and outlived four of them. After Robert entered a mental asylum and died a few years later, Clara was the family's sole supporter, which required nearly constant travel. This biography draws heavily from her childhood diaries and adult correspondence, and is beautifully illustrated with many contemporary pictures and photographs. A wonderful introduction to a remarkable musician.

Sills, Leslie. *Inspirations: Stories about Women Artists*. 1989. Hardcover: Albert Whitman. Ages 10–14.

This elegantly designed book discusses the lives and art of four women: the widely acclaimed Georgia O'Keeffe and Frida Kahlo and the lesser-known Alice Neel and Faith Ringgold. Full-color reproductions illustrate each chapter along with a few black-and-white photographs. Sills gives salient details from each artist's childhood and work, and comments on the factors that made art a difficult pursuit for them. Alice Neel spent years evolving her own dark painting style before she was recognized by the art world. An extensive bibliography and full notes about the reproductions appear at the back of this exemplary volume.

Sills, Leslie. *Visions: Stories about Women Artists*. 1993. Hardcover: Albert Whitman. Ages 10–14.

This companion volume to *Inspirations* is equally as elegant and interesting. It discusses Mary Cassatt, Leonora Carrington, Betye Saar, and Mary Frank. Each biographical sketch discusses the artist's childhood and influences, then goes on to describe her work. Mary Cassatt, the best known of the four, sets the tone with her decision to break from tradition and pursue her own vision of art. Leonora Carrington, born in England in 1917, rebelled against her proper upbringing and joined the Surrealists. Californian Betye Saar, who has experienced the dual pain of racism and sexism, uses objects from flea markets, nature, and everyday life to create sculptures. Last in the group, Mary Frank is a successful sculptor who has also worked in printmaking. Beautiful reproductions show the artists' work discussed in the text. Notes at the back list each piece of art, its size, and its location, and give bibliographies on each artist. Highly recommended.

Wolfe, Rinna Evelyn. *Edmonia Lewis: Wildfire in Marble*. 1998. Hardcover: Dillon. Paperback: Muse Wood. Ages 10–14.

Few readers will have heard of the nineteenth-century sculptor Edmonia Lewis, yet hers is a remarkable story. Born around 1844 in New York, Edmonia was the daughter of an Ojibwa mother, and a father who was a free African from the West Indies. Thanks to her brother's support, the future artist received formal education and eventually enrolled at Oberlin College in Ohio. The reproduction of a black-and-white drawing done in her teenage years indicates her artistic talent. After some painful experiences at the college, she moved to Boston intent on becoming a sculptor. She gained some success, then moved to Rome where her success increased. Black-and-white photographs show her busts of famous people as well as massive marble sculptures of classical themes. Although the prose is occasionally choppy, this biography introduces an artist well respected in her lifetime who deserves recognition today.

Sports Biographies and Nonfiction

Aronson, Virginia. *Serena and Venus Williams.* **2001. Hardcover: Chelsea House. Paperback: Chelsea House. Ages 9–14.**

Two of the great tennis players of our time are the sisters Serena and Venus Williams. This short biography describes their family background and tracks their careers in tennis through 1999. They grew up in Compton, a poor area of Los Angeles, and took up tennis at an early age. By the time they reached their early teens, it was clear that the sisters had a future in tennis. The family moved to Florida, and at age fourteen, Venus turned professional, followed by Serena the next year. Both have gone on to win Grand Slam tournaments in singles as well as victories together in doubles. This biography emphasizes the role of religion, education, and family loyalty in the sisters' lives, glossing over controversies and problems. Fans will probably not mind the author's uncritical enthusiasm for these outstanding athletes.

Blais, Madeleine. *In These Girls, Hope is a Muscle.* **1995. Hardcover: Atlantic Monthly Press. Paperback: Warner. Ages 13–14.**

Written for adults but accessible to teenagers, this conversational book honors a championship girls' high school basketball team. The members of the Amherst, Massachusetts, Regional High School team come to life through descriptions of their personalities and families, and through excerpts from their diaries and conversations. They forge strong bonds as teammates and friends, learning from their male coach and from each other. These strong-minded girls make the most of an experience previously reserved for boys. As one girl analyzes it, "The court is where you can be all those things we're not supposed to be: aggressive, cocky, strong." Dedicated to their team, they take the sport and themselves seriously, a spirit rarely captured in a book about girls and athletics.

Cooper, Cynthia. *She Got Game: My Personal Odyssey.* **1999. Hardcover: Warner. Paperback: Warner. Ages 13–14.**

Cynthia Cooper, one of the greats in professional women's basketball, was a star of the WNBA's Houston Comets. But as this highly readable autobiography reveals, her success never came easily. She grew up in a dangerous, poor section of Los Angeles in a single-parent family where her mother worked long hours to make life better for her children. Through grit and talent, Cooper made her way to the University of Southern California on an athletic scholarship, where she struggled with balancing intense basketball demands and studying, and lived with being the sixth person on a nationally winning team. She spent eleven years playing European pro ball, mostly in Italy. But her real chance to shine came with the formation of the WNBA. As her conversational writing explains, her religious faith and her family have proved to be enduring forces in her life over the years. Cooper gives advice to teenagers on how to succeed while maintaining strong values, as she herself has done so well.

Freedman, Russell. *Babe Didrikson Zaharias: The Making of a Champion.* **1999. Hardcover: Clarion. Ages 10–14.**

This excellent biography draws a lively picture of perhaps the greatest female athlete of all time, Babe Didrikson Zaharias, who died in 1956 at age forty-five. She excelled at baseball, basketball, tennis, and golf, and won many medals and broke records in different track-and-field events. She exuberantly proclaimed her talents and successes, drawing harsh words from critics who thought women should be demure, but also entertaining her thousands of fans. A natural athlete, she also practiced extraordinarily hard to develop her talents. Freedman uses wonderful black-and-white photographs and Babe's writing, newspaper articles, interviews with friends and colleagues, and other primary sources to convey her vibrant personality, amazing accomplishments, and, to a lesser extent, her personal life.

Hamm, Mia, with Aaron Heifetz. *Go for the Goal: A Champion's Guide to Winning in Soccer and Life.* **1999. Hardcover: Harper. Paperback: Quill. Ages 13–14.**

Mia Hamm loves soccer. Her enthusiasm pervades this book, which also gives a vivid picture of how hard she works at her sport. While the subtitle suggests the soccer star is offering advice on life, her focus is on playing soccer. Even the brief information about her personal life is couched in terms of her participation in the game. More than half of the text guides readers through ways to improve their game, with chapters on trapping, passing, dribbling, shooting, heading, and goal-keeping. Diagrams and step-by-step photographs demonstrate moves. Hamm acknowledges her own strengths, as well she should as one of the great players of all time, but she's also generous in her praise of her teammates. While not specifically published for young people, this straightforward book is clearly aimed at teenage soccer players, who will love it.

Hasday, Judy L. *Extraordinary Women Athletes.* **2000. Hardcover: Children's Press. Paperback: Children's Press. Ages 11–14.**

Nearly three hundred pages offer inspiring biographical portraits of female athletes from the United States and Europe. Starting with Ora Washington, a black woman who excelled in tennis and basketball in the first half of the twentieth century, and ending with gymnast Shannon Miller, forty-five individuals are profiled, with a few more chapters on broader topics, including the All-American Girls Baseball League, the impact of Title IX, and women's basketball today. The biographical sketches typically run from four to six pages, with a few black-and-white photographs. They give brief personal information but focus on the athletic accomplishments of these women from a wide range of sports: tennis, basketball, rowing, biathlon, track and field, skating, swimming, ice hockey, and more. Many of the women faced biases as females and athletes of color, and all worked extraordinarily hard to perfect their sport. A wonderful book for browsing, with more reading suggestions and Web site resources at the back.

Macy, Sue. *A Whole New Ball Game: The Story of the All-American Girls Professional Baseball League.* 1993. Paperback: Holt. Ages 11–14.

From 1943 to 1954, women played professional baseball in this country. Yet for the following thirty years, little was heard about these remarkable women. Finally in 1988 the National Baseball Hall of Fame in Cooperstown, New York, paid tribute to the All-American Girls Professional Baseball League with a collection called "Women in Baseball." This gracefully written history of the league sets women's baseball in the context of World War II and its aftermath. It brings the games and the players to life with intriguing details and anecdotes, conveying their intense love for the game and capturing their unique experience as women who worked and traveled together as a team. More than 550 women played in the league over twelve years and, during 1948 alone, drew more than 910,000 fans to their games. Photographs and memorabilia illustrate this readable account that will fascinate sports lovers and anyone interested in women's history.

Macy, Sue. *Winning Ways: A Photohistory of American Women in Sports*. 1996. Hardcover: Holt. Paperback: Polaris. Ages 11–14.

Fascinating photographs have been gleaned from many sources to illustrate this essay about the history of women in sports. The graceful writing delves into the biases and controversies that thwarted women as they tried to enjoy athletics, with anecdotes that will open the eyes of anyone who takes girls' sports teams for granted. Interviews and newspaper stories give an added dimension to this intriguing exploration of history. The priceless photographs, which convey a sense of the past and capture amazing moments in women's sports, will mesmerize readers and reshape their view of history. There are tennis players in 1886 in long skirts and petticoats; women boxers from 1912; a rodeo rider from the first half of this century; and a weight lifter from the 1930s. These women, who faced disdain and sometimes virulent opposition, paved the way for today. A fascinating social history, this unique photoessay is a pleasure to look at and read. Highly recommended.

Weatherspoon, Teresa. *Teresa Weatherspoon's Basketball for Girls*. 1999. Paperback: Wiley. Ages 8–14.

Basketball great Teresa Weatherspoon of the WNBA's New York Liberty has put together a fine resource for basketball players that covers the sport's basics in detail. The first chapter gives advice on warming up and stretching. Following chapters focus on dribbling, passing, shooting and individual offense, team offense, rebounding, individual and team defense, and conditioning. Black-and-white photos demonstrate the moves and also show the Liberty's workout routine. In the chapter about passing, for example, the text and photos guide players through the fundamentals, then specific passes such as the bounce pass, and finally several drills to improve the skills introduced. Weatherspoon adds personal information and motivational comments in frequent sidebars. An inspiring, informative guide for players.

More Dynamic Girls and Women

Ashby, Ruth, and Deborah Gore Ohrn, editors. *Herstory: Women Who Changed the World.* **1995. Hardcover: Viking. Ages 11–14.**

This inspiring volume tells the stories of 120 important women throughout history. The material is broken into three sections: prehistory to 1750, 1750 to 1850, and 1890 to the present. Written by nine contributors, biographical sketches of two or three pages highlight each woman's accomplishments, explain the obstacles she faced as a woman, and set her story briefly in context. Photographs or other portraits accompany many of the sketches, and sidebars add information on related topics. Some of the 120 women are famous, others more obscure. Even readers conversant with Western European history may not be familiar with such strong women as Vietnam's Trung sisters and India's Lakshmi Bai. *Herstory* is both a reference book and a volume for browsing through. It will transform many readers' understanding of history and the role women have played in creating it.

Bolden, Tonya. *And Not Afraid to Dare: The Stories of Ten African-American Women.* **1998. Hardcover: Scholastic. Ages 11–14.**

Twenty- to thirty-page chapters describe the accomplishments of ten impressive African-American women. The portraits include educator Mary McLeod Bethune, who founded a college in Florida, among other accomplishments; opera singer Leontyne Price, who broke down numerous barriers in the music world with her talent and perseverance; Nobel Literature Prize–winner Toni Morrison; athlete Jackie Joyner-Kersee; and others. These brave women faced racial bias as well as gender bias. Their determination comes through clearly in their stories, in a way that will inspire readers to aim high in their careers and their contributions to society. Photographs, or portraits, and quotations from the women's writings add to the collection's impact.

Chang, Ina. A *Separate Battle: Women and the Civil War*. 1991. Paperback: Puffin. Ages 10–14.

This exemplary book fills a gap in American history with its stories about women's roles in the Civil War. With photographs or drawings on every other page, it explains their work as abolitionists, nurses, soldiers in disguise, and spies. It describes the massive efforts by women—particularly in the North—to provide supplies for the army. Chang quotes from diaries and letters to give voices to the women of the time and uses well-chosen anecdotes and stories to make her points. Her writing is lively and full of intriguing details. Sidebars add information about certain important women and other topics such as wives who followed their soldier husbands from camp to camp. A top-notch book likely to interest not only history buffs but a wide audience of readers.

Colman, Penny. *Girls: A History of Growing Up Female in America*. 2000. Hardcover: Scholastic. Ages 11–14.

This substantial book gives a fine overview of U.S. history, emphasizing the roles girls played from pre-Colonial times to

1999. After an introductory chapter, each chapter of ten to fifteen pages describes life for girls during an era and shows how events like the Civil War affected them. The well-written text frequently quotes from girls' diaries and letters, and women's memoirs, giving a sense of their daily lives and emotions. Photographs of girls drawn from different ethnic groups and other illustrations such as book covers show girls over the years, what they wore, and some of their activities and jobs. Highly recommended for those who love history or who like historical fiction series like the "Dear America" or "American Girl" books.

Colman, Penny. *Rosie the Riveter: Women Working on the Home Front in World War II.* **1995. Paperback: Crown. Ages 11–14.**

Many of the women who worked during World War II lost their jobs as soon as men returned home. But "they never forgot that once there was a time in America when women were told that they could do anything. And they did." So concludes this outstanding history book about the six million brave, competent women whose work was vital to the war effort and kept the nation going. Excellent photographs portray women in their jobs from shipyards to farmyards, jobs previously closed to women, who were considered too weak or delicate for them. It is inspiring to read about the individual women who took on difficult work and succeeded at it, and heartbreaking to see them suddenly out of work when the war ended. The book's back matter includes an index, a bibliography, a chronology, and additional facts and figures. A well-crafted, exciting book about women's history.

Dash, Joan. *We Shall Not Be Moved: The Women's Factory Strike of 1909.* **1996. Hardcover: Scholastic. Paperback: Scholastic. Ages 10–14.**

In 1909 women workers in the garment district in New

York united to strike for better working conditions and recognition of their union. One out of every five factory workers was female and got paid a much lower wage than male workers. Organized and run by women, with little support from the big union officials, the strike peaked when thirty thousand workers walked out. Poor immigrant women, many of them Jewish, worked with college students and even some wealthy socialites to reach their goals. Young women who never expected it found themselves as leaders and public speakers. The strike, which was both exhilarating and difficult, lasted longer than expected and in the end achieved only some of its goals. But it got many women involved in union work and increased union membership enormously. Illustrated with photographs, this is an inspiring book about the power of women united in a cause.

De Pauw, Linda Grant. _Founding Mothers: Women of America in the Revolutionary Era_. Wood engravings by Michael McCurdy. 1975. Hardcover: Houghton. Paperback: Houghton. Ages 12–14.

Many books about American women's history start with the women's movement that began in 1848. This exceptional book concentrates instead on the women of Revolutionary War times, an era in which women had more freedom than they did in the next century. With fascinating details from newspapers, civic records, and contemporary writing, De Pauw paints a picture of a rougher, more informal time in which widows took over their late husbands' businesses and ran them successfully. One-third of the taverns were owned by women; women ran farms, plantations, stores, and even a few blacksmith and gunsmith shops. Although laws gave women little power, the times made it possible for women to leave bad marriages and still make a living. Chapters on black and Indian women highlight their accomplishments; other chapters detail women's roles on both sides of the war. A top-notch history book that will reward the reader again and again with fascinating information.

Frank, Anne. Translated by B. M. Mooyaart-Doubleday. *Anne Frank: The Diary of a Young Girl*. 1967. Hardcover: Doubleday. Paperback: Bantam. Ages 11–14.

Anne Frank wrote with epic courage in the face of evil and fear. Hiding from the Nazis in Amsterdam, she and her family heard repeatedly of the tragic fates of their friends, and they knew they might face the same. Nevertheless, this adolescent girl kept up her spirits and coped stalwartly with her problems. After almost two years in hiding, she admonished herself to quit grumbling and "Be brave!" She tried to view her family's confinement as a "dangerous adventure" and maintained her sense of humor. A talented writer with an ear for language, she chose apt anecdotes and snips of conversation to draw her pictures of her surroundings. She conveyed the personalities of those around her and made the details of their limited, everyday existence interesting. Her ability to draw the reader into her world is so extraordinary that the final note about her death in a Nazi concentration camp feels like a personal loss. A stunningly powerful work that everyone should read.

Gourley, Catherine. *Good Girl Work: Factories, Sweatshops, and How Women Changed Their Role in the American Workforce*. 1999. Hardcover: Millbrook. Ages 10–14.

Most American girls today would have a hard time envisioning the life of a factory girl in the 1800s and early 1900s, with inhumanely long days and terrible work conditions. The stories, statistics, and pictures in this social history effectively convey the life of factory girls, including children as young as six. The text moves chronologically from the early mills in New England, staffed by American-born girls, to the wave of nineteenth-century immigrant girls who worked to support their families, drawing on newspaper articles and books of the time. Chapters describe the long and difficult fights of social reformers and union activists in raising the age of workers and improving their situations. The book will open the eyes of those who assume women didn't hold jobs in the past, and will make them proud of the endurance and pride of the girls and women portrayed.

Ippisch, Hanneke. *Sky: A True Story of Resistance During World War II*. **1996. Hardcover: Simon & Schuster. Paperback: Troll. Ages 12–14.**

"The Dutch people were and are, in general, quite stoic," writes the author of this memoir about her teenage experiences in the Dutch resistance during World War II. In a matter-of-fact fashion, she writes of her remarkable exploits as a teenager escorting Jewish families and children to safe destinations, locating and preparing sites for the weekly meetings of resistance leaders, and spending months in a tiny prison cell with three other prisoners, knowing she might be executed. Ippisch describes her actions and the people and the places around her with well-chosen details supplemented by the necessary historical and personal background. Black-and-white photographs add information and atmosphere. The author's courage will stay with readers long after they close this memorable book.

Ketchum, Liza. *Into a New Country: Eight Remarkable Women of the West*. **2000. Hardcover: Little, Brown. Ages 10–14.**

As North America changed in the nineteenth century, so

did the lives and opportunities of women. This well-written collective biography describes eight women whose lives depended on those changes. It opens with a woman who kept a detailed diary as she and her husband rode the Santa Fe trail in 1846. The next woman, Lotta Crabtree, made her name as an actor, first during the California Gold Rush, then around the country, earning both fame and fortune. Biddy Mason, a slave who gained her freedom through a lawsuit, became one of the wealthiest women in Los Angeles. Two sisters of the Omaha tribe took on nontraditional roles, one as a tribe spokesperson and the other as a doctor. The first female doctor in Oregon, a resolute Chinese-American photographer and inventor, and a successful restaurateur during the Klondike gold rush round out these portraits, full of fascinating details, most illustrated with equally fascinating photographs.

Levinson, Nancy Smiler. *She's Been Working on the Railroad.* **Photographs collected and taken by Shirley Burman. 1997. Hardcover: Lodestar. Ages 10–14.**
The coming of the railroad changed the United States drastically, and women played various roles in that transformation. Starting in the nineteenth century, this straightforward history documents those roles, from telegraph operators to stewardesses to nurses and finally to a few engineers. The text combines railroad history with an overview of women's roles and profiles of specific women who made unusual contributions. Each of the World Wars merits a chapter, when men left to fight and women took over jobs usually reserved for men. The final chapter looks at the progress women have made since World War II in securing the more prestigious railroad jobs, helped by legislation and lawsuits that countered discrimination. Many black-and-white photographs

help bring the stories alive and highlight some fascinating women from the past.

Miller, Brandon Marie. *Buffalo Gals: Women of the Old West*. 1995. Hardcover: Lerner. Paperback: Lerner. Ages 10–14.

The plentiful photographs are the highlight of this book about women in the Old West. Although small, the pictures capture fascinating subjects: a female rodeo rider; newspaper women setting type in the 1880s; Wyoming pioneer women with their guns and animal skins; and two women dressed in long skirts, capering on a Yosemite peak. The history covers the trip West by covered wagon, frontier homes, women's work, entertainment, and the lives of Native American women. The dense text, with its many quotations from letters and diaries, is packed with surprising details. For example, in 1910, ten percent of the homesteaders on the Great Plains were single women, an amazing statistic. The writing is not as effective as the photographs, but will reward persistent readers with an unusual view of history.

Murphy, Claire Rudolf, and Jane G. Haigh. *Gold Rush Women*. 1997. Paperback: Alaska Northwest Books. Ages 11 and up.

Prospectors, entrepreneurs, Native women, dance hall girls—all kinds of women played roles in the Alaskan and Yukon gold rushes in the late 1800s and early 1900s. A terrific variety of black-and-white photographs show women and the rough country they inhabited. Biographical sketches of two to three pages describe twenty-three women, while chapter introductions give historical background about the gold rushes. Some women traveled on their own from the continental United States to escape their restricted lives and make their fortunes.

Others came with husbands, while yet others already lived in the area but found their lives changed by the discovery of gold. Women started hotels, restaurants, and trading posts. They hiked through wilderness and raised children in difficult conditions. Their stories add a dimension that is usually overlooked in this colorful segment of history. Sidebars, maps notes, bibliography, photo credits, and an index round out this fine book.

Myers, Walter Dean. *At Her Majesty's Request: An African Princess in Victorian England.* **1999. Hardcover: Scholastic. Ages 10–14.**

In 1848, neighboring warriors overran a West African village and kidnapped a young princess. She was saved from death by a British naval officer, Commander Forbes, who renamed her Sarah and took her back to England on his ship. During the voyage, she learned English from the sailors. Officially, six-year-old Sarah was a present to Queen Victoria from the African king who would otherwise have killed her. Queen Victoria, who enjoyed her meetings with Sarah, commanded Forbes to raise the girl while the queen herself paid the expenses. Myers effectively conveys the girl's celebrity and the problems it created, bringing her to life through anecdotes, photographs, drawings, and letters. A remarkable, moving story of a princess torn between two worlds.

Reit, Seymour. *Behind Rebel Lines: The Incredible Story of Emma Edmonds, Civil War Spy.* **1988. Paperback: Harcourt. Ages 10–13.**

Emma Edmonds was an amazing woman. She dressed as a man, calling herself Frank Thompson, and served in the Union army for two years. During that time, she acted as a spy for the North and went on eleven spying missions to gather information behind enemy lines about Confederate troops and plans. She successfully disguised herself as an old black man, a handsome Confederate sympathizer, and a matronly Irish peddler. During each venture into Confederate territory Edmonds risked her life, coming close to dying more than once. The only person who shared her secret was a chaplain's wife, who helped Edmonds in her disguises. Many years after the war, she secured a veteran's pension by a special act of Congress. Historians believe that Edmonds was one of more than four hundred women who disguised themselves as men to fight in the Civil War. An exciting fictionalized biography.

Schwager, Tina, and Michele Schuerger. *Gutsy Girls: Young Women Who Dare*. 1999. Paperback: Free Spirit. Ages 11–14.

Would you sky-dive? Try aggressive in-line skating? Do cartwheels on the back of a moving horse? This collective biography introduces young women who have done those deeds and more. Twenty-five biographical sketches, each illustrated with a few black-and-white photographs, introduce impressive girls and women, many of them in their teens, who have broken barriers and shattered stereotypes. The chapters include the highest-ranked competitive female rock climber in the United States, the fastest female drag racer in the world, a top high school surfer, and more remarkable champions. The uneven mix also features girls who have pursued goals available to almost anyone, such as working for Habitat for Humanity, or others whose stories depend on having money, such as world travelers. The last fifth of the book offers advice on pursuing goals and gaining confidence.

St. George, Judith. *Dear Dr. Bell . . . Your Friend, Helen Keller*. 1992. Paperback: Beech Tree. Ages 11–14.

Although the childhood of Helen Keller is well known,

her accomplishments as an adult are not. This elegant biography tells of both, with a focus on Keller's friendship with Alexander Graham Bell. Bell, who was deeply involved in issues concerning the deaf, was indirectly responsible for Annie Sullivan's role as Keller's teacher. With Sullivan's help, Keller, who was deaf and blind, succeeded at the seemingly insurmountable task of learning to understand language, to read and to write. Bell explained it as the "genius" of Sullivan and the "brilliant mind" of Keller. Keller went on to graduate from Radcliffe College and become a writer and activist whose impressive achievements broke stereotypes about what the disabled can do. Many quotations from their letters bring the personalities of Keller and Bell to life in this outstanding biography.

Weldon, Amelie. *Girls Who Rocked the World: Heroines from Sacagawea to Sheryl Swoopes*. 1998. Hardcover: Beyond Words. Paperback: Beyond Words. Ages 10–14.

This enjoyable paperback focuses on women who did something important as a child or teenager, and often continued that work as an adult. It tells thirty-three stories, starting with Cleopatra and ending with tennis player Martina Hingis. In between are biographical sketches of scientists, poets, political leaders, artists, musicians, and even a drag racer. The girls come from all around the world and have contributed to their fields in different ways. A photograph or portrait accompanies each sketch to personalize the subject. Small sidebars add interesting details about the heroines, while other short boxed paragraphs offer words from today's girls about how they plan to "rock the world." The writing style is upbeat, and the variety of women and what they have accomplished is truly inspiring. Followed by *Girls Who Rocked the World 2*.

6

Poetry

Only a handful of poetry collections for children focus on girls and women, but the ones that do, listed below, make wonderful gifts and provide inspiration to readers and future poets.

Glaser, Isabel Joshlin, selector. *Dreams of Glory: Poems Starring Girls*. Illustrated by Pat Lowery Collins. 1995. Hardcover: Atheneum. Ages 8–12.
The thirty short poems in this anthology are divided into three sections: Sports, Power, and Dreams of Glory. The sports poems are especially strong and include skiing, skating, horseback riding, baseball, track, and diving. Among the Power poems, "Abigail" is a particularly wonderful poem about a girl who doesn't fit in but who later writes a book that "would curl your hair," a happy revenge on a stifling life. There is a lack of poems about girls going on adventures or actually accomplishing something exciting. Far more concern hopes, dreams, and frustrations. But since few anthologies exist of poems about

girls, readers will find new material here. It is a good start that signals the need for more poems about girls.

Morrison, Lillian, compiler. *More Spice than Sugar*. Illustrated by Ann Boyajian. 2001. Hardcover: Houghton. Ages 8 and up.

This top-notch collection brings together more than forty poems about strong girls and women. Most fairly short, the poems celebrate important women and their accomplishments. One-third of the poems center around sports, with selections about Wilma Rudolph, Joan Benoit, Dorothy Hamill, and other famous athletes. Admirable women such as Harriet Tubman, Sojourner Truth, Amelia Earhart, Georgia O'Keeffe, Clara Barton, and many more merit their own poems. But other poems pay tribute to ordinary girls who break stereotypes in sports, music, training horses, and other diverse areas. Some of the poems are inspirational, others funny or joyous. Energetic black-and-white illustrations add to the book's spirit without overwhelming the poems. Highly recommended.

Paul, Ann Whitford. *All by Herself: 14 Girls Who Made a Difference*. Illustrated by Michael Steirnagle. 1999. Hardcover: Harcourt. Ages 9–14.

In this unusual collection, poems describe the deeds of fourteen girls throughout American history. Full-page oil paintings illustrate each poem with dramatic scenes in rich colors. The girls' accomplishments vary from Sacajawea guiding Lewis and Clark to Golda Mabovitch, later Meir, raising money for school books. Lesser known heroines include Violet Sheehy, who helped her family escape from a fire in 1894, and Harriet Hanson, an eleven-year-old mill worker who led her fellow workers to join a strike in 1836. The well-crafted narrative poems focus on a brave act or accomplishment during childhood or teen years. Inspiring as well as informational, this ends with a paragraph with more facts on each girl.

Philip, Neil, editor. *It's a Woman's World: A Century of Women's Voices in Poetry*. 2000. Hardcover: Dutton. Ages 12–14.

What was life like for women and girls in the twentieth century? The sixty-two poems in this collection give many answers to that question from women around the world. Seven sections divide the poems loosely into the topics of romance, babies, breaking free, life at home, power, surviving war, and old age. From a traditional Papago song for a young girl's puberty ceremony to poems by well-known poets such as Gertrude Stein, Stevie Smith, May Sarton, and Gwendolyn Brooks, the offerings vary in their accessibility and sophistication. Many speak to women's strengths while others ponder problems and lost opportunities. Elegant black-and-white photographs of women separate the chapters, just one feature in the elegant design. While dates for the poems and information on the poets would have added to the anthology's depth, it stands out for its range and focus on women and girls.

7

Nonfiction Books in Series

Some publishers issue books in series that focus on women. Since it would take too much space to describe each book, here are general descriptions of some good series arranged by age level.

Grandmothers at Work. Millbrook. Ages 8–12.
The three photo-essays in this series so far, which all begin with the phrase "Meet My Grandmother," show U.S. Senator Dianne Feinstein, Supreme Court Justice Sandra Day O'Connor, and deep sea explorer Sylvia Earle at work and interacting with the grandchild who narrates the book

You Can Be a Woman (name of career). Cascade Pass Press. Ages 9–12.
You Can Be a Woman Cardiologist is one of the books in this series in which women in each of the fields covered describes her work and answers questions. Careers include engi-

neer, Egyptologist, paleontologist, marine biologist, and architect, several sports fields, and more. The books, which end with a few hands-on activities, have uninspired illustrations but good information.

Female Skating Legends. Chelsea House. Ages 9–12.
Sixty-four-page photo-essay biographies of ice-skaters Baiul, Yamaguchi, Lipinski, Bobek, Kerrigan, Kwan, Witt, and Gordeeva.

Female Sports Stars. Chelsea House. Ages 9–12.
Sixty-four-page books with color photographs, by different authors. The titles begin "Superstars of" and include gymnastics, figure skating, golf, tennis, and track and field.

New Moon Books. New Moon Publishing. Ages 9–13.
An editorial board made up of girls, advised by adults, have put together attractive books on several topics: *Money: How to Get It, Spend It, and Save It; Friendship; Writing;* and *Sports.* Published in conjunction with *New Moon Magazine.* (*www.newmoon.org*)

Women in Profile. Crabtree. Ages 9–13.
Slim photo-essays that profile several women in an area, including athletes, leaders in medicine, humanitarians, explorers, and more. For an example, see *Entrepreneurs* on page 254.

Women Who Win. Chelsea House. Ages 9–14.
Eight volumes in this biographical sports series include Cynthia Cooper, Mia Hamm, Martina Hingis, Michelle Kwan, and others. For an example, see *Serena and Venus Williams* on page 355.

Girl Power. Lerner Publishing. Ages 12–14.

Four books of about one hundred pages each address challenges and stereotypes girls face in sports, the classroom, the family, and "the mirror." The books give advice, examples, and quotes from girls and women. For an example, see *Girl Power on the Playing Field* on page 271.

Cool Careers for Girls. Impact Publishing. Ages 13 up.

Each book includes profiles of women in careers including engineering, air and space, construction, working with animals, law, health, food, and sports, with information about the duties, salary range, daily routine, and training. Illustrated with color photographs.

Extraordinary People. Children's Press. Ages 13 up.

These collective biographies of more than two hundred pages each provide solid information on a variety of people in an area. Many of the titles begin with the words "Extraordinary Women" and cover science, medicine, journalism, athletes, and the American West. For an example, see *Extraordinary Women Scientists* on page 346.

8

Magazines and Web Sites for Girls

Magazines aimed at girls and women all too often emphasize clothing and beauty. They are filled with articles, fashion spreads, and advertisements that convey the message that females should measure their worth by their looks. The four print magazines listed below present girls in a different light. The recommended Web sites offer ideas, activities, and advice that encourage girls to expand their horizons.

American Girl

For girls 8 to 12. From the creators of the American Girls books, this bimonthly magazine includes historical and contemporary fiction and nonfiction. Despite the tie-in to commercial products and the polished looks of the girls in the photographs, this magazine compares favorably to more fashion-oriented ones. (*americangirl.com*)

New Moon: The Magazine for Girls and Their Dreams

For ages 8 to 14. This bimonthly forty-eight-page magazine is by and about girls and women. It includes fiction, essays, artwork, columns, and more on topics of interest to girls. Emphasizes strong, self-sufficient images of girls. (*newmoon.org*)

Sports Illustrated for Kids

For ages 7 to 13. Published monthly. A popular glossy magazine with articles and photographs about sports, including amateur and professional athletes. Includes many advertisements. (*sikids.com*)

Teen Voices

For teenage girls. A quarterly magazine that challenges the media's stereotyped images of girls. It publishes writing by teenage girls, too. (*teenvoices.com*)

agirlsworld.com

A Web site and free on-line magazine for girls 7 to 17, written and designed by girls. Covers a wide variety of subjects from technology to books to crafts.

girlpower.gov

A Web site sponsored by the U.S. Department of Health and Human Services "to help encourage and motivate 9- to 14-year-old girls to make the most of their lives." It offers ideas, activities, resources, sports information, and lots of useful advice in a jazzy design.

girlsinc.org

A Web site with one area for girls and another for adults who want to encourage "strong, smart, and bold" girls. The girls' area offers articles, ideas, and activities. Created by Girls Inc., a national nonprofit dedicated to improving life and opportunities for girls.

girltech.com

Although a bit heavy on promoting their own products, this Web site aimed at encouraging girls to master technology offers tips on inventing, profiles of successful women, information about sports, and much more.

jfg.girlscouts.org

The "Girls Space" section of the national Girl Scouts Web sites has well-presented information and activities, with book reviews, profiles of successful women, science projects, and more. Accessible even to non-scouts.

9

Resources and Tips for Parents

Locating Books

Libraries

Public libraries are a great resource for parents. They are free, and typically offer a broader and deeper range of books than bookstores do. Libraries are good places to find books that are out of print, an important service because many children's books go out of print quickly. Libraries are also more likely than bookstores to carry books from smaller presses.

Good libraries are increasingly easy to use, with computerized catalogs that tell if a book is on the shelf or in a nearby library. Many public library catalogs can be accessed from home through the Internet. Many libraries are part of a branch system or a large cooperative system, so you can use your card at more than one library. In such cases you can usually return books to the library closest to you, even if you checked them out elsewhere. Most libraries have bookdrops so that you can return books when the library is closed.

Interlibrary loan (ILL) is a convenient way to get access to many more books than your local library has in its collection. In many libraries, it is free to borrow a book through ILL, although some public libraries charge a small fee per book. Some computerized catalogs allow you to input your library card number if you want to request a book from another library. Your local library will call, e-mail, or send a notice through the post when it arrives, often in a few days.

While you are signing out books, find out what other programs and services your local library offers. You may discover storytimes for younger children, summer reading programs for a wide range of ages, book clubs for older children, programs on parenting, and more. Many libraries carry books on tape and videos, too.

School libraries come in all sizes, and the large ones will probably have many of the books in this guide. Some school libraries are open during the summer, although most are not. Whether parents can sign out books depends on the school.

Bookstores and Catalogs

Bookstores vary enormously in their selections of children's books. Some offer a wide array of books, usually with an emphasis on paperbacks. Others have only a small selection, or carry mostly books in popular series. Some cities have bookstores devoted just to children's books, a treat for children's book lovers.

It is important to realize that most bookstores will order a book for you for no charge if the bookstore doesn't carry it but can get it easily from another source. If you don't see the book you want, ask about placing such a special order.

Bookstores are increasing the services they offer for families, adding storytimes, author book signings, and other programs.

On-line bookstores such as amazon.com and barnesand noble.com are increasingly popular. They are especially helpful for getting obscure books that a local store might not carry, or for people who don't live near a bookstore. Their Web sites offer an easy way to survey what books an author has written and if they are available for purchase. They may also offer an out-of-print service to get books that a publisher no longer supplies. It is discouraging how many children's books go out of print quickly, as you can easily see on these Web sites.

Take the recommendations of on-line bookstores and the information they provide with caution. While some of the recommendations come from knowledgeable staff, most of the recommendations are not reliable. "Subject" searches on amazon.com, for example, to find books on a certain topic don't display the books based on quality. Worse, a search for fiction on a subject most often turns up nonfiction as well and results in a huge number of series books rather than a few well-chosen novels.

Most catalogs and book clubs typically offer such a small selection that they carry only a few books about strong girls and women. One exception is *Chinaberry Books*, an outstanding catalog of more than five hundred children's books, with thoughtful descriptions of each title. It covers toddlers through adolescents, with a section on parenting books and a small selection of novels for adults. Chinaberry Books, 2780 Via Orange Way, Suite B, Spring Valley, CA 91978. 1-800-776-2242. *www.chinaberry.com*

Keeping Up with Children's Book Publishing

If you are interested in keeping up with what's new in children's books, here are some recommended magazines, review journals, and Web sites. Also keep an eye on your local newspaper, which may have regular or occasional articles on new children's books. Libraries often provide booklists that highlight recent recommended books. For example, each year the American Library Association publishes an annotated list of approximately seventy-five Notable Children's Books, a useful resource available in most libraries and on the American Library Association Web site in the following list.

The Horn Book Magazine, 11 Beacon Street, Boston, MA 02108. 1-617-227-1555. *www.hbook.com*

The Horn Book Magazine is a well-established bimonthly journal about children's books. It prints insightful reviews of recommended books and well-written articles about children's literature. Available at bookstores and libraries, and by subscription.

Book Links, 434 W. Downer, Aurora, IL 60506. 1-708-892-7465. *www.ala.org/BookLinks*

Book Links is an attractive, useful magazine of great interest to children's librarians and educators, published by the American Library Association. It highlights books on selected topics and authors, geared toward curriculum needs. Available by subscription and in many libraries.

Book: *The Magazine for the Reading Public*, 252 West 37th Street, 5th Floor, New York, NY 10018. 1-212-659-7070. *bookmagazine.com*

BOOK: *The Magazine for the Reading Public* is a glossy bimonthly magazine aimed at the general public that carries a column and a limited number of reviews of children's books, both written by Kathleen Odean.

Children's Literature Web Guide from the University of Calgary. *www.ucalgary.ca/~dkbrown*

This is an outstanding site that provides information as well as links to many other good sites.

Fairrosa Cyber Library of Children's Literature. *www.dalton.org/libraries/fairrosa*

This Web site is an enthusiastic collection of information, links, and booklists.

American Library Association. *www.ala.org*

The American Library Association's Web site provides links to ALA journals, Web site picks for families, book lists, award information, and a limited number of book reviews.

Tips on Reading Aloud

Reading aloud well does not come naturally to everyone. Here are techniques you can practice until they come easily. *The Read-Aloud Handbook* by Jim Trelease offers more ideas about how to go about it, as well as numerous reasons that reading aloud is beneficial.

- If you haven't read the book already, scan it to get a sense of its content before you start reading aloud.
- Choose books you are excited about or your child is excited about. It is hard to read a book you don't enjoy, especially a long one.
- Read with expression. A monotone is hard to listen to. Children need to hear changes in your voice to indicate when you are reading dialogue. Vary your pace, too. Slow down to build up suspense, and speed up during exciting scenes.
- Create voices for different characters if you enjoy it, but it isn't necessary for a good reading. A story can be read effectively in a straightforward manner as long as you have expression and enthusiasm.
- Read at a moderate pace, not too fast. Listening is a challenge for many children, and you don't want to leave them behind as you speed ahead. Picture-story books require time for enjoying the illustrations.
- Feel free to stop and discuss the book if you and your listener want to. Answer questions as they come up. How much you want to stop and explain new words is up to you. If they can be understood in context, you may want just to

keep reading. Stopping too often to explain can undermine the story's impact.

- Keep in mind that children can look bored or restless and still be listening. Some children need to be moving around or fidgeting with something. The real question is, are they following the story? If so, let them squirm or even draw pictures as they listen.
- Sometimes a book will lead to conversations afterward, sometimes not. Play it by ear. Either way is fine.
- If your child wants to read to you sometimes, great. Beginning readers especially enjoy their new skills. You can trade off pages or chapters, or just sit back and listen.
- If your child is not enjoying a book, you are not obliged to finish it. This is most likely to come up with chapter books. You don't want to abandon a book quickly, but if a book has not sparked interest after several sessions, try another one. If this is a pattern, you may want to switch to shorter books and build up to longer ones.

Reading aloud has a host of educational benefits, but it works best if it isn't approached as an educational exercise. Parents have been known to have children repeat each word after them, as a device to teach reading. Such a tedious approach is more likely to dampen enthusiasm for books than to promote learning. Just enjoy the books together; the increased vocabulary, understanding of story structure, exposure to correct grammar, and other benefits will follow naturally.

Activities with Books

Books stand on their own as art and entertainment, and sometimes the best approach is simply to read a book and savor it. In other cases, discussing the book enriches the experience. But it can also be fun to pair books with activities such as crafts, trips, cooking, and more. Most of the following ideas are geared toward picture-story books and biographies, but reading a novel together can also lead to shared activities. Brainstorm with your child about other possibilities, with the goal, as always, to make reading a wonderful experience.

My guide to children's books by subject, *Great Books about Things Kids Love* (Ballantine, 2001), offers even more activities and ideas for using books with children.

- Take a low-key field trip in conjunction with a picture-story book. Read *Pond Year* and then take a walk at a pond. Read *Emeline at the Circus* before going to a circus or *If Anything Goes Wrong at the Zoo* before a trip to the zoo.
- Add props to your reading of a picture-story book. Get a squirt gun or set of Groucho Marx glasses for reading *Chester's Way*. Find a metal Band-Aid box and fill it with coins before reading *The Purse*.
- Read *Get Set! Swim* before going swimming or starting swimming lessons.
- Read *How to Make an Apple Pie and See the World*, then bake together. Cooking is a wonderful combination of math, such as fractions and measuring, and reading.
- Read *Zin! Zin! Zin! A Violin* before going to hear instrumental music.

- Read *Owl Moon* and go out on an evening hike to look for birds.
- Read *June 29, 1999* and try a science experiment. Libraries have many science experiment books for children.
- After reading a book illustrated with collage, try making a collage. Or paint with watercolors after seeing watercolor illustrations in a book.
- Encourage your child to write and illustrate her own books. She can dictate the words to you if she doesn't know how to print yet. Remind her to add an About the Author paragraph.
- Read a biography about a woman artist. Take a trip to a museum and point out art by women. Paint a picture or make a sculpture together.
- Since children's books have a limited number of reproductions of paintings, find a book for adults with even more pictures to look at.
- Read a folktale from another country together and then locate the country on a map. Find a book with photographs of that country.
- Read a folktale, then a parody of the tale, such as *Cinderella* and *Cinder Edna*. Talk about the similarities and differences.
- Read about a female athlete. Go to a local girls' sports event, such as a high school or college game or track meet.
- Read a novel together that has been made into a video. Watch the video and compare the two.
- Read about a marine biologist, such as Eugenie Clark or Sylvia Earle, in conjunction with a visit to an aquarium.
- With a child who can read independently, start a mother-daughter book group, or help your daughter start a book group with her friends.

- Before a space shuttle launch, follow the stories in the newspaper together and read about a female astronaut.
- Read *Sarah, Plain and Tall* together. Then each write a letter such as Sarah wrote, describing yourself to someone who has never met you.
- Read a novel in conjunction with a trip to a geographic region: *Caddie Woodlawn* for Wisconsin; *Our Own May Amelia* for Oregon; *The Missing 'Gator of Gumbo Grove* for Florida; and many more.
- Visit a place on vacation connected with important women. For example, read about the history of women's rights before going to the Women's Hall of Fame in Seneca Falls. Or visit the National Museum of Women in the Arts in Washington, D.C.
- Donate a book that you both like about a strong female to your daughter's school or your public library.
- Alert teachers and librarians to books about strong females that you and your daughter especially enjoyed.
- Read about an important woman in conjunction with Take Our Daughters to Work Day.
- Listen to a book on tape together on a long trip. A number of the novels in this guide have been recorded and are available at your library or for rental through the mail. Audiobooks offer many of the same benefits as reading aloud. They expose listeners to new vocabulary with correct pronunciation and good grammar. They also make it possible for children to listen to stories above their reading level, which is especially wonderful for those who read below grade level, and who can now enjoy books written for their age group. Two good sources for audiobooks are Blackstone Audio Books (800/720-2665; *www.blackstoneaudio.com*) and Books on Tape (800/882-6657; *www.booksontape. com*).

- Read about a female author whom your daughter admires. The following Web sites provide links to children's writers as well as other useful information about children's books:

  —Children's Literature WWW Guide, University of Calgary *www.acs.calgary.ca/~dkbrown/*
  —Internet School Library Media Center—Index to Children's Authors and Illustrators *http://falcon.jmu.edu/~ramseyil/biochildhome.htm*

Further Reading for Parents

Here are some recommended books and Web sites about raising daughters, gender issues, and related topics.

Bingham, Mindy, and Sandy Stryker with Susan Allstetter Neufeldt. *Things Will Be Different for My Daughter: A Practical Guide to Building Her Self-Esteem and Self-Reliance from Infancy through the Teen Years.* **1995. Paperback: Penguin.**

Packed with information and ideas, this nearly five-hundred-page volume addresses many aspects of girls' development and needs, and what parents can do to support them. Practical exercises and step-by-step plans included.

Brown, Lyn Mikel, and Carol Gilligan. *Meeting at the Crossroads: Women's Psychology and Girls' Development.* **1992. Hardcover: Harvard University Press. Paperback: Ballantine.**

Based on interviews with one hundred girls, this important book provides insights into the problems girls face at adolescence. By well-known experts in education and human development.

Eagle, Carol J., and Carol Colman. *All That She Can Be: Helping Your Daughter Achieve Her Full Potential and Maintain Her Self-Esteem During the Critical Years of Adolescence.* **1993. Hardcover: Simon & Schuster. Paperback: Simon & Schuster/Fireside.**

Detailed, useful information on girls' social and psychological development. Full of examples and specific suggestions from a psychologist whose practice is geared toward adolescent girls.

Elium, Jeanne, and Don Elium. *Raising a Daughter: Parents and the Awakening of a Healthy Woman.* **1994. Hardcover: Celestial Arts. Paperback: Celestial Arts.**

The authors reflect on the special challenges facing parents of girls in today's world, offer parenting advice, and take the reader through each stage of a girl's development. Also authors of *Raising a Son: Parents and the Making of a Healthy Man.*

Fine, Carla. *Strong Smart & Bold: Empowering Girls for Life.* **2000. Hardcover: HarperCollins/Girls Inc.**

This useful book, written in conjunction with Girls Inc., gives practical advice with specific examples on raising daughters to resist stereotypes, speak out, take risks, achieve goals, accept and appreciate their bodies, and more.

Gilligan, Carol. *In a Different Voice: Psychological Theory and Women's Development.* **1982. Hardcover: Harvard University Press. Paperback: Harvard University Press.**

The groundbreaking book by a Harvard psychologist about girls' and women's psychological development. Readable and thought-provoking.

Godfrey, Joline. *No More Frogs to Kiss: 99 Ways to Give Economic Power to Girls.* **1995. Paperback: HarperCollins.**

An exceptionally useful guide to helping girls look at the world around them in terms of business and economic opportunity. A fine combination of practical ideas and inspiring stories.

Mann, Judy. *The Difference: Growing Up Female in America.* **1994. Hardcover: Warner.**

Reporter Mann takes a sociological look at the forces that hold girls back. Based on interviews with experts in different fields and on the experience of her daughter and her daughter's friends, this accessible volume is full of interesting insights and observations, with some thoughts about how to change society.

Pipher, Mary. *Reviving Ophelia: Saving the Selves of Adolescent Girls.* **1994. Hardcover: Putnam. Paperback: Ballantine.**

This compassionate bestseller addresses parents' fears and concerns about raising an adolescent daughter in a threatening world. Using examples from her practice as a clinical psychologist, Pipher examines the problems and offers guidance to parents and their daughters.

Rimm, Sylvia. *See Jane Win: The Rimm Report on How 1,000 Girls Became Successful Women.* **1999. Hardcover: Crown. Paperback: Three Rivers.**

Child psychologist Rimm describes the findings from her research about successful women and translates them into helpful advice for parents in this long, informative volume. Also see Rimm's companion book *How Jane Won*, which describes the experiences of fifty-five successful women.

Sadker, Myra and David. *Failing at Fairness: How America's Schools Cheat Girls.* **1994. Paperback: Simon & Schuster/Touchstone.**

A landmark study of sexism in our schools and what can be done about it. Readable and inspiring.

Books for Children on Sex and Growing Up

It is vital for children to understand the changes that will take place in their bodies when they become adolescents. They need accurate information about sex, and reassurances about puberty and its effects. Here are some recommended books with age guidelines.

Cole, Joanna. *How You Were Born*. Photographs by Margaret Miller. 1993 revised edition. Hardcover: Morrow. Paperback: Mulberry.

For ages four to seven. Color photographs and diagrams show the development of the fetus and the birth process, and the welcome arrival of newborn babies into several families.

Brown, Laurie Krasny, and Marc Brown. *What's the Big Secret? Talking about Sex with Girls and Boys*. 1997. Hardcover: Little, Brown. Paperback: Little, Brown.

For ages four to nine. Cheerful pictures create a relaxed mood in this useful book about sex and development that answers many questions that younger children have about sex, but with only a brief mention of puberty.

Andry, Andrew C., and Steven Schepp. *How Babies Are Made*. Illustrated by Blake Hampton. 1968. Paperback: Little, Brown.

For ages five to eight. Simple information for younger children about sexual reproduction in flowers, animals, and humans. Illustrated with cut-paper illustrations.

Harris, Robie H. *It's So Amazing: A Book about Eggs, Sperm, Birth, Babies, and Families.* **Illustrated by Michael Emberley. 1999. Hardcover: Candlewick.**

For ages eight to eleven. Cozy pictures of real-looking children and adults (naked and clothed) illustrate this discussion of human bodies and reproduction with an emphasis on how families are created, including adoption, with an overall spirit of celebration. Highly recommended.

Gravelle, Karen, and Jennifer Gravelle. *The Period Book: Everything You Don't Want to Ask (But Need to Know).* **Illustrated by Debbie Palen. 1996. Hardcover: Walker. Paperback: Walker.**

For ages nine and up. A simple, conversational discussion of the changes puberty brings for a girl, illustrated with humorous cartoon drawings. A solid introduction.

Harris, Robie H. *It's Perfectly Normal: Changing Bodies, Growing Up, Sex & Sexual Health.* **Illustrated by Michael Emberley. 1994. Hardcover: Candlewick. Paperback: Candlewick.**

For ages nine and up. A well-crafted book that answers children's questions about their bodies and sexual reproduction. The straightforward text is balanced by funny, apt cartoon drawings, many of nude figures.

Madaras, Lynda, and Area Madaras. *The What's Happening to My Body? Book for Girls: The New Growing Up Guide for Parents and Daughters.* **2000 3rd Edition. Hardcover: Newmarket. Paperback: Newmarket.**

For ages nine and up. A comprehensive, readable handbook filled with useful information, mainly about females, although some facts about male puberty are included. Madaras has written a companion volume for boys.

Jukes, Mavis. *It's a Girl Thing: How to Stay Healthy, Safe, and in Charge*. **1996. Hardcover: Knopf. Paperback: Knopf.**
For ages ten and up. An upbeat, honest approach to adolescence that covers sexual issues; drugs, alcohol, and smoking; and staying safe. Written in a personal, good-humored tone to make readers feel comfortable and reassured.

Empowering Your Daughter

I have gleaned these ideas from many sources. Try some you haven't considered before, keeping in mind that no parent can expect to be doing all of them all the time. For excellent suggestions to introduce business and entrepreneurial thinking into your daughter's everyday life, see *No More Frogs to Kiss*, listed on page 392.

- Let your daughter get dirty. Children need to explore the world around them and be physically active. Science, nature, sports, arts and crafts—all these important parts of growing up entail getting dirty.
- Give her time to try to do a task herself rather than "rescue her" by giving advice or doing it for her. Encourage her to be persistent in working out her own solutions.
- Encourage your daughter to state her opinions and thoughts, and listen respectfully to what she says. If she has trouble speaking out in class, practice with her at home and help her plan strategies for the classroom.
- Notice how you compliment girls. Typically girls get compliments on what they wear or how they look, while boys get compliments on what they do. Try to give compliments on specific accomplishments, not general qualities. "Your speech had a powerful opening," not "You are a good speaker."
- Encourage her to participate in sports. Give her the support to join a team sport. Show her you value physical fitness and strength in girls and women.
- Watch television together and discuss the portrayal of women, how realistic it is, what messages it sends. Extend this to movies, videos, magazines, and computer games.

- Find ways to help your daughter develop math, science, and computer skills. Provide games that develop spatial skills such as puzzles, model kits, checkers, and chess, etc. For older girls, look into after-school classes or summer camps on math, science, and computers.
- See that she learns some mechanical, building, and repairing skills, and becomes familiar with tools. Give young girls blocks and simple tools. Have older girls learn to repair their bicycles and encourage them to take apart old appliances, etc.
- Emphasize the importance of developing talents and interests. Such pastimes give girls pleasure and a self-image that doesn't rely on appearance, popularity, or relationships. Girls need to be good at doing things as well as at dealing with people.
- Examine your expectations for girls and boys. Do you give boys more leeway to be rowdy, physically active, outspoken? Do you expect girls to be more domestic, caring, polite, thoughtful? Do you expect boys to help with outdoor tasks and girls with indoor ones?
- Introduce her to strong female role models. Expose her to a variety of career possibilities and women who enjoy their work. Teach her to assume she will have to make her own living someday, like most women do. Participate in Take Our Daughters to Work day in April. For more information on Take Our Daughters to Work, contact the Ms. Foundation for Women, 120 Wall Street, 33rd Floor, New York, NY 10005. 1-800-676-7780. (*www.takeourdaughterstowork.org*)
- Support your daughter in pursuing her interests and in taking risks. Be ready to help but encourage her to make her own decisions and choices. Praise her for her intelligence, abilities, and initiative as well as her hard work and dedication. Most of all, believe in her.

Author Index

AUTHOR INDEX

AUTHOR INDEX

Title Index

TITLE INDEX

TITLE INDEX

TITLE INDEX

411

Subject Index

About Kathleen Odean

Kathleen Odean has been a children's librarian for seventeen years in public and school libraries. She chaired the 2002 Newbery Award Committee, and has served on a previous Newbery Committee, the Caldecott Award Committee, and the American Library Association's Notable Children's Books Committee. Her other two guides to children's books are *Great Books for Boys: More than 600 Books for Boys 2 to 14* and *Great Books about Things Kids Love: More than 750 Recommended Books for Children 3 to 14*.

Ms. Odean is a contributing editor for *BOOK: The Magazine for the Reading Life* as well as a reviewer for *Kirkus Reviews*. She frequently speaks to parent and teacher groups about books for children and teens, and how to encourage reading. She lives in Barrington, R.I.